The Helping
Professions in the
World of Action

The Helping Professions in the World of Action

Edited by I. Ira Goldenberg
Harvard University

Lexington Books
D.C. Heath and Company
Lexington, Massachusetts
Toronto   London

Library of Congress Cataloging in Publication Data

Goldenberg, I.   Ira, 1936-
    The helping professions in the world of action.

1. Social service – United States – Addresses, essays, lectures.
2. Social action – Addresses, essays, lectures. 3. Community mental
health services – United States – Addresses, essays, lectures. I. Title.
HV91.G57   361'.973   73-11660
ISBN 0-669-88955-5

Published simultaneously in Canada.

Printed in the United States of America.

International Standard Book Number: 0-669-88955-5

Library of Congress Catalog Card Number: 73-11660

This book is dedicated to the memory of one of its authors, Harold I. Lewack — and through Harold to the countless others who struggle, often unheralded and unrewarded, to leave this world a little better than the way they found it.

Table of Contents

Preface

The central theme of this book is simple: to demonstrate, through the concrete experiences of a number of different "helping professionals," both the truth and implications of the statement that *no scientific discipline (or profession) develops independently of, or is unaffected by, the social and political realities of its time.* And by social and political realities we mean the changing manner in which human problems are defined and the particular ways in which these definitions are perceived (or are not perceived) as related to the existential contradictions characteristic of our society as a whole. Even more, however, this book attempts to share with the reader the struggles of some of those professionals who sought to engage themselves more directly in efforts to deal with those contradictions on a community or institutional level.

The impetus for this volume can be traced fairly directly to my own experiences as a rather traditionally-trained and academically-based clinician who, for a variety of different and as yet only partially understood reasons, became involved in the problems of community action. In 1965, I together with a small group of so-called nonprofessionals from the inner city of New Haven, Connecticut, became engaged in a process which eventually led to the development and implementation of the Residential Youth Center (RYC). The RYC was a neighborhood-based, indigenously-staffed facility whose "public mission" was to "work with" (i.e., rehabilitate) those youth (males between the ages of sixteen and twenty-one) who were not only "out-of-school and out-of work," but had also been termed incorrigible by most of the existing social, legal, educational, and mental health related agencies in the city.[a] This public mission notwithstanding, our own concerns as a group went far beyond questions of how best to continue patching up what were clearly the victims of an essentially dehumanizing matrix of social institutions. It was clear, at least to us, that the mandate of the times demanded much more. What was needed was both a reassessment of existing conceptions of, and helping approaches toward, the inner city, coupled with the development of patterns of action that were more

---

[a]The Residential Youth Center was funded as an experimental and demonstration (E&D) project by the U.S. Department of Labor (Office of Manpower Policy, Evaluation and Research) administered through New Haven's community action agency (Community Progress, Inc.), and run in conjunction with the Psycho-Educational Clinic of Yale University. Readers wanting a more detailed description and analysis of the Residential Youth Center are referred to Goldenberg. *Build Me A Mountain: Youth, Poverty, and the Creation of New Settings.* (Cambridge: Mass., MIT Press, 1971).

consistent with the aspirations and goals of its understandably alienated and chronically disaffiliated people. These aspirations were relatively concrete; they included an increasing sense of self-determination, the acquisition of power, and the desire to finally begin to control those events and forces which had for so long gone unchallenged in the shaping of their lives and destinies.

In addition to the above, however, it soon became clear that many of us involved in the project had become a part of the group for other, far more personal reasons — reasons not directly or apparently related to the Center's contractual goals or implicit ideological underpinnings. We were, both as individuals and as a group, far from happy (indeed, often increasingly bitter) in the settings, programs or institutions in which we were already engaged and from which we earned our livelihoods. Thus, whether we were truck drivers, professors at an Ivy League university, rock 'n roll singers, ex-policemen, or employees of the local community action agency, we were people who had begun to become increasingly concerned about the relationship between how we were leading our lives and the context of the values and life styles that dominated the settings in which we were employed. Put another way, each of us, independent of our varying skills, interests, levels of formal education or particular competencies, had arrived at that point in time when questions concerning the quality of life — the quality of our own lives — could no longer be separated from the nature and ideologies of the systems of which we were a part. In short, what had supposedly begun as an attempt to rehabilitate others was quickly transformed into a project with an additional focus: to develop for its rehabilitators a setting that was very different from the ones out of which they themselves had recently emerged.

Given the above, I think it would be fair to say that our entrance into the community, initially in the form of developing another in a long line of War on Poverty related helping settings, created a sequence of events which, in today's terminology, was definitely of the consciousness-raising variety. First, of course, there were the "victims," and the reality that individuals (in this case "hard-core" youth) needed help if they were going to be able to survive the personal ravages of poverty and powerlessness. Second, there was the realization that patching up the victims, laudable an enterprise though it might be, was certainly not enough — that what was needed was an attempt to both understand and deal more directly with the broader and more pervasive institutional sources of victimization. Finally, there was the growing awareness that we ourselves, by virtue of the kinds of lives we led and the institutions of which we were a part, were also an important variable in the social equation — that we too were in a sense being caught up in a set of institutional arrangements that mitigated against growth.

For me, the years between 1965 and 1970 were dominated by the development and implementation of a variety of community-based projects, each of which sought, in its own way, to address itself to one or another of the issues described above. After the Residential Youth Center there came another, somewhat different facility developed to meet the needs and problems of inner-city adolescent women. This was followed by the development of a Training and Research Institute for Residential Youth Centers (TRI-RYC), an institute through which the attempt was made to replicate the original Youth Center concept in five different states across the country. And finally, in 1970, we became involved in the problems of the Neighborhood Youth Corps and the issues of drug addiction and alcoholism in manpower training and opportunity programs. These years of involvement in the problems of community action were in many ways very good ones, years during which programatic triumphs and tragedies became deeply personalized within the context of an ever-increasing consciousness of the scope and intensity of the issues associated with social change. Moreover, they were years during which questions of personal competence (let alone, effectiveness) could not be divorced from the still-fresh memories of the content of one's own professional preparation. Ultimately, however, they were years of action in the most direct sense of the word — for it was a time in which sacrifice and commitment became the handmaidens of personal and communal indentity.

In 1970, after more than six years of relatively full-time involvement in the "world of action," I "semi-retired," returned (both physically and psychologically) to the university, and began the process of sorting out the varying and often conflicting themes that had characterized my professional life. Much to my surprise, this period of time devoted to reflection turned out to be neither calm in nature nor conducive to developing a satisfying sense of closure concerning the previous years of activity in the community. In part, this was due to the fact that each and every attempt to analyze a particular experience, rather than serving to significantly decrease ambiguity, actually raised as many new questions as it apparently answered. Thus, for example, in thinking through my role in various projects, it became clear that there was a fairly low correlation between the kinds of functions and responsibilities I had assumed and the nature of my professional or clinical training. Similarly, I became increasingly aware of a profound discrepancy between the ways in which I had been conditioned to conceptualize problems and the day-to-day realities of life in the community. But most importantly, I began to experience a sense of puzzlement, a feeling of having become disconnected from the experiences and concerns of many of my university-based colleagues.

While it is undeniably true that the experience of uniqueness is an important part of one's overall sense of identity, it is also a fact that one needs to feel a part of some reference group with which one can share a particular affiliation and communality of intent. For me this meant seeking out those who, for one reason or another, had both been engaged in activities similar to mine and were willing to share their experiences with others. But even more, it meant asking those individuals not only to relate their experiences, but to reflect upon them very critically — the assumption being that what might initially appear to be a host of unique and atypical experiences could, upon being shared and analyzed, become the data out of which there emerge new and more helpful patterns of professional thought and action. This volume is the result of that process.

Given the above, this book obviously belongs to many people. Thus, while we shall later offer the reader brief biographical information concerning each of the contributors to this volume, we would like at this point to acknowledge them individually and thank them for their patience in putting up with the often inexcusable delays (mea culpa) that have marked the preparation of this book for publication. I should like to think that their experiences in the world of community action — where delay and distraction are often the order of the day — prepared and fortified them for the experience. So, with the apologies now made, we again thank the authors: Michael Domenico, Irving H. Frank, Anthony M. Graziano, Benjamin S. Hersey, Edward S. Katkin, Murray Levine, Harold I. Lewack, Thomas W. Mahan, A. Verne McArthur, Linda M. Michlin, Lawrence Paros, Paul M. Quinlan, N. Dickon Reppucci, Seymour B. Sarason, Brian P. V. Sarata, J. Terry Saunders, Ralph F. Sibley, Alan P. Towbin, and Steve Tulkin. Special thanks are also extended to Elsie B. Keatinge and Debbie Spitalnik who, in addition to preparing the final manuscript for publication, were constant and invaluable sources of help and constructive criticism.

Introduction: The Purpose, Context, and Organization of this Volume

I. Ira Goldenberg
Harvard University

The major purpose of this book is fairly simple: to provide the baseline data out of which, hopefully, there can begin to emerge a profession (perhaps one should call it a movement) less concerned with protecting and perpetuating its own orthodoxy and more committed to addressing itself to those institutional arrangements and contradictions that have adversely affected the quality of life in our society.

All of the papers included in this volume are accounts of projects undertaken and developed during the 1960s. This is certainly not accidental, for the decade of the sixties was a period of time replete with the rhetoric of reawakenings, new commitments, and innovation. Future historians will place the "action sixties" in proper and critical perspective. Were the Kennedy and post-Kennedy days symbolic of the initial stirrings of a long dormant Camelot? Or were those years merely another prelude to the long night that signifies the end of the "American Century"? It is too early to tell, and it is certainly difficult to experience any coherent sense of unity between Camelot and Cambodia, affluence and Appalachia, the moon and "Welfare Moms." But a few things are relatively clear. The decade of the sixties began with purpose and ended with pain. For a few highly visible moments America seemed poised, ready to undertake the awesome task of transcending its own historical consciousness. Instead, almost as if guided by some faceless archetypical reflex, it recoiled from the existential moment and destroyed the very people who came to symbolize its approaching liberation. But in between those two points in time attempts were made to affect the quality of life in a society undergoing acute social change. To be sure, those concrete beginnings were neither grand in scale nor Herculean in impact. This is not to say, however, that they were unimportant, for they addressed themselves, however hesitantly and timidly, to the profound discrepancies between our national myths and community realities. This book is about those attempts.

In many ways the legislative and personal ground out of which the projects to be described in this book arose was sown during the guilt-ridden days that followed the assassination of President Kennedy. Two congressional acts, the Community Mental Health Act of 1963 and the Economic Opportunity Act of 1964, were particularly important in providing the impetus for a host of new beginnings in the area of human and institutional renewal. In both instances there was a similar public intent: to marshall and provide the resources for the development of bold new approaches to the problems of America's disadvantaged and disaffiliated citizenry. In both instances there was a similar private concern: could this country, operating once again within a reformist tradition, deal simultaneously with both the victims of the system as well as the institutional sources of their victimization? The problem was as clear as it was compelling. Individuals needed help. But the reasons why they had not previously received help (or, in those cases where they had received it, why it had been inappropriate either in form or in focus) invariably involved the helping institutions and their relationship to, and embeddedness in, the socio-political fabric of our society as a whole.

For the helping professions, the "challenge of the sixties" brought with it the need for an agonizing reappraisal. The searing implications of the War on Poverty, no less than the implied indictments behind the advent of the Community Mental Health movement, forced the mental health professions (including the universities to which they looked for intellectual nourishment and professional manpower) to take a long, hard look at what they were doing, who they were doing it with, and, by implication, what they were generally *not* doing to alter and influence the human condition. For some, perhaps the greater majority of mental health professionals, the response involved little more than the repackaging of old services and outworn mythologies in new containers bearing bright new labels. For others, this reappraisal resulted in action, the impact of which was to change personal conceptions and professional alliances. This latter group, with few allies and even fewer institutional supports, having thrust itself into that cauldron so simplistically referred to as the community, now had to address itself, if for no other reason than survival, to some of the very same issues and forces that had on other days and in other ways succeeded in creating the very victims they were now trying to help. Finally, perhaps in many cases for the first time, it became all too clear just how pervasive and binding — how mutually defeating — a social matrix had been allowed to become. It was indeed true that the same forces which prevented even one man from being fully free kept all men part slave.

How Is this Book Different?

In recent years a number of books have appeared in the area of community psychology and/or psychiatry. In most of these publications the attempt has been made to legitimize the existence of a "new" field in rather traditional ways; that is to say, by quickly offering examples of the linkages between existing clinical theories and community practice, by defining the field in terms of an accepted clinical perspective, and/or by hastily pointing to some "hard research" as evidence of the worth (if not validity) of the entire enterprise. More often than one would have hoped (or expected), there has been a self-congratu-

latory tone to these offerings, almost as if the professions involved had discovered, rather than reacted to, the events that had called their prior behavior
into question in the first place. And finally, too many recent publications
seem to have fallen prey to the push for closure, thus prematurely defining
(and confining) the field of community mental health as exclusively clinical
in both its membership and allegiance.

We think, naturally, that the present volume differs significantly from the
description offered above. To begin with, we have consciously sought to
include the work of people not typically considered to be clinicians. Rather,
by focusing attention on the helping professions, we have attempted to
broaden the field to include people (e.g., educators, administrators, "Feds,"
etc.) whose efforts, independent of formal or professional label, have been
directed toward problems and settings characterized by the limitations they
placed on human freedom and growth. It should be clear, however, that our
list is far from inclusive. The concept of "helping," if taken seriously, might
well include the work of anyone whose focus it is to examine critically, develop
alternatives to, and attempt to implement new models or modes of person-
institution relations. We hope that this will eventually be the case. Perhaps
this volume marks a beginning in that direction.

A second difference, perhaps related to the first, is the fact that this book
does not pretend to have as its goal the presentation of a theory of community
practice. It is not intended to provide the reader with closure. Indeed, the
opposite would be closer to the truth. The concept of the community (especially with respect to the practices of the helping professions), far from being
ready for definition, is in need of continuing differentiation. The premature
push for closure invariably retards the attempt to develop anything more than
novel approaches to the handling of symptoms. Options are reduced and
problems (as well as solutions) become defined narrowly and with little self-
critical analysis. This book, therefore, seeks to contribute to the development
of a field by trying, as it were, to slow it down. It offers basic experiential
data under the assumption that the tendency to disregard such data in the past
(a tendency, we might point out, deriving from some rather truncated views
concerning the trustworthiness of personal experiences) has resulted in the
diminution of creativity in the name of professional continuity.

Finally, with very few exceptions the papers in this volume were all written
specifically for inclusion at this time. This is significant for two reasons. First,
because as original accounts that have not appeared elsewhere, they offer the
reader new and personal analyses of the dimensions of the problems of public
practice. And second, and perhaps more important, is the fact that the papers
were not sought out or included on the basis of the success of the particular
project involved. Many (if not most) of the accounts included in this volume
were "failures" of one kind or another. However, the author's analysis of what
some people might label a failure is what we consider to be the essential data

calling for public awareness and reflection. A new field, especially one whose goal it is to question, understand, and change the human condition (including its own) is rarely developed on the basis of triumphs and successes. It emerges through conflict, confrontation, defeat, and doubt. Whatever personal victories are achieved along the way are usually small in scope and generally of a kind that merely "keep you going." We hope this book will help to keep its contributors going and entice others to join them.

The Organization of this Book

This book has been organized into three separate but related sections. This section, Part I, is devoted to an analysis of the historical, phenomenological, and personal dimensions of social intervention, particularly intervention of the mental health variety. In it the attempt is made to describe the development of clinical psychology (and, by implication, all other professions in the area of human renewal) from a socio-political perspective. In addition, attention is directed toward the phenomenological correlates of action, the goal being to make clear how psychologically and professionally ill-prepared clinicians are to deal with the demands and problems of a world that lies beyond the private consultation room or university. In short, Part I of this book poses the existential question: Is it possible, given the history of the helping professions, to posit the integration of one's personal and professional stances in the world, one's public and private modes of existence?

Part II constitutes the heart of the book in terms of the issues it seeks to raise as well as the data it attempts to make available. It consists of a series of case studies of attempts at social intervention of one kind or another. The projects vary, ranging from attempts to influence and change existing institutions, to the creation of totally new settings. They address themselves to what might appear, at least on the surface of things, to be wholly different problems and populations (e.g., welfare mothers, underachieving but high-potential high school students, Job Corps enrollees, prison inmates, chronically hospitalized mental patients, adjudicated youthful offenders, elementary school children, the aged, etc.). Finally, they summarize work undertaken through local community action programs, federal and state agencies, and/or universities. All of the cases, however, are bound by similar formats and intents. In each case study the author attempts (often by writing in the first person) to share with the reader the particular events which led him to become engaged in the project for which he initially or ultimately had to assume prime responsibility. Each project is described as fully as possible, care being taken to provide the information needed to understand the project's background, goals, processes, and outcomes. Major emphasis, however, is placed not on justifying the particular project (or in rationalizing its ultimate fate) but on communicating the essence of the experience of seeing it through. Attention, therefore, is focused on the problems and demands each project presented, and on how these issues were dealt with from the perspective of the "interventionist." Finally, and most important, each author reflects upon his experiences, and attempts (at least for himself) to develop a coherent framework for thinking about the dimensions of public practice — and more specifically, the kinds of preparatory experiences future helping professionals will have to have if they are to avoid some of the mistakes of their predecessors and, by implication, decrease the overwhelming odds against effective social change.

In Part III we turn our attention to the implications of the previous two sections for the development of this new profession (or movement) we have chosen to call "Mental Health Intervention." The papers in this final section of the book are all quite specific in focus. They address themselves to the ways in which our traditional training, research, and service perspectives must change if we are, indeed, going to commit ourselves and our resources to the task of developing a new field, a field whose conceptions and practices are more appropriate to the needs of a society in which the issues of pluralism and change remain essentially unresolved. In addition, attention is directed toward that institution — the university — which has heretofore assumed the primary responsibility for the preparation of scientist-practitioners. The university, particularly in terms of its relationship to, and embeddedness in, the community is reviewed from the perspective of the "regularities" that have come to define each setting's stance toward, and expectations of, the "other."

We have tried in this chapter to do two things. First, to convey much of the ground out of which this book emerged as figure; and second, to share with the reader some of our own disquiet concerning the response of the mental health professions to the problem — the unfinished business as it were — that the sixties placed before us. If the chapters that follow succeed in making us even more uncomfortable than we already are, if they confront us with the need to examine once again our own values, ideologies, traditions, and allegiances, they will certainly have served one of the book's primary purposes.

Part I

The Unresolved Past: The History, Politics
and Phenomenology of Action

1

The Helping Professions in Times of Rapid Social Change: The Development of Clinical Psychology as a Case in Point

I. Ira Goldenberg
Harvard University

*It is the profound tendencies of
history and not the passing excitements
that will shape our future.*
John F. Kennedy

No scientific discipline develops independently of, or is unaffected by, the social and political realities of its time. What men do and think, how their ideas and practices change or remain the same — these things are as much matters of historical imperatives as individual choices, and it is often difficult to tell where one leaves off and the other begins. Professions, no less than individuals, are shaped by the same "profound tendencies of history" that mold the societies of which they are a part. Their orientations and practices are more often than not a reflection of the prevailing values and attitudes of the greater society in which they are embedded. They change as the needs of their societies change, and accept as inevitable that through this process of change they will be continually defining and redefining themselves.

What we have said above is undoubtedly true to one degree or another for all professions, but it is particularly true of what we call the helping professions (e.g., psychiatry, clinical psychology, social work, education, etc.). There are probably two reasons for this, both of which have to do with the uniquely human character of the goals and processes of the helping professions. The first is that as clinicians of one kind or another our primary focus of concern is to understand the exigencies of what we call the human condition. This being the case, our primary reason for being is to help people, and to utilize the helping relationship to develop and increase our knowledge of human behavior, all in the hope that we will someday come to better understand ourselves and others. However, unlike members of other professions, the clinician (no less than his clients) is a part of and is affected by the same human condition he seeks to understand. The simple fact of life is that no clinician can hope to be maximally

This is a revision and updated version of a chapter in my book, *Build Me a Mountain: Youth, Poverty and the Creation of New Settings.* (Cambridge: MIT Press, 1971).

helpful unless and until he begins to understand the myriad pressures, both inside and outside of the individual, that influence behavior. But once this process begins the clinician and the client become bound in one way or another by the same values, attitudes, and even inequities of the society in which they both live. The longer the clinician practices the more he realizes the degree to which what he says and does is a reflection of his own participation in a societal process. Such is the fate (even, perhaps, the legitimate paradox) of the helping professions: the truth-seeker is inevitably the subject of his own quest — a situation which makes the luxury of disengagement well-nigh impossible.

The second reason is best stated in the form of a working assumption: a science's vulnerability to society's demands that it change its basic orientations and techniques is directly proportional to its level of theoretical and technological sophistication at that point in time. The helping professions, unlike their more highly developed brethren in the physical sciences, have not evolved a technology sufficiently precise to hide behind or use as a buffer against the relentlessly shifting influences and needs of society. Rubinstein and Parloff, after reviewing the progress in research on psychotherapy, the most prestigious of the helping professions, conclude as follows:

> Much has been done, but there has been relatively little progress in establishing a firm and substantial body of evidence to support very many research hypotheses. Basic problems in this field of research have remained essentially unchanged and unsolved. There is no simple, reassuring, authoritative principle which clearly supports one approach and demonstrates the invalidity of the others. (1959, p. 292)

Whether we wish to speak in terms of theoretical or methodological maturity it is clear that we are far more infantile, both in age and in level of development, than our colleagues in the physical sciences. As such, our theories and techniques, the ways in which we conceptualize problems and how we go about dealing with them, are much more likely to be deeply affected by the political and social upheavals through which our society is passing (Levine, 1967).

With this as our point of departure, it would seem appropriate that we describe in some detail just how closely our own professional behavior and development has mirrored what might be called the temper of the times. If, as we would like to believe, all that is past becomes prologue, then it is to the past that we must look if we are to understand the present and illuminate the future. For the field of clinical psychology the past was not so long ago.

Clinical Psychology in the 1940s

Clinical psychology was a "war baby," the bastard child of parents called Emergency and Need. It was born at a time and under conditions which threatened the very existence of what we think of as the American society. Its birth was accompanied by havoc and its early development took place in an atmosphere of frenzy; World Wars I and II saw to that.[a] Not having natural parents it was adopted by — rather it grafted itself onto — that discipline (i.e., psychiatry) which needed it, wanted it, and was willing to provide it with a home in which to grow up. What happened from that point on is now history, but for the present what is important to note is that even in its earliest years clinical psychology functioned as would anyone conscripted into service; doing the kinds of things and thinking the kinds of thoughts that were appropriate to facilitating the war effort. The fact that the crisis-ridden 1940s were not the kind of years which guaranteed a period of professional development that was stable, calm in nature, or conducive to reflective thinking is not the issue. Not very many people or professions were, or could afford to be, stable, calm, and reflective during that time. Stability and reflection are luxuries and, like all luxuries, they are subject to rationing during a period of national emergency. A society caught in a crisis in which its very fate is in question knows only one thing: to survive, and in order to survive, people do what they have to do rather than what they want to do. In retrospect, what was most interesting about the 1940s was the degree to which clinical psychology grew up doing the kinds of things it had to do in a way that was, in principle, no different from what was characteristic of our society as a whole.

War has a way of making instant experts out of self-proclaimed amateurs. A society engulfed in a battle for survival must often suspend its usually held criteria for expertise in recruiting and mobilizing its human resources to fill vital manpower needs. Often, of necessity rather than choice, it must lay aside, hold in abeyance, or temporarily cease to indulge itself in many of its ancient and sometimes treasured sexual and racial prejudices. The 1940s were a time when anyone, often regardless of sex, race, age, or experience became fair game for performing the kinds of jobs heretofore denied them. It was a time when women became welders and riveters in heavy industry war plants; when black people and other chronically oppressed minority groups suddenly found themselves in demand; when the aged and the young donned air raid warden helmets and scanned the evening skies; and when city-dwellers and residents of our urban ghettos suddenly became farmers, tending their Victory Gardens with the same infinite love as their mythified rural brethren. The war had succeeded, albeit unintentionally, in proving once again that under conditions of emergency and need people could learn to function in ways that had not been fully anticipated or imagined.

---

[a] Sarason et al. (1966) offer a detailed description of the impact of the world wars on the development of clinical psychology as a helping profession. Their analysis shows how the remedial and rehabilitative needs generated by these wars led to specific governmental policy decisions and actions that had significant consequences for the field of mental health in general, and for the development of clinical psychology in particular.

But just as the war made heroes out of cowards and patriots out of cynics, it also made clinical practitioners out of psychologists whose pre war world was the world of academia and whose major prewar goal was to become a part of that crusading army hotly in pursuit of the holy grail called Pure Science. It is important that we do not underestimate the difficulties or problems that this transformation entailed, for, as Sarason et al. point out:

> It would be correct to characterize American psychology before World War II as 'academic,' but this would not convey the fact that it was also anti-clinical in orientation. The Ph.D. was treasured as a symbol of scholarly and research performance untainted by practical or professional considerations (1966, p. 3).

But wars, as we have already pointed out, have a funny way of making the improbable almost commonplace and, just as anyone who could walk was a potential soldier, so too was anyone who had ever had a course in psychology a potential clinical psychologist. If women could make planes and if children could collect paper and cardboard for the war effort, it was not too much to expect academicians to leave their universities, temporarily put aside some of their research interests, and become instant mental health workers. And that, essentially, is what happened. Clinical psychology, which had lived a relatively cloistered and serene life prior to World War II, emerged from its comfortable home in the Halls of Ivy and thrust itself into the world of practical and clinical concerns. Clinical psychology was in sense reborn as a war psychology, as a psychology of emergency in the "frantic forties."

What followed was the same adolescent exhuberance and functional self-definition that characterized the activities of so many people during those years of trial and turmoil. With little preparation, and even less supervision, clinicians began to function in ways that, heretofore, had been almost unthinkable. They began doing things (e.g., psychodiagnostics, individual and group therapy) and assuming responsibilities (e.g., making clinical decisions, developing and administering programs of rehabilitation) as needs calling for such behaviors arose, rather than because their own traditions had prepared them for this work. It was a time when clinical psychologists "learned while they earned" in what for all practical purposes was an OJT (on-the-job training) experience.

World War II, which placed the stamp of finality on so many lives and institutions, and changed so many others, also irrevocably altered the field of clinical psychology. A profession had, like to many other citizens, responded to a national crisis; it had, like so many others, functioned in a variety of different ways and undergone a host of new experiences, and would, like so many others, never again be the same.

Clinical Psychology in the 1950s

If the 1940s were frantic years, the 1950s had to become silent ones, for no society can battle endlessly without itself becoming a war casualty. A society must rest, and begin to consolidate rather than continue to innovate. And so it was in the 1950s. Americans had emerged from the war victorious, but not a little tired and disillusioned, and certainly with the full realization that the "American Century" had ushered in The Bomb and the Age of Anxiety.

Under these conditions the decade of the fifties became a period of quiet desperation. It was a time of dullness and Dulles, mistrust and McCarthy (Joe, not Eugene), tailfins and torper, security-seeking, and above all else – silence. We became a people who either joined in the endless quest for status or withdrew into some purposely disorganized band of muted rebels and quiet insurrectionists. Schlesinger describes well this "generation which had experienced nothing but turbulence": ". . . in the fifties some sought security at the expense of identity and became organization men. Others sought identity at the expense of security and became beatniks. Each course created only partial men" (1965, pp. 113-114).

The affluent years were upon us and some – those who became members of *The Lonely Crowd* (Riesman, Glazer, and Denny 1950) or *The Status Seekers* (Packard 1959) – sought in their new suburbias and packaged villages that measure of security and permanence that the world situation could no longer offer or pretend to guarantee. These were the "organization men," men who, denied a sense of historical continuity, reached out for the instantaneous "belongingness" offered them by the beneficent organization. Whyte puts it this way:

> Listen to them talk to each other over the front lawns of their suburbia
> and you cannot help but be struck by how well they grasp the common
> demoninators which bind them. Whatever the differences in their or-
> ganization ties, it is the common problems of collective work that
> dominate their attentions, and when the DuPont man talks to the re-
> search chemist or the chemist to the army man, it is these problems
> that are uppermost. The word 'collective' most of them can't bring
> themselves to use – except to describe foreign countries or organizations
> they don't work for – but they are keenly aware of how much more
> deeply beholden they are to organizations than were their elders. They
> are wry about it, to be sure; they talk of the 'treadmill,' the 'rat race,'
> of the inability to control one's direction. But they have no great sense
> of plight, between themselves and organization they believe they see
> an ultimate harmony and, more than most of their elders recognize,
> they are building an ideology that will vouchsafe this trust. (1956, p. 4).

Others, those who chose the not-so-quiet refuge offered by Kerouac's *Subter-*

raneans (1959) and Lipton's *Holy Barbarians* (1959), sought "non-alignment" and became the alienated hipster who, as Holmes described it:

> . . . moves through our cities like a member of some mysterious, non-violent Underground, not plotting anything, but merely keeping alive an unpopular philosophy, much like the Christian of the first century. He finds in bop, the milder narcotics, his secretive language and the night itself, affirmation of an individuality (more and more besieged by the conformity of our national life), which can sometimes only be expressed by outright eccentricity. But his aim is asocial, not anti-social; his trancelike 'digging' of jazz or sex or marijuana is an effort to free himself, not exert power over others. In his most enlightened state, the hipster feels that argument, violence and concern for attachments are ultimately Square, and he says 'Yes, man, yes' to the Buddhist principle that most human miseries arise from these emotions. I once heard a young hipster exclaim wearily to the antagonist in a barroom brawl: 'Oh man, you don't want to interfere with him, with this kick. I mean, man, what a drag.'
>
> On this level, the hipster practices a kind of passive resistance to the Square society in which he lives, and the most he would ever propose as a program would be the removal of every social and intellectual restraint to the expression and enjoyment of his unique individuality, and the 'kicks' of 'digging' life through it. (1957, pp. 18-19).

Schlesinger, perhaps better than anyone else, has captured the essential quality of the fifties, and describes it in the following way:

> In the fifties the young men and women of the nation had seemed to fall into two groups. The vast majority were the 'silent generation,' the 'careful young men,' the 'men in the gray flannel suits' – a generation fearful of politics, incurious about society, mistrustful of ideas, desperate about personal security. A small minority, rejecting their respectable world as absurd, defected from it and became hipsters, 'rebels without a cause.' Pervading both groups was a profound sense of impotence – a feeling that the social order had to be taken as a whole or repudiated as a whole and was beyond the power of the individual to change. David Reisman, hearing, undergraduate complaints in the late fifties, wrote, 'When I ask such students what they have done about these things, they were surprised at the very thought they could do anything. They think I am joking when I suggest that, if things came to the worst, they could picket! . . . It seems to me that students don't want to believe that their activities might make a difference, because, in a way, they profit from their lack of commitment to what they are doing.' (1965, pp. 739-40).

Clinical psychology's quest in the 1950s was not discernably different in either its orientations or its tactics from the rest of society's goals in the postwar era. Just as security and status dominated the thinking and behavior of the vast majority of postwar Americans, so did they come to characterize the actions of many clinicians. With the guns now silent and the battlefields finally deserted, clinical psychology began its own silent war for recognition, prestige, and professional parity. The new adversary was psychiatry and the prize at stake was the right to first-class citizenship in the field of mental health. It was a quiet war — even a humane one — for clinical psychologists wanted little more than to become as much like their adopted fathers as possible. Clinical psychologists were not so much concerned with developing a professional image and identity of their own. The war years had already provided them with a ready-made image with which to identify, for by doing the kinds of things psychiatrists did, psychologists had for a long time been incorporating their values and introjecting their life styles. All that psychologists wanted (and eventually got) was "official" recognition that the practice of psychotherapy was now one of their inalienable rights rather than a temporary privilege that had been bestowed upon them by psychiatry.

In short, clinical psychology in the 1950s was a profession concerned with insuring its own safety and status. The "war for psychotherapy" was only the most obvious vehicle by which this security and prestige could be guaranteed. While most of our citizenry was obsessed with the ideas of keeping up with the Jones, installment buying, and a house in the suburbs, clinical psychology was obsessed with the idea of consolidating its wartime gains in a nation that was still converting to a peacetime economy. That clinical psychology should have had these goals, or should have pursued them with such laudable restraint, needs no retrospective justification or apology. Our own professional values and practices in the 1950s were no more or less a reflection of the attitudes and behaviors of so many of our war-weary fellow Americans.

Clinical Psychology in the 1960s

If the forties were frantic years, and the fifties silent ones, the decade of the sixties sought its root in action. The 1960s began as a time when personal visibility, social responsibility, and the quest for a self-critical autonomy replaced the aimless and egocentric quietude of the previous decade.[b] America

---

[b] We are acutely aware of the fact that by labeling periods of time in the manner we have been doing, we have been speaking in the categories of a guiding fiction. No single classification of an age — even more importantly, of a mere decade — can accurately reflect the upheavals and dislocations of human thought and action that took place during that span of time. Our description of the temper of the 1940s, 1950s, and 1960s is little more than an attempt to employ an historical shorthand in depicting the feeling-tone of a limited number of years. It is, therefore, of necessity, a description that is somewhat arbitrary, unreal, and incomplete. In point of fact, none of these decades existed in and of themselves without continuity or overlapping.

was entering a new decade, and its entrance was gradually giving birth and form to a new style, an altered orientation, and a new perspective in the conduct of public affairs. A nation once more began to examine itself with unsparing objectivity and candor and to understand how great a discrepancy there was between the image it tried to project abroad and the harsh imperfections of the society within its own borders. The doubting and challenging of institutions and established ways of thinking were no longer luxuries and were no longer interpreted as acts of treason: they became an imperative, an obligation, a sacred trust. There was now nothing inherently wrong with being imperfect, either as an individual or as a nation. What was morally wrong was the inability to admit imperfection and the unwillingness to do anything about it. Thought became coupled with personal action, and a nation of young people began to understand that risk-taking and the acceptance of peril in the service of ideals were the causes, rather than the effects, of freedom. More than anything else, a generation of Americans began viewing themselves as cheated so long as they lived in a society which, for all its apparent affluence and wealth, was still incomplete and unfinished.

Kennedy, the man and the president, became a symbol of the time, for, as Schlesinger put it,

> He voiced the disquietude of the postwar generation — the mistrust of rhetoric, the disdain for pomposity, the impatience with the postures and pieties of other days, the resignation to disappointment. And he also voiced the new generation's longings — for fulfillment in experience, for the subordination of selfish impulses to higher ideals, for a link between past and future, for adventure and valor and honor. What was forbidden were poses, histrionics, the heart on the sleeve and the tongue on the cliche. What was required was a tough, nonchalent acceptance of the harsh present and an open mind toward the unknown future. (1965, p. 114).

A nation began responding to a man, and through their responses gave concrete meaning to his words: "I do not want it said of our generation what T. S. Eliot wrote in his poem, *The Rock* — 'and the wind shall say these were decent people, their only monument the asphalt road and a thousand lost golf balls.' " (John F. Kennedy, Columbus, Ohio, October 17, 1960)

The early 1960s was a time when direct action became the vehicle for the attainment of individual and group identity, autonomy and fulfillment. Selfhood was now defined in terms of one's willingness and ability to act, and through this action to alter and influence the condition of man. It was a time when three young men (Michael Schwerner, Andrew Goodman, and James Chaney) would die, not only *with* each other, but *for* each other, realizing that so long as one of them was not fully free all of them were part slave.

The atmosphere that was once more making individual action a meaningful thing — an atmosphere in which, as Schlesinger puts it, ". . . even picketing no longer appeared so ludicrous or futile" — was also infusing old movements with a new and youthful dynamism; a dynamism which their elders found at once both awe-inspiring and not a little frightening. College campuses once again began seething with political and intellectual unrest and the movement for civil and human rights was born anew. In both cases there was a new insistence and an impatience to wait that amount of time which had so often in the past resulted in the conversion (or subversion) of high ideals into more "mature" forms of reflection and non action. The concepts of partial fulfillment, half-victories, and "wait, take your time, don't go too fast" were relegated to the past, to the dung-heap of worn-out ideas and retarding cliches: "Freedom Now!" was the chant of the present.

It was in this climate of insistence and action that a plethora of new programs were born, each one, in piecemeal fashion, seeking to fill an unfulfilled need, each one serving as both an indictment of past neglect and a challenge to prevailing orientations. In a relatively short span of time the Peace Corps, VISTA, Operation Headstart, and, most importantly, the War on Poverty made their appearances. In each case, despite differences in emphasis, there was a communality of intent: each program was an attempt to change something and to provide a vehicle through which individual action could become an instrument (albeit a limited one) for social change. The concern was now with the condition of man both at home and abroad. The overall focus became the community of man and, by implication, the communities in which people lived.

Clinical psychology in the sixties, no less than in the preceding decades, could not long remain unaffected by, or impervious to, the social and political changes through which our society was passing. If the "zeitgeist" of the sixties, and the programs it was giving birth to — especially the War on Poverty — were breathing new life into a society that had been too quiet too long, it was also succeeding along with several other factors in providing the mental health professions with a mirror through which the social bankruptcy of their own traditional modes of practice could be reflected back to them. In making this statement we are acutely aware of the fact that what we have said is somewhat inflammatory both in tone and implication. To label much of our traditional clinical efforts as "socially bankrupt" has the appearance of a blanket indictment devoid of any real appreciation of the exigencies, goals, and processes that go into the formation and maintenance of that particularly delicate human situation we call the clinical relationship. Nothing could be further from the truth. The attempt to use the psychotherapeutic situation to help a troubled individual — any individual — needs no justification: it is, in and of itself, an important, laudable, and necessary clinical-human activity.

What we are saying, however, is that in the process of wedding ourselves so completely to the psychotherapeutic model of help a very important thing occurred: we, as mental health professionals, became parties to a process which both restricted and limited our modes of conceptualization and patterns of service, and simultaneously excluded us from thinking about, and dealing effectively with, a large part of our society — namely, the poor and the oppressed — with whom we might or should have been joined. In short, psychotherapy (and more importantly, the patterns of thinking and behavior it both required and rewarded) had little to say and less to do about the gut problems confronting twentieth century America — the problems of institutionalized poverty, racism, violence, and sexism.

In making these statements we have done little more than echo what some clinicians have known or felt for some time. Reiff for example, in a paper stressing the adverse affects of our exclusively psychotherapeutic focus of treatment on the understanding of institutions as sources and influencers of behavior, put it in the following way:

> ... there has been a long history of persistent alienation from mental
> health professionals of the lower socioeconomic groups in this country.
> This alienation represents a critical failure. It is not merely the failure
> of each individual mental health professional, although there is the ele-
> ment of the individual's social responsibility involved here. Neither is
> it primarily a matter of tools and skills, although, again, this element
> is also involved. Basically, the problem is an ideological one. The
> roots of this alienation from the low-income populations lie primarily
> in the middle-class ideology of contemporary mental health services
> and secondarily in its technology. (1966, p. 548)

Gordon, writing from the point of view of the vocational counselor who tries to deal with the problems of culturally disadvantaged youth, came to a similar conclusion:

> ... counseling generally assumes that the locus of problems is in the
> individual client, rather than in the conditions to which he has adapted.
> This kind of counseling, as an instrument for changing lower class
> boys, will at best have an up-hill battle because it seeks to make them
> maladapted to the conditions of their lives while those conditions
> remain unchanged. At worst, such counseling will simply temporize
> by 'taking the edge off' obstreperous behavior and directing it back
> at the individual as the locus of his problems, without revising the
> causes or conditions of his discontent. Most benignly, such counsel-
> ing may be a palliative, helping a few individuals to move a little, but
> if there is no enduring structural change in the factors creating an
> infinite future supply of clients needing counseling, there will be
> no end to the counseling, and no possibility of anything but limited
> success. And what success is achieved will be at the price of deepen-
> ing the self-blame for failure which is already so deeply enmeshed
> in the problems of the poor, by agreeing with the premise that the

causes lie in the individual and his responses, rather than in the conditions to which he is responding.

Thus my position is that though counseling is necessary for those who are already the products of the forces indicated, the more important task is structural socio-economic change to end the production of disadvantagement, and that this goal represents a better and more productive use of the resources of counselors than a continued palliative effort to patch up the mistakes of the past without preventing the mistakes from recurring. If counselors are to be seriously concerned with the plight of the disadvantaged, they should bend their efforts toward changing the societies in which the boys grow up disadvantaged.

The vocational counselor stands at the crucial intersection of individual behavior and the structure of opportunities available to the individual. If he sees his job as primarily working with the individual, so that he is presumably better able to take advantage of the limited opportunities that are available, he will be doing only half his job, and that the easier half, since it manipulates the weak and the powerless while leaving the dominant majority safe, unchanged, and protected in its preservation of the better opportunities for itself and its own children. Thus it seems to me that it is only if the counselor also sees himself as an agent of social change in the wider community of which he is a part that he can take pride in carrying out the mandate of his profession. For it is only then that he will be stimulating natural and adaptive change in his clients, instead of engaging in psychological minipulation of them; it is thus the pre-condition of honesty in his profession. (1967, pp. 71–73).[c]

Focusing their attention more directly on the impact and meaning of the War on Poverty for the mental health profession, Rae-Grant, Gladwin, and Bower concluded that:

The helping professions are facing a crisis, although some professional groups seem more aware than others that their moment of truth is at hand. For mental health programs the crisis may contain the seeds of a major revolution. Like all revolutions this one could readily go too far, rooting out the good along with the bad. This is, then, a time for very careful charting of our future strategies.

The crisis with which we are faced is being precipitated by the President's declaration of War on Poverty. The reason this represents a crisis for mental health agencies is simply that the target population in this war is composed precisely of those people whom the 'helping' professions have not yet figured out a way to help. If mechanisms

[c]Jesse E. Gordon, "Counseling the Disadvantaged Boy," in William E. Amos and Jean Dresden Grambs, Eds., COUNSELING THE DISADVANTAGED YOUTH, ©1968. Reprinted by permission of Prentice-Hall, Inc., Englewood Cliffs, N.J.

for helping them were already available and in use, the acute distress
to which the President points would already have been relieved.
(1965, p. 1)

Clearly, the "action sixties" were forcing the mental health professions to
take a long, hard look at what they were doing, who they were doing it with
and — by implication — what they were more generally not doing to alter and
influence the social conditions of man. This agonizing reappraisal brought many
of us face-to-face with ourselves and with some rather painful and distressing
facts that could not easily be dismissed. As much as all other profession, we
were the products of our history, the victims as well as the beneficiaries of our
past. It was indeed a fact that the poor in this country had been largely ignored
by and had become alienated from the mental health professions (Smith and
Hobbes 1966). It was a fact that the poor, even when "treated," may have been
treated in a way and with the kinds of assumptions that were irrelevant to the
problems they were having or the needs they were experiencing (Kelly 1966).
And, perhaps most important, it was a fact that the mental health professions
had taken a basically passive stance with respect to the social, economic, and
institutional inequities that existed in our society (Yolles 1966) — the very
conditions which exacted such a heavy toll in human misery and contributed
so much to our mental health problems. In short, the movement that was
not making the eradication of poverty a respectable crusade served as both an
indictment of and challenge to the mental health professions, and provided
these professions with a new opportunity to direct their attention and talents
to the wider community of which they were a part and to which they bore
a responsibility.

The early 1960s saw the mental health professions begin to respond to these
challenges. Attention was now focused on the community and on the ways in
which clinicians could utilize existing resources and develop new ones to provide services which were more efficient and appropriate to the needs of the communities in which they lived or worked. What had begun as a long, hard look
at existing clinical practices — as a reappraisal almost forced upon the mental
health professions by events in the society as a whole — culminated in the passage of the Community Mental Health Acts of 1963 and 1964. These acts,
coupled with the events that led up to them and the processes they gave rise to,
resulted in the community mental health movement, a movement which was
heralded as the "bold new approach" to the prevention and treatment of
mental illness in our society.[d] Levine (1967) has summarized some of the

---

[d] It would indeed be a mistake to interpret the phrase community mental health
movement as implying anything even bordering on revolution. Like its counterpart, the
War on Poverty (the war that never was a war, or was ever really intended to be one),
the community mental health movement was, and continues to be, more rhetoric than
reality. The gap between what might be called the movement's public vs. private intentions will be explored in later chapters of this book.

specific social and professional pressures that facilitated the development of the community mental health movement. He describes them in the following way:

> The community mental health movement had its origins in a specific set of historical facts and in a set of social and professional pressures. These pressures had to do with the demand for new patterns of treatment which would not remove the mentally ill or the deviant from the community (Joint Commission, 1961), with the demand for preventive patterns of help (Eisenberg, 1962), with the inevitable shortage of professionally trained treatment personnel (Albee, 1959), with dissatisfactions with the efficacy of current patterns of diagnosis and therapy (Meehl, 1960; Eysenck, 1952), and with dissatisfactions concerning inequities in the distribution of services to all levels of society (Hollingshead and Redlich, 1958).

In summary, the mental health professions as a whole, in their own right and in a manner consistent with their own histories, became a part of the movements of change that were sweeping the country in the early 1960s. To be sure, there were rumblings of change among mental health workers long before the War on Poverty ever came along, and the field probably already was beginning to change or at least question some of its traditional directions and orientations. But the emergence of the action programs of the sixties certainly facilitated this process of self-scrutiny and, more than likely, made it imperative that much of this questioning be translated into programs of service within a relatively short period of time. More than anything else, the spirit of the times brought the mental health professions face-to-face with the necessity of developing new programs to meet chronically unmet needs, and, above all, with its professional and ethical responsibility to the community as a whole.

Clinical psychology in the 1960s, in addition to responding to the pressures for change being directed at the mental health professions as a whole, was simultaneously dealing with a second crisis, a crisis most aptly termed an identity crisis. This identity crisis was the natural result of a developmental process wherein clinical psychology, from almost the very moment of its birth, was both dependent upon, and ultimately scornful of, the field of psychiatry. No profession, especially one whose parentage is in doubt and whose development was accompanied by the chaos of having to function as an adult too soon, can long endure without a viable sense of self. Now in the 1960s, clinical psychology, perhaps spurred on by the movements for independence and freedom taking place all around it, left its childhood (and its father) to seek an identity of its own; an identity freed from second-class citizenship and its attendant ancillarly existence.

In summary, then, clinical psychology in the 1960s, both as a part of the mental health professions and in response to its own needs to develop a meaningful and independent identity, was seeking new directions. To be sure, the search is far from over, and it is still too early to assess the long-term effects of current social crises on the changing practices or identity of clinical psychology. But some things are fairly clear. Born as a war psychology, clinical psychology in the 1960s was still developing in the context of upheaval. Only now the setting for conflict had shifted from foreign soil to our own native land. The war was now against poverty, racism, sexism, and those forces and institutions which were depriving a significant number of our citizens (and by implication, us as well) from full and rightful participation in society. The same sociopolitical process which had produced instant mental health workers in the 1940s, and silent psychotherapists in the 1950s, was now creating the conditions and making it imperative for clinical psychology to begin to explore, and become a part of the world of the action sixties — and the disquieting years that would follow.

REFERENCES

Albee, G. W. *Mental Health Manpower Trends.* New York: Basic Books, 1959.
Eisenberg, L. "If Not Now, When?" *American Journal of Orthopsychiatry.* 32 (1962).
Eysenck, H. J. "The Effects of Psychotherapy: An Evaluation." *Journal of Consulting Psychologists.* 16 (1952).
Gordon, Jesse E. "Counseling the Disadvantaged Boy." In William E. Amos and Jean Dresden Grambs, Eds., *Counseling the Disadvantaged Youth.* Englewood Cliffs: Prentice-Hall, Inc., 1968.
Hollingshead, A. B. and Redlich, F. *Social Class and Mental Illness.* New York: John Wiley & Sons, 1958.
Holmes, J. C. "The Philosophy of the Beat Generation." In S. Krim (ed.), *The Beats.* Connecticut: Fawcett Publications, 1960.
Joint Commission on Mental Illness. *Action for Mental Health.* New York: Basic Books, 1961.
Kelly, J. G. "Ecological Constraints on Mental Health Services." *American Psychologist.* 21 (1966).
Kerovac, J. *The Subterraneans.* New York: Avon Publications, 1959.
Levine, M. "Some Postulates of Community Mental Health Practice." Prepublication report, Yale University, 1967.
Lipton, L. *The Holy Barbarians.* New York: Messner, 1959.
Meehl, P. E. "The Cognitive Activity of the Clinician." *American Psychologist.* 15 (1960).
Packard, V. *The Status Seekers.* New York: David McKay, 1959.
Rae-Grant, G. A.; Gladwin, T.; and Bower, E. M. "Mental Health, Social Competence, and the War on Poverty." *American Journal of Orthopsychiatry,* 1965.
Reiff, R. "Mental Health Manpower and Institutional Change." *American Psychologist.* 21 (1966).

Reisman, D.; Glazer, N.; and Denny, R. *The Lonely Crowd.* New Haven: Yale University Press, 1950.

Rubinstein, E. A. and Parloff, M. B. (eds.). *Research in Psychotherapy.* Washington, D.C.: American Psychological Association, Inc., 1959.

Sarason, S. B.; Levine, M.; Goldenberg, I.I.; Cherlin, D.; and Bennet, E. *Psychology in Community Settings: Clinical, Educational, Vocational, Social Aspects.* New York: Wiley & Sons, 1966.

Schlesinger, A. M., Jr. *A Thousand Days: John F. Kennedy in the White House.* Boston: Houghton-Mifflin, 1965.

Smith, M. B. and Hobbes, N. "The Community and the Community Mental Health Center." *American Psychologist.* 21 (1966).

Whyte, W. H., Jr. *The Organization Man.* New York: Doubleday, 1956.

Yolles, S. F. "The Role of the Psychologist in Comprehensive Community Mental Health Centers." *American Psychologist.* 21 (1966).

2

The Phenomenology of Action: An Unresolved Problem in Mental Health Intervention

I. Ira Goldenberg
Harvard University

We are deeds
You have left undone;
Strangled by doubt,
Spoiled ere begun.
         Henrik Ibsen

For an individual, to be "strangled by doubt" involves much more than the pain experienced upon suddenly finding oneself at the mercy of competing drives. It is also the inability (or unwillingness) to resolve the ensuing conflict in any way except through the exercise of "bad faith"; that is to say, by refusing to create oneself anew, and choosing, instead, to fall back on the least common denominator and determiner of available response – namely, tradition. Professions, no less than individuals, can be similarly strangled by doubt, and in the case of the helping professions, the strangulation has occurred over the meaning and interpretation of the concept of action.

As indicated in Chapter 1, the events of the 1960s placed squarely before this nation both the nature and extent of America's unfinished business. Poverty, racism, sexism and violence – in short, the myriad causes, manifestations and consequences of one or another form of growth-inhibiting oppression (both for the oppressed *and* the oppressors) had been laid before a public in ways and with an intensity previously either unknown or only dimly approximated. The data were clear, compelling, and hard. A significant proportion of America's citizenry was actively and consciously being prevented from exploring and realizing the full limits of their creative potential. In addition, those not *actively* a part of this preventing phenomenon were themselves being dehumanized by virtue of their unwitting participation in or nonresistance to the process that was destroying others. In both instances the effects on the human spirit were profound. For the poor as well as the affluent there was a loss of self, a feeling of rage coupled with powerlessness, and an overwhelming sense of futility, of being controlled and regulated by an oftentimes impersonalized system fast approaching "perfect madness." The decay of the cities was rivaled only by the barrenness of the suburbs; there was, indeed, at least some existential continuity between the numbing life in Appalachia and the empty one in Middle America. In both cases, the symptoms were almost classic: withdrawal (into drugs or some other form of chemical dissociation), violence (toward those either similarly oppressed or randomly selected as symbolic of the oppressors), and despair (the deep, unabating sense of the meaninglessness and arbitrariness of life).

25

And so, the stage was set. And the helping professions, whether they liked it or not, and whether they would have preferred to or not, found themselves at a point in time when they had little choice but to begin to respond to the social and political pressure that was emanating both from the community and from those liberation movements which had begun to gain momentum and visibility in the grief and guilt-ridden days that followed the assassination of President Kennedy. Amid cries for relevance, calls for rededication of energies, and the promulgation of a new mandate to create the Great Society, the helping professions emerged from their relative isolation and sought, often timidly and with more reluctance than we would now like to admit, to engage themselves in a world no longer content with being viewed from the relative comfort of the therapist's private office or endlessly studied from the antiseptic laboratory of the non-tax-paying university. The helping professions, which had for so long been involved in attempts to *study* and *understand* the human condition (often without being called upon either to make an impact upon it or to go beyond the rendering of assistance to individuals caught up in it), were now being asked to do something about *changing* that human condition. In short, whereas in years gone by clinicians had always been able to act privately, thereby putting themselves at the disposal of personal and professional history, they were now being pressured to act publicly, thus placing themselves at the disposal of social history.

However, the ability to shift from a basically private to a more-or-less public mode of dealing with the world and its problems requires much more than good will or external pressure. The successful transformation from private to public practice is predicated on a willingness to significantly change one's professional behavior and, in the process, to fundamentally change oneself. This process of change, always difficult even under the best of circumstances, was in the present instance further complicated by the fact that their previous life-style as private or individual entrepeneurs was neither dissatisfying nor unexciting both financially and professionally.

Ultimately, however, there was the question of *action*, what it meant, what it involved, and how it could be defined in ways that were clearly anchored in common perceptions and shared experiences. This was (and still is) the issue around which many potential helpers found themselves strangled by doubt, for, as we shall try to indicate in the pages that follow, it is an issue whose roots are inextricably embedded in the very fundamental human dilemma concerning the relative balance of man's responsibility to himself as contrasted with his obligation to other men.

The World of Action

Any analysis of the problem of action and the clinician must begin with the observation, admittedly overgeneralized, that there exists a persistent and as yet unresolved conflict between the traditional conception of what constitutes relevant and appropriate clinical behavior on the one hand, and the demand characteristics of the world of action on the other. The conflict we speak of takes many forms and has been argued on many different levels, but it invariably involves such questions as: whether or not it is appropriate that clinicians become directly involved in action settings (i.e., in settings not typically clinical in orientation, design, and leadership); whether or not our training or traditions have prepared us for such involvement; and, in the final analysis, whose agent we really are, the troubled individual's or the troubled society's?

Let us begin by assuming that the conflict is no longer a real one, that the relentless press of historical imperatives has taken the decision out of our hands, and that the question is no longer one of whether or not we wish to become involved but rather how we might effectively begin to re-tool our profession so that it can meet its new and shifting responsibilities in a society undergoing acute social change. We begin then with the assumption, as Krasner (1965) puts it, that the clinician has "no place to hide" and that he can no longer perpetuate those "professional myths behind which he can take refuge in denying role responsibility."

Perhaps the best way of approaching the problem would be to admit the fact that in trying to relate traditional conceptions of clinical behavior to the demand characteristics of social action we are really trying to forge an alliance between two phenomenologically different stances in the world. In other words, any structural analysis of the worlds of the clinician and the social activist would reveal important differences in attitudes, orientations, and, perhaps most significantly, fundamental differences in the modes and conceptions of relatedness deemed necessary for the attainment of certain ends. Action, for example, is above everything else a particular mode of being in relation to the world, a stance one assumes with respect to the exigencies of change. Phenomenologically, the world of action is a world of personal visibility, public risk, and unselfconscious partisanship — the kind of partisanship that is both scornful of neutrality and suspicious of compromise. Moreover, it is a world boardering on absolutes, where "winners" and "losers" are willingly pitted in battle, the ultimate outcome of each struggle being an incremental but concrete, observable, and measurable shift in power and resources. It is a Right Now! world, forever restless, often chaotic; a world whose basic dimensions are those of commitment, direct impact, and the unequivocal acceptance of responsibility. It is, in short, a condition of being in which there is an identity between one's own sense of incompleteness and the imperfections that define the human condition.

By contrast, the traditional world of the professional helper is a relatively quiet world, almost a tender one; a world in which two people meet, the silent agreement being that one will nourish the other's growth. The clinician does not seek, he is found; he does not impose, he enables; he does not dictate, he perseveres. When change occurs it is not usually characterized by volcanic eruptions;

rather, it unfolds organically, much like the blooming of a flower whose soil is rich and whose roots become stronger with the passage of time. It is a world unbounded by nonnegotiables and uncluttered by social history; a world where catastrophe is individualized and where man, no longer mythified as Everyman, reveals himself in all his subtlety and complexity. Under these conditions, where the nightmare is but a suicide away, movements become intrusions and causes become absurd.[a] The clinician's world, in short, is a world of personalized concern and self-conscious neutrality a world in which confrontation, precisely because of its awesome absolutistic implications, is handled with infinite care and practiced caution. Where a single life is the sole object of concern one does not deal with humanity in the abstract.

The consequences of living in two phenomenologically different worlds are amply reflected in the behavior of the social scientist. The clinician, for example, has always made clear the distinction between his role as a functioning professional and his role as a concerned private citizen: as a professional he is committed to helping an individual lead a fuller, more self-enhancing life independent of the shifting political and social realities that define the human condition as a whole; as a private citizen he may become engaged in causes or movements which seek to change those realities independent of the individuals involved. By so compartmentalizing his life he has been able to participate in what are, for all intents and purposes, two different worlds, and to participate in them without allowing the demand characteristics of one to alter the life style required by the other. It is a situation not unlike most human situations; a single human being lives in multiple worlds, worlds that often coexist in intention but are rarely fused in experience.

The Problem of Control and Power

But even beyond the philosophical (and perhaps almost mystical) issue concerning one's overall stance in and toward the world, there is the very concrete problem of *control*; and by control we mean the helper's ability to both define and determine the physical and psychological limits of his encounter with the individual or group needing help.

The power to "orchestrate" the helping situation has always resided with the credentialed professional. By both training and tradition, the professional

---

[a] Parenthetically, we might point out how difficult it is to examine however briefly, the world of the clinician without making referrence to what Camus (1959) has called the "one truly serious philosophical problem," the problem of suicide. It may well be this concern for the problem of suicide, coupled with clinical psychology's roots in the values and traditions of science, that has produced a profession which can still encourage, even demand, detachment and passivity in the midst of a relationship replete with the most personal and private of dynamisms.

has generally assumed the right to develop and implement the therapeutic context within which participants engage each other. Despite the fact that his own behavior in the situation is essentially passive in nature (i.e., restricted to offering certain specifically timed verbal interpretations and/or nonverbal feedback of some other kind), he retains and exercises virtual control over the essential variables governing the ongoing character of the interaction. Thus, for example, the time for each meeting, while sometimes open to limited negotiation, cannot regularly occur outside of certain clearly defined office hours. The place where the protagonists meet is not negotiable — it occurs on the helpers "turf," either in his office or in the institutional setting out of which he operates. Similarly, the cost factor (both financial and psychological) of each encounter is essentially regulated by the therapist. He (or she) determines what is manageable and tolerable for the client. It is in many ways a closed system; for once the client commits himself to the therapeutic relationship he relinquishes (most often quite willingly) any direct claim or access to the levers that will govern his future interactions with the helper.

Clearly related to the problem of control are the issues surrounding the exercise of *power*; and by power we mean the ability to summon and utilize all available resources for the purposes of maintaining and/or enhancing one's position and influence in a given situation. The professional helper is always in the preferred position with respect to the question of power, and whether he wishes to acknowledge that fact or not, the reality of the traditional therapeutic situation is such that his actions are rarely open to review (let alone change) during the treatment hour. Oftentimes the therapist's position of actual or perceived power is conceptualized as the very subject of treatment itself — as, for example, in the work of Haley (1971) — but this fact alone serves to highlight the degree to which the imbalance of the traditional helping situation has come to be accepted as part and parcel of the therapeutic context. Naturally, the manner in which the helper exercises his power, or the degree to which he recognizes and focuses attention on the philosophical implications of a situation in which equals meet as unequals is often used as a basis either for assessing the competence of an individual therapist or for differentiating one school of therapy from another. In all cases, however, what is accepted as assumptively true is a situation characterized by the unequal allocation and distribution of power.

At least two factors, in combination, account for the unequal allocation of power and control in the traditional helping situation. The first simply has to do with the fact that it is the client who must present himself to, and request help from, the therapist. As previously indicated, the therapist does not seek, he is found — and being found means that the initial decision to render help (to alleviate suffering, if you will) rests with the professional. His decision to help, to intervene in the life of someone who is at that moment experiencing profound personal distress, is indeed an extremely potent one. It is a decision which, for all its explicit humanity and caring, both defines and legitimizes a condition of ongoing encounters between symbolically unequal individuals. The second factor, perhaps related to the first, revolves around the lingering analogy between the kind of help that is made available through the psychotherapeutic situation and the help more generally associated with the clinical-medical setting. The latter situation is one in which we consciously and purposefully place ourselves in the doctor's hands. Phenomenologically, we turn ourselves over to the other, thus (at least temporarily) becoming objects to be ministered to or otherwise manipulated. The mystery surrounding our bodies couple with the aura surrounding the medical profession is sufficient to prepare us to willingly assume the dependent position. What further facilitates this volitional dependence is the fact that we do not generally define our interactions with the medical practitioner as constituting a relationship in the sense that we use the term to depict most of our other ongoing human encounters. Rather, we tend to view our being with the physician as a period of time characterized by clear and objective goals, goals which are primarily medical rather than psychological in nature. What is at stake is the integrity of the body, not the viability of our existential souls. Clearly however, and with far less objective data to justify or support the appropriateness of the carryover, we tend to view and enter into the psychotherpeutic situation with similar attitudes and behavioral expectations. The client is "sick" and the therapist is "healthy" (not to mention perceived as equipped with a set of mystifying skills somewhat comparable to those possessed by the medical practitioner). Consquently, the client is prepared, both socially and personally, to assume the position of the dependent patient. Irrespective of the important relational differences that distinguish the psychotherapeutic situation from the physical-medical situation, the client approaches his treatment fully ready to relinquish much of the power and control that he would normally regard as important (if not sacred) in many other human relationships.

However, once the professional helper leaves his office or usual place of business and enters, as it were, the community, he often loses much of the power and control he has been able to exercise and command as part of his traditional mode of operation. To begin with, he is no longer on his own turf, nor can he often successfully transform the new and relatively unfamiliar community settings in which he is forced to operate into the older, more comfortable ones he has left behind. Community Action Agencies are not mental hospitals, Citizens Advisory Groups do not stand still long enough to be studied in the fashion of undergraduate students in laboratory-based social psychology experiments, and Neighborhood Youth Corps enrollees rarely abide by the rules that govern the behavior of clients who present themselves for treatment to therapists in private offices. Both the clients and settings are significantly different from the ones the professional helper has become accustomed to in the past. What is more, they rarely show any interest in accommodating themselves to the needs or expectations of the helper. Rather, the reverse is often the case and, psychological interpretations aside, it is the helper who must perform and produce before an oftentimes cynical and impatient consumer or community group. One need only read the work of Hersch (1972) to begin to appreciate the problems encountered by mental health professionals who attempt to work with neighborhood groups, especially those grass roots organizations which take the concept of community control seriously. Furthermore, the credentialed helper who chooses to become engaged in the world of action often finds himself involved in settings where the dynamics of federal, state, and local bureaucratic traditions are at least as strong, pervasive, and influential as those of his own professional traditions — and, like the client in the therapeutic situation, he may finally begin to experience (albeit unwillingly) the essence of being powerless and dependent.

Thus it is that participation in the "outside world" — especially if that participation is going to be productive and meaningful — confronts the professional with the need to rethink the dimensions and implications of the concepts of control and power. This is especially true since one's entrance into the community often coincides with a cancellation of one's exclusive policy to unilaterally orchestrate both the structure and content of the helping situation.

The Problem of Skills

In a very real sense the professional helper's power and control in the traditional helping situation is derived from a public acceptance of the usefulness of his *skills* and the exclusive manner in which he possesses and exercises those skills. This "mystification of the profession," independent of hard data supporting (or challenging) either the validity of those presumed skills or the legitimacy of the ensuing process of canonization, is certainly an important factor in understanding the degree to which the helping professions have assumed such a prominent and prestigious place in our society. This is, of course, especially true in the private sector of the economy; that is to say, among those who both have the means and have already been socialized to view and accept the professional and his skills as something special. Thus, in a manner of speaking, one might view the world of action (the public sector of the economy as it were) as somehow lagging behind the rest of society in terms of participation in the process through which the skills of the professional helper have become the object of veneration. This phenomenon, coupled with the kinds of issues that present themselves to professionals who begin to work in the hitherto unfamiliar world of nontraditional community settings, can prove highly unsettling if not downright ego-deflating. But one way or another, it raises anew the question of the kinds of skills needed to function effectively in public settings.

At the present time there are two general areas of involvement available to professionals who elect to work in action settings. The professional helper can choose to become involved in the direct provision of services to clients, or he can assume broader planning, programatic, and/or administrative responsibilities.

The important thing to point out, however, is that in neither instance are the skills required for effective performance identical with (or, at times, even directly related to) the kinds of skills which the private practitioner brings with him to the work situation. In other words, while it is undoubtedly true that the mystification of the skills attributed to the helping professions has raised those professions to a position of some prominence in the general field of human renewal, it is also true that the particular and traditional skills with which the clinician is equipped are not ipso facto of the sort that would allow one to predict (with any certainly) a high probability of success once the behavioral context has shifted from the private office or university to the community. But let us be more specific.

If, for example, the professional chooses to become engaged in providing direct services, it is quite likely that he will not long be able to get away with a pattern of being with the client that is essentially (if not exclusively) passive, analytic, and/or reflective in nature. Even the most clinical of one-to-one relationships in many community settings are governed by the rhetoric (and often the reality) of advocacy — and by advocacy is meant the process by which the helper does much more than merely listen to and interpret the client's verbalizations: he (the helper) must be prepared to actively engage himself in the client's problems and the client's world, to advocate, as it were, for the client's rights be it in the schools, with the Welfare Department, or on the job. Simply put, an advocacy relationship, predicated as it is on the assumption that a client's problems are not solely in his head, but are, indeed, in large part the result of malfunctioning social institutions, makes it imperative that the helper join directly with the client in actively combating or otherwise intervening in those situations where institutional unresponsiveness is contributing to the client's hardships. Thus, in many important ways, an effective advocacy relationship requires helping behaviors which are certainly not of the usual kind, and it is more than possible that the traditionally-trained professional (at least when he first enters the world of action) possesses neither the skills nor the overall orientation essential to such a relationship.

If, on the other hand, as is so often the case, the professional finds himself either volunteering or being called upon to design and administer a program of help, he is again faced with a situation in which there is no clear-cut correlation between his prior training and the demands of the job. Indeed, if there is one area in which the helping professions have not distinguished themselves it is in the development and implementation of effective and responsive mental health delivery systems. The particular skills and perspectives required of the planner and the administrator — skills such as community analysis, the evaluation of existing and potential resources, the coordination of services, budget preparation, the development of political and community constituencies, the negotiation of a viable organizational framework, etc. — have never entered into the process by which clinicians have been trained. If anything, the professional preparation of clinical practioners has made it a point to steer clear of such issues, preferring to view such experience as at best ancillary to the clinical enterprise and at worst downright interfering with the objectives of the therapeutic relationship. But be that as it may, the reality of the situation is that the professional helper who enters the world of community action in a planning or administrative position currently does so with little preparation and even less experience.

Clearly, the situations described above are almost guaranteed to produce feelings of conflict, anxiety, and uncertainty in professionals who seek to transform themselves from private into public practitioners. On the one hand they may be perceived (at times even by the most militant and vocal of consumer groups) as people possessing secret or magical skills which, if and when applied, will significantly and positively alter the conditions under which people live. On the other hand they cannot avoid the experience of some form of culture shock: the gradual if not sudden awareness that their skills are either inappropriate to the problems they are called upon to deal with or, even worse, nonexistent with respect to the roles they may be expected to assume. The danger here, of course, is that the professional, faced with the need to fulfill conflicting demands and expectations (both his own and those of the people around him) in this decidedly new and unfamiliar situation, will succumb to the tendency to fall back on his repertoire of traditional behaviors. By so doing, he often attempts to turn the new situation into what for him is a more comfortable one, one much more like the kinds of situations he has experienced in the past. This process of "retransformation" often does little but further exacerbate an already difficult situation. For the professional helper it results in a semblance of immediate personal security at the expense of long-range growth; for the community it results in the illusion of increased clinical service, albeit of the kind previously found wanting. In both cases what remains essentially unexamined (and unchanged) are the issues surrounding both the definition and development of the skills required to enhance community self-sufficiency.

The Problem of Ideology

We come now to what may in the final analysis turn out to be the most important and least understood problem of all. And yet, for all its ambiguity, the problem of ideology is probably the fundamental issue confronting professionals who seek to begin to relate themselves to community settings. It is, at least from our point of view, the issue which, depending upon its final resolution, ultimately determines both the form and content of the professional's behavior in the world of action.

For purposes of the present discussion we shall define ideology as the specific dimensions around which an individual chooses to organize his perceptions of the social world so as to form a personally meaningful sense of the broader causes and consequences of specific human problems. Put somewhat differently, it is the overall socio-political framework within which one interprets the essential meaning of social events and through which one defines the existential limits of one's own response to those events. Thus, in the final analysis, the problem of ideology involves much more than "simple" politics or "pure" philosophy; one's ideology serves as the conceptual bridge between one's analysis of the human condition and one's actions in and toward that condition.

Given the definition developed here, it would appear important that we begin to examine very carefully the particular ideology implicit in and attendant to the theories and practices of the helping professions. It is important that we do so for at least two reasons. First, because we must begin to understand the relationship between the manner in which professionals are trained and the ways in which they ultimately come to view the human condition; and second, because nowhere are the consequences of a particular kind of ideological conditioning more readily apparent than in the attitudes and behaviors of professionals who seek to become involved in community settings.

By and large the professional helper enters the world of action with an ideological set which Levine and Levine (1969) have termed "intrapsychic supremacy." The doctrine of intrapsychic supremacy holds that an individual's problems, independent of the social realities and options which define the limits of his existence, are essentially "in his head." Moreover, it views the problem of change (and, by implication, the only legitimate role of the professional) as somehow involving the process by which "one's head gets straightened out," hopefully in a manner so as to enable the individual to become more acutely aware of the ways in which his feelings and beliefs have been the major source of his difficulties. Most importantly, however, the doctrine of intrapsychic supremacy, predicated as it is on the assumption of psychological causality, assigns primary responsibility – "original sin," if you will – to the deceptive and often devious machinations of the human mind. Thus, while members of the helping professions may indeed "know" at some deeply personal level that most of the "individual deficits" they are called upon to deal with are both symbolic and symptomatic of an oppressive social fabric, their built-in professional armamentarium is composed of clinical conceptions and orientations which invariably lead them to treat these deficits as if their authorship resided solely in the persons (i.e., client's) experiencing the difficulty (Goldenberg and Keatinge 1973).

The ultimate expression of the doctrine of intrapsychic supremacy is the practice of what Ryan (1970) has called "Blaming the Victim." Ideologically, the process of blaming the victim rests on an exceptionalist analysis of social arrangements. According to Ryan,

> Such arrangements imply that problems occur to specially-defined categories of persons in an predictable manner. The problems are unusual, even unique, they are exceptions to the rule, they occur as a re-

sult of individual defect, accident, or unfortunate circumstances and
must be remedied by means that are particular and, as it were, tailored
to the individual case. (1971, p.17)

Even more importantly, the ideology of blaming the victim invariably sanctions
and gives intellectual legitimacy to forms of help (e.g., interventions of an exclusively individual or small group psychotherapeutic nature) which seek to reduce or eliminate individual deviance under the assumption that deviation from
existing behavioral norms and societal standards are instances of failed or incomplete socialization. Thus, in a variety of often gentle but equally perverse ways,
the ideology of blaming the victim can serve what Ryan calls the "dominant interests of society by principally functioning to block social change." This occurs,
for example, when we treat what are called social problems, such as poverty, disease, crime, civil disorder, and mental illness, in terms of the individual deviance
of the special, unusual groups of people who have and/or manifest those problems. Ryan summarizes both the pervasiveness and implications of the blaming
the victim mentality in the following manner:

> In defining social problems in this way, the social pathologists are, of
> course, ignoring a whole set of factors that ordinarily might be consider-
> ed relevant — for instance, unequal distribution of income, social stratifi-
> cation, political struggle, ethnic and racial group conflict, and inequality
> of power. Their ideology concentrates almost exclusively on the failure
> of the deviant. To the extent that society plays any part in social prob-
> lems, it is said to somehow failed to socialize the individual, to teach
> him how to adjust to circumstances, which, though far from perfect, are
> gradually changing for the better. (1971, p. 14)

Another, perhaps more subtle but no less important aspect of the problem
of ideology revolves around the helping profession's commitment to the concept
of self-actualization as opposed to self-determination. And while the implications
of this distinction may not at first be readily apparent, it is, at least in our opinion, of sufficient importance to warrant some special attention. Basically, the
problem is again one of focus and emphasis, and again some explanation is necessary.

By and large, the clinically-oriented therapeutic interventions utilized by
most professional helpers are derived from the theories that have been developed
for and about white, middle-class populations. Historically, this has meant dealing with problems properly defined as self-actualization in nature; that is to say,
problems having to do with the individual's attempts to fully realize his or her
creative potential. However, focusing therapeutic attention on the "full-flowering
of one's essential humanity" implies (and quite rightly so) that the individual
client already possesses some control over the social and economic resources

through which this humanity seeks to express itself. Moreover, it also implies that in a host of very important and fundamental ways the client already experiences himself (or herself) to be a human being who has a definite stake in, concern for, and place within the total societal process (Goldenberg 1966). That this is simply not the case for people who are poor and/or black (or are members of some other socially or economically oppressed minority) is by now an accepted if only dimly appreciated fact of life. Thus, it has only been recently, primarily through the work of Cloward (1965) and Reiff (1966), that the helping professions have become aware of the lack of fit between traditional self-actualization oriented therapeutic practices and the concrete needs of people who are either poor or similarly disenfranchised. Put another way, problems and ideas concerning self-actualization are almost a luxury to people who are dealing daily with issues of survival, people whose prime concerns revolve around gaining (let alone maintaining) some minimal sense of economic and social viability. Rather, as Reiff (1966) has pointed out, the disenfranchised are dealing with problems more accurately defined as self-determination in focus and in origin; that is to say, problems of gaining a modicum of control and power over the institutional resources that have heretofore either been denied them or been used in ways that guaranteed their continued subjugation.

The problem, of course, of the professional's exclusive ideological commitment to the concept of self-actualization, is that it can result in practices that continue to blame the victim, however different and dignified the rhetoric. Similarly it can lead to a form of help which, either wittingly or unwittingly, serves to further alienate the professional from the client. In part, this is due to the professional's belief — directly derived from his acceptance of self-actualization as the universal goal of all people, independent of their particular social and eco‑ nomic circumstances — that somehow, in some vague, unspecified, almost mystical manner, the truly healthy person will naturally and with little difficulty deal with the problems of survival on his own. Traditionally trained (and conditioned) professional helpers, for all their exposure to the dark and brooding passions that supposedly lurk within the human spirit, remain incorrigible and splendid optimists. For them, there is virtually nothing that the man (or woman) whose "head is together" cannot accomplish. A productive and well-paying job? No problem at all for the person who has learned how to cope. The demonstrated racism and sexism behind industry and organized labor's exclusionary policies? A mere inconvenience to the person who has begun to resolve his inner conflicts. The lack of quality education, or the absence of truly equitable and viable avenues for the redress of historic grievances? Little difficulty for the person who has his "shit together." In short, the heroic view that most professional helpers have of man's infinite capacity to actualize himself makes it virtually unnecessary for the therapeutic or educational process to address itself to questions of survival in any direct or central manner. The ideology is as clear as it is ultimately self-defeating: the healthy man can fend for himself — or so say those whose relative comfort makes personal heroism unnecessary.

We have tried in this chapter to describe some of the issues and problems that confront the helper who seeks to become meaningfully engaged in the world of action. Some of the problems are certainly external in nature; that is to say, a part of and endemic to that mosaic of interlocking interests we call the community. Others, however, cannot be attributed to seemingly uncontrollable factors in the external world: they are part and parcel of the helping professions themselves. Consequently, they may be even more difficult to deal with, for they are intimately connected with our own professional identities, the certification processes to which we have been subjected, and the training rituals through which we have willingly passed. Ultimately, the degree to which the helping professions become a viable part of the struggles for liberation that will continue to characterize our society will in large part depend on the honesty with which we are able to deal with the contradictions that define our own lives both as professionals and as citizens. The primary purpose of this chapter was to begin to define some of the dimensions of those contradictions. In the chapters that follow we shall see how a variety of different helping professionals sought to deal with them.

REFERENCES

Camus, A. *The Myth of Sysyphus and Other Essays.* New York: Vintage Books, 1959.

Cloward, R.A. Poverty, Power, and the Involvement of the Poor. Testimony before the Senate Select Subcommittee on Poverty. Washington, D.C., June 29, 1965.

Goldenberg, I.I. "Psychotherapy: Its Underlying Assumptions and Possible Modification." Paper presented at the Meetings of the American Psychological Association, New York, 1966.

Goldenberg, I.I. and Keatinge, E. "Businessmen and Therapists: Prejudices Against Employment." *Journal of Contemporary Drug Problems,* 1973.

Haley, J. *The Power Tactics of Jesus Christ.* New York: Avon Books, 1971.

Hersch, C. "Social History, Mental Health and Community Control." *American Psychologist* 27, 8 (1972).

Krasner, L. "The Behavioral Scientist and Social Responsibility: No Place To Hide." *Journal of Social Issues* 21, 2 (1965).

Levine, M. and Levine, A. *A Social History of Helping Services: Clinic, Court, School and Community.* New York: Appleton-Century-Croft, 1969.

Reiff, R. "Mental Health Manpower and Institutional Change." *American Psychologist* 21 (1966).

Ryan, W. *Blaming the Victim.* New York: Random House, 1971.

Part II

Case Studies in Community Action and Social
Intervention: Experiences, Reflections, and
Analyses

3 From Old Mythologies

Thomas W. Mahan
The Citadel

[Editor's Note] : *The use of busing as a means of achieving racial integration and/or quality education remains an essentially unresolved and conflict-ridden issue. Emotions continue to run high, and many people (both black and white, "liberal" and "conservative") have suddenly found themselves allied with others, with whom on other days and with respect to most other issues, they would have little in common. This chapter concerns the development, in 1966, of the nation's first city-to-suburb busing project involving inner-city youngsters. Thomas W. Mahan was the project's first director. In order to implement the project, he left what he describes as his "enjoyable life-style" at the University of Hartford, where he was then a professor of education. In part, his chapter deals with the concerns and conflicts that surrounded even the earliest plans and attempts to bus children from one school to another. Clearly, those concerns and conflicts have not diminished with the passage of time.*

I had made a reasonably comfortable adjustment to my return to the academic world. As an associate professor in the Department of Special Education at Boston University, I had the opportunity to pursue my clinical inclinations by serving as co-director of a very exciting psycho-educational clinic; at the same time I was able to enjoy the life style of a professor who moved comfortably among ideas and theories, had the stimulation of student contact, and obtained considerable satisfaction in the conviction that what he was doing was helpful to some children in particular and to society in general. There were the frustrations that go with faculty status; there remained the desperate sense of futility that colored all faculty meetings, but at the same time there was growing awareness that much could be done if one merely went about and did it and ignored some of the formal mechanisms of academia. And so it was professionally a comfortable life with the prospects of research and writing on the immediate horizon. Into that context there came a telephone call that was the harbinger of a dramatic change in my status.

A call came from Hartford, Connecticut. At the other end of the line was Dr. Alexander J. Plante, then the executive director of the Office of Departmental Planning. The Connecticut State Department of Education, and Sandy Plante's voice boomed across the telephone line to Boston with this message: "Tom, you said if I ever needed you in Hartford, that all I need do is call and you would come. I'm calling." It was true that I had made some such statement to Sandy as I fled from the bureaucracy of the State Department of Education to where I thought the action could be — to the university. I am uncertain now as to why I had made such a pact, but in retrospect it seems to me that I was trying to say to Sandy, "Thanks for being a colleague and a friend." Now I was startled and his statement struck me in a piercing fashion.

In spite of the anxiety into which I was plunged by Sandy Plante's initial comment, I was also flattered that he would think of me for some task as yet undefined. And as I mumbled something into the telephone, he began to explain in more detail what he had in mind. Sandy had undertaken the task of developing a school integration plan that was novel in many respects. Essentially it called for the placement of black and Spanish-speaking youth from Hartford's inner city into upper-middle-class suburban white classrooms. And it called for this to be done on a random basis so that there might be some research data to support the hypothesis which would be a major focus of the soon to be released "Coleman Report"; namely, that the achievement climate of the classroom is a major determinant of the achievement level of those placed in that classroom.

As the skeleton of the plan came to me through the telephone, I was immediately excited by the idea, but frightened by the prospect. It seemed clear to me that there really was no reason why I should be chosen to direct such an undertaking. It was true that I was concerned (and had been for a number of years) with how children learn and how youngsters who had been having difficulty in learning could be helped. It was also true that I had been involved only a few years earlier in the development of legislation for Connecticut children who could be classified as "disadvantaged." But my sphere of involvement had been that of a consultant, that of a person involved in the ideological aspects rather than the operational ones. Now the demand was for an operational leader and Dr. Plante was making his request of me in direct fashion.

My response, evolving from both anxiety and pride, ran like this: "I'll come if you need me, but it will be necessary that I clear this with the university and also I will need some assurance that the black and Spanish-speaking communities in Hartford will accept me." In a sense, those conditions were reassuring, because it seemed to me unlikely that either, never mind both, could be met. My contacts with the black community had been that of a typical white liberal professor. I had a few black friends, but most of them were professionals also. I had had some limited involvement in projects that touched on the black and Spanish-speaking communities, but I would have been the last to consider myself knowledgeable about the dynamics of these neighborhoods. And yet the die was cast and it fell to me to get clearance from the university while Sandy would arrange for my introduction to Hartford's black neighborhoods.

The university reaction came swiftly. It was helped a great deal by the fact that Boston, too, was thinking about a similar plan (called METCO). As the approval came through without a hitch I was jarred that much closer to the reality with the thought that my whole training in clinical school psychology and special education might be totally inadequate to the task. I spent hours conjuring up images of the demands of the role and the images that arose again and again were those of administrator, counselor, politician, and researcher. And even this last in which I felt most comfortable caused considerable trembling because I was well aware that the arena in which research would take place was one where the voice of professional concern would have to be balanced against other, more insistent voices.

And so it was in that frame of mind that I journeyed down to Hartford in April 1966 to be "interviewed." Sandy Plante met me and we went to lunch with two members of Hartford's black community. One was a sensitive, intelligent driving woman dedicated to exerting all her energies toward gaining as much as possible for her people; the other was an equally intelligent man whose style was much more shrewd and realistic. Both Mrs. Gertrude Johnson and Mr. William Brown, my two interviewers, asked few questions. Rather, they let me talk and they listened to Dr. Plante. At the conclusion of the session, I was uncertain as to their reaction. Somehow I felt that they had been searching me out very carefully; the criteria for their decision were unclear to me. I was convinced that my naiveté was obvious. I had some reservations as to how much my deep philosophical commitment to the project mattered to them or how impressed they were by my faith in the human being's ability to learn and adapt. I went back to Boston somewhat shaken by the episode and wondering what the outcome would be. Sandy had assured me that things had gone very well, but I suspected that it was his enthusiasm that colored his perception.

It was only a short time later that I heard that I was acceptable, but never did I learn why this was so. As I think about it now, it seems to me that there were probably basic criteria that I satisfied: (1) I was a person in whom Alexander Plante had faith and he was willing to "guarantee" my performance; (2) I brought the requisite respectability (academic, that is) which the project needed if it was going to gain the support of superintendents of schools, board of education members, and the media. Those, I suspect, were the real bases for my selection as director of Project Concern. They flowed much more directly from my reputation than from my training. In fact, it seems that areas of expertise and training were considered to be almost irrelevant, that very pragmatic guidelines established my acceptability. This is a somewhat sobering thought and it was one that escaped me in the excitement of the moment.

Throughout the spring months, Dr. Plante had remained as the spear of the project. He had developed a prospectus; he had gained supporters and he had made enemies. But he had also done what many had considered impossible; he had brought the idea to reality. As June came, five suburban boards of education had agreed to participate with the city of Hartford in the program. There had been vehement discussions in each of these suburbs, but in the last analysis an affirmative vote had been taken and the contract drawn. In a sense, the program was a simple-minded one. It avoided any conscience-seering questioning of the philosophical bases of the public school system; it took the present status and accepted the fact that many youth (particularly black and Spanish-speaking youngsters in the Northeast) were not obtaining equality of educational opportunity. And it looked for a strategy whereby the inequality of educational opportunity might be decreased. It accepted as prima facie evidence the unsatisfactory results of compensatory programs, half-hearted though they might have been, in either their conception or their funding. But it took in equal prima facie fashion the evidence of learning that the inner-city child shows in his daily living and moved from that basis to the conviction that he could show a similar degree of learning within the formal context of the school if he were placed in a situa‧tion that stimulated him in that direction.

There were a number of objections raised to the Project Concern approach to dealing with this issue. Some of these objections were openly bigoted; others stemmed from deep human concern. Each objection placed a further constraint upon the development of the project itself. For example, the objection that the problem was Hartford's and not that of its neighbors brought with it the requirement that Hartford find a way of providing financial support not only for the actual cost of the program, but also for a tuition charge for each pupil accepted which would result in a healthy net profit for the suburban community. In similar fashion, the research questions were broadened to encompass a number of areas that were voiced as concerns by those who either resisted or doubted. It was into this process of give and take, into a developing struggle of who would control the project that I came.

I struggled through the early summer session at Boston University, making occasional trips to Hartford, and then, as the summer session ended, terminated my responsibilities there. Suddenly it was August and the opening of school was only a few weeks away — yet nothing had been really accomplished beyond the political miracle of obtaining the previously described agreement from the five suburban boards of education. The youngsters who would be going into the grades (K-5) had yet to be selected and all of the mechanics of getting them there had yet to be designed. In a sense, two quite different problems pressed immediately upon me: (1) how to develop the theoretical framework and research design so as to achieve credibility and respectibility; and (2) how to cope with the political realities and the logistical problems that demanded resolution if the program was to become operational. And hovering in the background there was a third concern which Dr. Plante of the State Department of Education had agreed to monitor, but which could not be ignored — the quest for funding. With the program about to begin, with staff coming on the payroll, with contracts signed for tuition agreements and transportation, it was still unclear whether the verbal assurances received from Washington for federal support would be translated into official documents.

Nonetheless, life goes on and an early lesson for me was one that insisted on action in the face of obstacles rather than on a sequential, logical process. I suppose that in an ideal world it would make more sense to have financial resources before making fiscal commitments (yet I suspect my personal style of living on the expectations of the future is not uncommon), but this was not an ideal world. Either we began the operation or it would be too late; to wait for assurance was to doom the entire program. And so the staff was employed — and once again the crude realities were in the forefront. It was getting later by the day and staff who could break free in time had become increasingly scarce. Thus, competence was but one of a number of criteria that had to be considered, and the foremost criteria had to be availability, willingness to take a chance on the program, and some degree of ethnic mixing.

As these decisions were made in the hot, stuffy 10' x 10' office (begged from a neighborhood center) that was to house the seven members of the central office staff, the dimensions of my task began to come into focus. The following areas demanded my immediate attention: (1) planning the random selection of participants; (2) developing the plan for data collection; (3) developing the research design; (4) providing staff orientation and training; (5) evolving policy in regard to placement, assessment, and intervention issues; (6) planning the procedures for parental contact; (7) planning the bus routes; (8) responding to parental concerns and questions; (9) responding to teacher concerns and questions; (10) neutralizing the political issues; (11) providing emotional and/or professional support for staff; (12) managing the fiscal aspects; and, (13) dealing with public relations and media. The first five of these tasks seemed to fall directly within my area of training, but even here I quickly learned that my preconceptions had to be modified by variables which fell beyond my control. For example, the rigors of a sample selected randomly from all pupils (K-5) who were in Hartford public schools with 85 percent or more nonwhite population had to be modified such that intact classes were randomly selected rather than individuals. This tactic became necessary when it was decided that a certified teacher would accompany every twenty-five youngsters going out to a community so that additional professional support would be available if needed. By selecting intact classes it was expected that Hartford teachers would therefore be released from prior responsibilities and a pool established from which such teachers could be assigned to the suburban systems. (As it turned out, there were a number of flaws in this argument, but these again became known after the fact.) And then there was the ever present political sensitivity — the need to emphasize again and again credibility; consequently, members from the black and Spanish-speaking communities were involved as participants in the initial use of the tables of random numbers for selecting the classrooms.

But I had no such sense of professional competence when it came to some of the very important and very basic responsibilities such as maximizing the probability that the parent of a randomly selected youngster would agree to have the child participate or planning bus routes such that youngsters would not find themselves spending an inordinate amount of their lives on the bus and the schools would find them arriving at an acceptable time for class. Somehow these problems were dealt with, and by drawing upon the ideas and knowledge of others many were dealt with effectively. In this fashion, 96 percent of the youngsters who were chosen in the random selection were allowed to participate by their parents. Also, in an area which may seem of little importance in retrospect, but which haunted us day and night in the initial weeks of the project, a plan was evolved which required no Hartford youngster to spend more time on a bus than did many of the suburban youngsters while traveling within their own community. But probably the greatest demand on the program — and one which continued to be great throughout the two year experimental phase — was that for open communication and responsiveness. There was fear on all sides; Hartford minority children were frightened, not knowing how they would be received or how they should react; suburban teachers were frightened — uncertain as to whether they could be successful in teaching "these" children; suburban parents were frightened — some of them worried about what might happen to their children, others worried about what might happen to the Hartford children. In this climate of fear rumors bred rapidly and inquiries were constant. It was immediately obvious that every question, every inquiry, every concern had to be treated quickly and sincerely. That became a goal designed to give a sense of coherence to the operation and a philosophical climate to the project. It seemed to be the natural thing in light of the title which had been selected for the program — Project Concern.

Two years as the director of Project Concern in its initial development, in its implementation, and in its further growth leaves many marks. Above all else there is the sense of exhilaration that comes from this involvement, and the awareness that probably never again will there be the professional satisfaction that arose from this opportunity. But there is another side to this coin also; there is the aspect of the need to seriously question the professional training and resulting self-concept which were at most moments a mixed blessing. I like to see myself (and did then as well) as a student of human behavior, as one much interested in knowing about and learning about how institutions and individuals interact. Over the years, like anyone else, I have developed some hypotheses about this whole field and some intuitions as to how individuals and institutions can assist each other in their own growth processes. In many ways, this self-perception was a definite asset in the performance of my duties as a project director. Lying behind the list of all of the responsibilities which I had, there remained three basic functions which I served: I was a catalyst; I was an advocate; I was a channel of communication. Over the years I had been taught — and then taught myself further — how important it was to observe behavior and to observe it carefully. I suspect that this prepared me for the role of a listener, for being one who could hear the fears and anguishes of others that lay behind their words and attempt to deal with this more relevant, more personal communication. It was a short step from that operation to one where I became a kind of interpreter, an individual who attempted to make people available to each other. But the next step seemed to me the dangerous one — the step from becoming an interpreter to becoming a spokesman. And it was here that I have the greatest reservations about the professional preparation that we as psychologists have received in terms of the demands of the role. In the advocate role it seems easy to forget one's constituency and to move toward becoming the advocate of one's own beliefs and aspirations and desires. The dogmatism of science (and the theories that arise from science) intrude themselves quickly upon a methodological approach which is essentially nondogmatic and basically open to modifications based upon new observations.

Yet I have seen in myself some of the signs of a willingness to become a social engineer rather than a catalyst and an advocate. It is so much faster, and frequently so much easier, to bring about change directly rather than to assist others to work through a situation for which they ultimately will take responsibility. This fear has been intensified by a number of encounters with other professionals who are willing to judge this project (or any other project) on what *they know* the people served really want. My own conviction is that my level of success was related directly to my ability to observe and listen, to find cues which made possible the bringing about of dialogue among desperate groups and to avoid taking on the cloak of a Messiah. Perhaps there is a better way to put this aspect of a director's function: to the extent that I was able to learn, I was able to be effective. The arena of operation was instantly that of human sensitivities and expectations with the realities and distortions that that brings. The ultimate task was one of organizing the human element so that individuals who had had years of experience in confronting service agencies that were impersonal, unresponsive, and inflexible would *not* find themselves now facing a similar institution equally impersonal, unresponsive, and inflexible, but perhaps a little bit more benevolent.

From this perspective psychology seems to me the ideal training ground in which to develop administrative leaders. Unfortunately there seems to be in the traditional training program a number of tendencies that may serve to block this sort of development. Most important among them is the tendency to develop ideological allegiances and perhaps even ideological purity, an inclination to equate objectivity with uninvolvement and impersonality, and a reluctance to take the responsibility for action that cannot be supported from an adequate data base. In other words, it is my fear that we may be training for the social action arena eunuchs, useful perhaps as consultants but impotent in the face of the crises of human living where they have to be willing to reveal themselves as persons investing in an experience.

Equally inadequate are some of the golden calves of the scientific tradition. In Project Concern, for example, the research design and the final statistical results possessed great symbolic significance. But their actual impact on action was extremely limited. The research data provided a basis of support for believers, but it seems to have had little efficacy in terms of conversions. Rather, conversions seem to come about from the actual living experiences of people who saw and observed — and even this experience was not free from distortion. This discovery brings to the psychologist or to any other professional a much more healthy and realistic appreciation of the role of power. Perhaps the most critical area for observation and analysis of social reality in terms of social action programs is that of power: the locus of power, and the use and abuse of power. This in no way suggests any deification of power; on the contrary, it emphasizes power as a dynamic, human phenomenon. It is no more magical or mystical than other human phenomena. Early in 1967 when we were first attempting to gain legislative support for our on-going Project Concern (support in terms of legislative sanction and fiscal resources), we drafted a bill and submitted it to the Connecticut General Assembly. The bill, we knew, would be a controversial one — after all, it advocated busing in a situation which would be threatening to many people who had recently fled from city life. In our naiveté we expected that we would easily gain the support of liberal legislators on the Education Subcommittee who might then rally for us support from other areas. Contrary to this hope, we found ourselves blocked by a few key legislators — known as "ultra-liberals" — whose objections were always technical rather than substantive. It took us some time to discover that our proposal ran counter to a prime concern of the leadership; namely, to avoid any new taxation. Once this knowledge was obtained, the strategy for implementation of the legislation shifted from one of working through liberal legislators who would be ideologically in favor of the program to demonstrating rather wide-spread support in critical voting areas to more conservative legislators who controlled the purse strings of the budget. In this fashion the ultimate goal — passage of Public Act 611 — was obtained without the martyrdom of the personal ambitions of liberal legislators who found themselves caught between their ideology and their loyalty. Again, the intent here is not to underestimate the rigidities of our institutional society, but rather to underline the pervasiveness of the human element and the necessity for maintaining flexibility and openness within one's own system.

As I walked down the stairs from my office carrying the last box of my personal materials in August of 1968 and terminated my formal relationship with Project Concern (the informal relationship continues vigorously even to this day), I found myself feeling a number of strange emotions. Among these were two that directly affected my professional career: first, there was a feeling that the formal training in the field of psychology needed a much clearer orientation toward practical application in the sphere of social action; and second, there was the conviction that the university ought to become the sponsor and stimulant for action in this direction. The feeling of weariness — the sense of just being tired — had begun to weigh heavily upon me for a number of months. And the desperate need for colleagues to whom one could turn for inspiration, for new ideas, and for support – both professional and personal – went unmet in the hurly-burly of daily activities. Still, all around me there were a number of universities, filled with professionals whose interests bordered upon mine, but who found themselves cut off from direct involvement. This struck me as the base from which relevant and adequate resources could be provided for the meeting of a number of our social needs in today's society. The university, so long the patron of learning, and the guardian of individual freedom, could now distinguish itself in a role that called for the implementation of both of these previous concerns. And so, feeling burned out, I fled back to the university, hoping for the opportunity both to recharge myself professionally and to continue the tasks which I had begun. This double aspiration led me toward accepting an administrative position in the university hierarchy in the belief that from such a vantage point it would be more possible to increase academia's involvement in the community, not in terms of obtaining funds nor in terms of using the community as a large research reservoir, but rather as a collaborator with the community in the joint learning process of discovering ourselves through interaction with others.

From this experience I have drawn a number of conclusions, but none of them really provide the basis for spelling out in detail and fashion what I feel an appropriate training program would be for the helping professions. I am convinced that the helping professions are burdened by needs that are neurotic themselves; I see us frequently engaging in activities that are designed to define us rather than to help others. And I suspect that the two most dangerous ailments of man in relation to other men are common to us: the danger of the doctrine of the immaculate perception and the assumption of omniscience. I think the time has come for psychologists to be as skilled in the observation of behavior as they are in the analysis of theories; to be as conversive with the complexities of their own inner workings as they are with the complexities of multivariate analysis; to be as open to learning as they are willing to teach. Yet, in no way do I wish to play down the importance of theories, of research skills, or of teaching. These are assets that bring a breadth and a discipline to methodology that is essential if it is to be effective. But somehow the humanity of the psychologist in relationship to mankind needs to have greater impact. The demands of today are for professionals willing to face real issues, not academic ones. Perhaps in the long run basic research in the area of behavior may have far reaching impact upon society and the profession – but at this moment the plea is for professionals who will help to assure that there is a long run. And these professionals must come as helpful persons – alert, perceptive, and imaginative – but these qualities will not be enough in themselves. To them must be added the courage to dream of what is possible for men generally or man individually, and the added courage to pursue that dream. This willingness to act, this bold plunge into risk taking, demands an even more vigorous sequence of experiences in the training process. It calls not only for a thorough knowledge and analysis of the literature, it calls not only for highly developed skills in terms of methodology, it calls not only for the ability to work with and through people; in addition, it demands that the psychologist be aware of himself as the instrument being used in this process. Somehow the training sequence must include not only the acquisition of knowledge and skills, not only the field testing of one's theories, but perhaps even more important, the opportunity to explore one's own behavior and its impact upon others in an atmosphere of both support and confrontation. From the old mythologies of the helping professional as the expert to whom one could turn for assistance we need to move to a new model where the psychologist is a naked explorer, a provocative adventurer calling upon wide knowledge and intense discipline in his collaborative quest for a goal. In this fashion, he can cast aside the garb of the magician, of the paternally guiding figure, or the devious, subversive observer and be what his field should teach him to be: an effective catalyst in an emotionally charged dialogue, an accurate and perceptive spokesman for those who desire one, a builder of channels of communication, and, above all else, the imaginative dreamer who constantly keeps in view (and forces others to do likewise) what is possible rather than what is probable in the realm of human behavior.

4

Prepping the Poor: The Yale Experience

Lawrence Paros
Alternate Learning Project

[Editor's Note:] *In this chapter, Lawrence Paros describes the efforts of a small group of educators — "kindred spirits", in Paros' terms — to develop an innovative educational setting for disadvantaged youth at one of the most prestigious and powerful universities in our country. He details, often in moving and eloquent terms, the problems that confront people who attempt to deal directly with the educational implications of racism on both an institutional and personal level. Paros' experience at, and analysis of, the Yale Summer High School in 1967 and 1968 is clearly open to varying and often conflicting interpretations. Yet, his work represents and remains a crucial exploration in the problems inherent in both "compensatory education" and the creation of truly liberating alternative educational contexts.*

Introduction: The Person

I was fortunate to experience early in life the perfect metaphor for my future work and life style. The occasion came while I was employed in an ice cream factory. There I functioned as an integral part of a highly sophisticated operation accountable for the daily production of some one thousand dozen popsicles, fudgicles, or creamsicles.

I was responsible for Phase 2. I stood before a massive tank filled with water, into which a steady flotilla of "barges" rushed — hundreds of metal mold trays filled with the appropriate ices. My task was to reach into the water, retrieve a tray, and with one unbroken motion, immerse it in a tub of hot water to my left, press an appropriate lever releasing the ices from the bottom, and lift the remains onto a moving conveyor belt that hung above me to my right. The belt then carried the product down the line for a dip into the syrup (when required), bagging, and ultimately packaging.

A certain unthinking rhythm developed to the job — at times threatening to induce a sleep-like state. I had to *always* keep a careful eye upon the conveyor belt itself. Most of the bobs on the belt were black, except every thirteenth which was painted bright red. I was *never*, under any circumstances, to hang the ices on the *red* bob.

The first few days I quietly and efficiently managed to negotiate Phase 2, but I was continuously haunted by the red bob and its meaning. The third day I

51

I could no longer resist the temptation. I cautiously, but determinedly, lifted my product to the conveyor belt and let it rest gently upon a *red* bob.

In the space of fifteen seconds, a magnificent geyser of chocolate syrup erupted, together with a steady stream of invective from the women at the other end of the line whose sanitary white costumes were now swathed in sticky brown goo. A siren wailed; the conveyor belt ground to a halt; and dozens of unfinished eskimo bars fell to the floor.

That afternoon I was relegated to the freezing compartment, at thirty degrees below zero, taking inventory of the past months' work.

The following ten years were spent in another industry of sorts — education, the processing of the young, but I never quite lost my affinity for the red bob.

Context and Setting: The Yale Summer
High School

The Yale Summer High School was very much the product of the early nineteen sixties, a time when such works as Michael Harrington's *The Other America* (1962), awakened America to a "culture of poverty", previously invisible, in her midst.[a] It was in response to "the crusade against the other America," launched under the aegis of the Office of Economic Opportunity, and to President Kennedy's request that our universities bring their resources more effectively to bear on the problems of poverty and discrimination, that Yale University initiated its Summer High School in 1964.

Initially a six-week program (operated at the Yale Divinity School) for 100 academically talented but economically and educationally disadvantaged boys, the Yale Summer High School's fundamental purpose, as set forth in its proposal for the 1965 session was:

> . . . to develop a model program which might be utilized by colleges, universities, school boards and private secondary schools all across the country in enabling young people to lift themselves out of the conditions of cultural impoverishment and educational shortcomings. (YSHSP 1965)

----

[a] It was Harrington's thesis that the poverty of the sixties differed from earlier forms in that it formed a whole in such a way that efforts to eradicate it by attacking isolated components were doomed to failure. Harrington recommended, therefore, a "comprehensive campaign" against contemporary poverty, and stressed the need for a coordinating center from which to launch and administer what he then termed a "crusade against the other America." The "comprehensive campaign" which was eventually launched and administered through the Office of Economic Opportunity became known as the War on Poverty.

More immediately, Yale hoped to sensitize the participants to the potential value of higher education and the intrinsic pleasure of learning by exposing them to the life of a great university. At the same time, by means of a curriculum tailored to their needs, talents, and interests, and taught by the finest group of teachers Yale could assemble, they sought to provide students with the academic skills needed to succeed at a quality college.

Although other colleges and universities initiated programs of compensatory education for high school students, the Yale Summer High School was the only program which both drew its students nationally and returned them to their home schools during the academic year. The decision to draw students nationally resulted from the belief that the program should seek the relatively rare student with sufficient academic and leadership potential to make him a realistic candidate for admission to Yale or a college of similar quality. Political, educational, and practical reasons prompted this view. In 1964 there was a growing need for individuals who could bring the nation's resources more fully to bear on the problems of poverty and discrimination. In the light of her traditional role as an educator of leaders, it seemed appropriate for Yale to undertake to identify and train talented students with roots in poverty, since first-hand experience with the conditions of deprivation would both enhance a commitment to the effort to eliminate poverty and injustice, and provide an expertise individuals from other backgrounds lacked.

The academic curriculum of the Yale Summer High School, as it was elaborated over the first four years, was composed of two different kinds of courses, one addressing the motivational problem supposedly characteristic of the students sought, the other the skill deficiencies from which they were thought to suffer. The standard disciplines (English, social studies, mathematics and science) were offered, supplemented (beginning in 1965) by elective courses such as drama, logic, and international relations, allowing students to pursue subjects generally not found in the high school curriculum. These courses were made as exciting and as rigorous as possible in order to challenge the student to make the fullest possible use of his potential. Complementing these were "skill" courses including composition, speech, and study skills, intended to compensate for deficiencies in the verbal areas and to enable the students to handle the academic aspect of the curriculum with increasing facility over the course of the summer.

It was recognized from the outset that special pains had to be taken to ensure that the academic aspect of the summer experience was relevant to the personal concerns the students would bring with them. It was the function of the "tutor-counselor" to guarantee that this gap be bridged. Predominantly Yale and Harvard undergraduates, the tutors were not only to help eight to ten students who comprised their tutor-group with their academic work, but were also to serve as counselors, supervisors of athletic events and afternoon activities, and as teachers of electives. Perhaps their most important function, however, was to stand as models for what the Yale Summer High School student might someday hope to become.

While the primary function of the summer phase of the program was to motivate and prepare talented students from poor backgrounds for the nation's most competitive colleges by enabling them to function more effectively in their home schools, it was also expected to serve, in a purely practical sense, as a vehicle for the identification and placement of talented students. Many Yale Summer High School students attended schools during the winter which rarely sent their graduates to the more competitive colleges. Most college admissions officers had no way of knowing how to interpret and evaluate their grade transcripts. In addition, deceptively low standardized test scores further decreased serious consideration by admissions committees, unless supplementary information from sources considered reliable was available. It was hoped that the Yale Summer High School recommendations, written for all students who requested them, would insure careful and serious consideration of their high potential.

After a careful reading of the Yale Summer High School's history, I was excited by the possibilities the program had as an experimental institution and as a contributor, albeit limited, to the war against poverty. I was also elated by the prospect of employing the resources of Yale University as leverage for change in the New Haven school system, and the hope that a university, such as Yale, might provide for reflection and personal clarification of matters educational. Seemingly, what better place from which to question the basic assumptions that underlie American education than from one of its great universities? Consequently, it was with both joy and anticipation that I accepted the job as director of the Yale Summer High School.

The Summer of 1967

Summer '67 was relatively tranquil, but it soon became clear from conversations with students that there was considerable turbulence beneath the surface. For the first time that summer, there was a small group of students actively and openly questioning members of the administration and faculty as to the validity of the purpose of the Yale Summer High School. When told that the purpose of the school was to ensure them access to colleges commensurate with their high ability, and to give them the academic tools and skills they would need in order to succeed at top colleges, they questioned why they should want to go to, much less succeed at, the "prestige colleges." They argued that these institutions were an integral part of the same system which had discriminated against them in the first place, and made remedial programs like the Yale Summer High School necessary.

When reminded that there were considerable differences between Wallace's

Alabama and Yale, they agreed, but claimed that the difference was that Yale
was worse — that at least in Alabama they knew where they stood, whereas at
Yale "phoney white liberals" pretended to care about them in order to salve
their consciences and, more practically, to "buy them off" in order to "keep the
lid on the ghetto." When asked why they came to Yale, if they knew it was part
of the system, these students informed us that it was their intention to turn the
tables on us by "using" us to put into effect the changes they considered necessary within society at large, and even within the immediate setting of Yale and
the Yale Summer High School.

The main interest of the more disaffected students of all races during the
summer of 1967 seemed to fall in the area of race and race relations. It was at
first unclear, however, what dimension of the problem made it such a profound
concern to these students. The more militant black students seemed to see the
problem primarily in practical political terms; thus their concern with the notion
of black power. This perspective on the problem led a number of them to suggest that the Yale Summer High School be transformed into an all-black institution which would serve the overtly political function of enabling blacks to get
together so that they might engage more effectively in the kind of direct social
action they saw as the only way out for the black man.

Other students, more often white, tended to view the race problem in highly
ideological terms, as just one more symptom of the contradictions implicit in the
liberal establishment. They were particularly sensitive to the paradox of the establishment's attempt to help those against whom it had discriminated in the
past, and felt that those who were a part of the system couldn't help anyone until the system itself was changed by a revolution of one kind or another. The
growing interest of such students in the critical approach to history and social
problems led us to include in the 1967 curriculum a course focusing, in a concrete way, on the problem of Vietnam; but conversations with these students revealed that while they enjoyed this course, they wished to study a manifestation of the problem which was closer to home.

Still other students, primarily those who were members of minority groups,
saw the problem in cultural or anthropological terms, and expressed the wish
that more "blackness," "redness," or "browness" be included in the curriculum.
In order to satisfy this demand, a seminar on the experience of minority groups
in America was established. At the end of the summer, these students informed
us that the Yale Summer High School would be more relevant to them if such a
course were made a permanent feature of the curriculum.

The event which first suggested why students of all races and outlooks now
found the problem of race so relevant was the performance toward the end of
the summer of the play *Masquerade*, a psychodrama, written by the students
themselves, in which blacks, whites, and Indians interchanged roles and acted
out scenes of various acts of racial discrimination. The play, which represented
the emotional culmination of the summer, had the important effect of helping

the school as a whole face the race issue more openly, and of realizing the extent
to which the problem had not been honestly dealt with earlier. This indicated to
us that students found this issue relevant, not so much as it related to their political, ideological, or cultural concerns, but because it addressed their immediate
and personal concern with such issues as *interpersonal communication, honesty,
and the authenticity of human relationships;* that is to say, *the problem of the
nature and origin of the discriminatory attitude itself.* These issues were present
with peculiar intensity at the Yale Summer High School because, while it was a
fully and self-consciously integrated institution explicitly devoted to the eradication of poverty and discrimination, the question of the origin and nature of the
discriminatory attitude itself appeared, for some reason, to be a taboo subject
for classroom discussion.

Also of particular interest to us were a group of students, generally cited as
"psychological problems," who, for the most part, had been excluded from the
Yale Summer High School student body. However, conversations with other students, their families, and school personnel, suggested that the "problem" students' academic difficulties sprang from different sources. It was not that these
students *could not* adjust to the traditional demands of school, but *would not.*
School simply failed to inspire their commitment. Consequently, we finally concluded that the underachievement of these students was a function of what we
came to term *existential alienation.* Appalled by the meaningless and irrelevance
of life as they experienced it, these students dared not accept themselves and
their existence because of the risk of disappointment and hurt they felt full engagement in life might involve. *Yet they felt the existential need to commit
themselves to something so strongly, that, unable to choose to be, they chose re-
solutely not to be* – in fact or in effect. Their dilemma was nowhere so well expressed as by a scorned and jilted Richard III:

> *Why I in this weak piping time of peace,*
> *have no delight to pass away the time,*
> *Unless to see my shadow in the sun,*
> *And descant on mine own deformity,*
> *And therefore, since I cannot prove a lover*
> *To entertain these fair well-spoken days,*
> *I am determined to prove a villain,*
> *and hate the idle pleasures of these days.*
> (Shakespeare, *Richard III*, 1.1. 24[N]-32)

In school the "problem" student found himself implacably at odds with the
value system implicit in the curriculum, pedagogical procedures, and the social
and political structures of his high school. In short, he had decided it was not
worth his effort to try to succeed in terms of traditional criteria. He seemed to
feel that the price of academic success, as measured by the standard criteria, was

his personal integrity and that, as such, it was too high. Thus, while his poor schooling and the economic poverty of his background might contribute to his academic difficulties, for the most part he was underachieving for the same reason as his "alienated" middle-class counterpart.

It was clear to us that this student would not be motivated by being placed in a better school, insofar as the value system used to judge the superiority of the better school is the very one against which he is reacting. We drew this conclusion from a variety of sources, but especially from conversations with alienated Yale Summer High School students who had dropped out of, or done poorly at, excellent independent schools to which we had helped them gain admission. Their claim was that these schools perpetuated the same practices which had turned them off in relation to their "bad" high schools, only in a more subtle and efficient manner.

What particularly bothered them was the basic assumption which seemed to underlie every aspect of both types of school that "because the faculty and administration knew more about certain academic subjects than you and had had more experience, they also had the right to impose their values on you and legislate your future." These students were quick to acknowledge differences between their "bad" high schools and the preparatory schools, allowing that whereas in their high schools teachers and administrators openly moralized about what was best for them, and backed up their convictions with threats of disciplinary action, at prep school they tried to "psyche you out" using marks, the lure of getting into a top college, and other gentler forms of persuasion "to try to get you to do well in those subjects they said you had to do well in, in order to get into the colleges they said were best. If you didn't finally come to agree with their way of doing things, they didn't threaten you; they just left you alone."

Judging from such comments and our own visits to both the high schools and the preparatory schools, we concluded that in spite of their obvious differences the "bad" and the "good" schools had two crucial points in common: both presumed to know what is best for students in certain important respects; and both discouraged serious and open dialogue about the value assumptions which determine their basic structures and pervasive ethos – the "bad" school by making such issues the subject of dogmatics, the "good" school by its insistance that since value assumptions always, in the end, turn out to be relative and subjective, everyone has to decide value issues for and by himself. The result is the overwhelming willingness of the "good" school to let every individual "do his own thing," effectively discouraging discussion about *what should be done.*

What struck us as strange about this tendency of the schools to discourage the discussion of value issues was that all our experiences with adolescents, and particularly with the alienated adolescent, indicated that what he wanted more than anything else was: first, to be left free, but *not alone,* to make such basic personal value decisions as whom, when, or whether to marry, how much education he should seek, or what work he should engage in; second, to be able to clarify in conversation with adults and peers fundamental questions about life, the world, society, and himself on which these basic decisions must ultimately be based; and finally, to feel assured that the commitment of adults and peers to him is not contingent on his following their advice with regard to these questions, advice which he, nonetheless, would both probably seek and desperately need.

Our Thinking and Directions Begin
to Change

In the light of these considerations, it was clear to us that even if the existentially alienated student were a member of an ethnic minority he would not be significantly helped by being placed in a local compensatory education program whose purpose was to demonstrate to him and to his school that his cultural values and those of the dominant society were not necessarily mutually exclusive. For his problem resulted not so much from the lack of "anthropological" sensitivity of his teachers to his special needs as a member of an ethnic minority, as from the contrary fact that he and his teachers sensed all too clearly the contradictory value systems from which one another was operating, and that no reconciliation was possible until one, the other, or both changed.

Finally, we concluded that the alienated student would not be helped by any form of psychological therapy which required him to view himself as a patient. For, since it was his claim that it was not he but society which was sick, the only form of therapy which could touch him was one which could authentically acknowledge the possibility of the partial correctness of his position. We suspected, on the other hand, that the Yale Summer High School might provide the ideal setting in which to work with this student, provided certain changes were effected in the ethos and curricular structure of the program.

Additional deliberation on the larger American crisis of poverty, discrimination, and racial and ideological conflict led us to the conclusion that the aspect of the system at once most responsible for the current unrest, yet with the most potential to provide a "way out" was the school system itself. We came to agree with Friedenberg (1959) that "the crucial lack in American society is . . . intimacy." It became our conviction that *the kind of intimacy required was not to be obtained by a political revolution predicated on the necessity of destroying the necessarily and properly impersonal political and economic structure, but by a new turning toward one another possible only through a rediscovery and regeneration of those values which define and bind people.*

It seemed to us, moreover, that the schools were ideally suited to play a central role in the required regeneration of values by stimulating an awareness of the basic existential and normative problems, particularly those raised by a consideration of the ideal definition of human nature. Yet, as we noted earlier, schools presently systematically discourage the treating of such value issues.

It was widely acknowledged after the summer of 1967 that there was something seriously wrong with America. But the American habit of seeking political solutions to all problems seemed to be so deeply ingrained that the only changes proposed were essentially politico-quantitative: the "system" should "let in" more of the poor by making more of an effort to provide them with the better job and educational opportunities to which they had been hitherto denied access. The schools were to play a major role in this redistribution of economic opportunity, resulting in a significant increase in compensatory efforts.

It struck us, on the other hand, that the existing framework of the Yale Summer High School was ideally suited to function as the context for the development of a new kind of school which would directly address the students' quest for meaning and social involvement. We would design a curriculum which would enable students, staff, and administrators to explore together the question, "What ails America?" Not only would such a program permit students and staff to consider this question "academically," but insofar as we were correct in our hypothesis that the heart of America's sickness was in the schools themselves, to the degree that we, together, successfully generated a new educational ethos, we would all be participating in a politically "revolutionary" act.

There were several unique advantages which we felt we possessed by virtue of both our national character and our association with Yale University. Our Yale affiliation, we hoped, would provide us with the necessary support for bold and important educational experimentation — free from those restraints which tend to be imposed on programs operating at the more conservative colleges and universities.

Our national constituency in contrast to that of the local program, would provide us with a student body representing both a *homogeneity* of talent and a high racial, ethnic, and geographic *diversity*, seldom found on a local or regional level. We assumed that both components would be critical for the kind of student with whom we chose to work.

As regards the homogeneity, in order for our student to confront and attempt to resolve the problems of our times, thrust upon him by his critical awareness, he must first be convinced that he is not alone in his condition — hence the need for kindred spirits, peers of similar sensitivity and talent with whom he might share his awareness. Without such support he might too easily excuse himself from his responsibility on the grounds that the actions of any one person can only prove futile.

The variety of the student body — which included such disparate spirits as the Indian from Rosebud Reservation in South Dakota, the black from Bedford-Stuyvesant, and the white from rural New Hampshire — would in turn help dispell any feelings he might have that either human inferiority or superiority, or his own existential plight, is a function of race, background, or region; as well as allay any suspicions that he has been chosen for the program because of some "problem" he might have. Most important, it would help convince him of what is actually the case, that he has been selected because he possessed those qualities which would enable him to learn from and teach in the kind of educational context we hoped to create.

Finally, association with Yale University would also have important pedagogical advantages, for it would provide students with the opportunity to confront potentially sympathetic adults perceived to be part of the establishment and engage with them in dialogue about the fundamental value assumptions which underlie their behavior. This would have the effect of breaking down stereotypes on both sides, provided authentic and honest dialogue occurred.

This last would be crucial, for the failure of authentic communication could only result in further disillusionment on both sides. We therefore intended to develop a curriculum consistent with the new aims we saw for the school, one which would explicitly address the mutual concerns of students and staff involved: the concern of the staff to discover the relevance of knowledge and thought to the suffering of their students and the nation; and the concern of the students to discover the relevance of learning and knowledge to their suffering. Only such a curriculum might facilitate the mutal learning of wisdom, which we saw as the end of the school.

Summer of '68: The Core Curriculum

The most concrete result of our extensive analysis and deliberations was the development of what was called the core curriculum. This curriculum, adopted for use during the 1968 session of the Yale Summer High School, focused attention almost exclusively on the question of race (and racism) in contemporary American society. Employing a spectrum of materials from the western intellectual tradition, we sought to address ourselves, as directly as possible, to the issue of racism and American values. In truth, students had not overtly asked to examine the race question in this way; as noted earlier, they expressed interest only in the political, ideological, and cultural dimensions of the question. However, the core curriculum grew out of our realization that an expressed interest can often point to an unexpressed concern. The ambiguity of the word itself suggests our meaning: those things which concern us touch us whether we like it or not.

The core curriculum itself rested on a number of assumptions, the most important of which was that the concern of the militant students with "black power" was less an expression of their immediate interest in the general powerlessness of blacks in America, especially as regards their efforts to gain access to economic opportunity, than an expression of their concern with their sense of personal impotence in interpersonal situations involving whites, and especially, white adults, in which their special sensitivities and concerns are constantly and steadfastly ignored and disparaged.

On the other hand, we did not intend to ignore the student's *expressed* interests. Thus, spun off the core curriculum were nineteen electives including such titles as "Racism and Revolution," "Violence," "Love and Death in Poetry," and "Utopias" — electives intended to provide students with the opportunity to pursue in greater detail a topic of individual interest, a topic perhaps only briefly considered in the core seminar. It was our hope that these variegated explorations would add depth to the ongoing discussions and encounters that would necessarily characterize the core seminar, since students would have benefited from readings which might make them more knowledgeable than the core teachers on some points.

Finally, we intended to use the core curriculum, as far as possible, as the unifying principle for our program of informal social and cultural activities. Thus, speakers and films would be chosen (always with the full participation of students in the decision-making process) in terms of the extent to which they might illuminate the particular race-related issues then under discussion in the core seminar. Intramural sports, expressionistic dance, dramatic presentations, and individual projects, geared to problems generated through the core curriculum or seminar, would be undertaken in tutor units, and all would culminate in a festival which would include playoffs in the sports leagues, faculty-student "all-star" games, dramatic presentations, and essay competitions.

The gains, we anticipated, would be twofold. First, students would learn to participate in a decision-making process and would become more conscious of themselves as active members of a group. Second, through the essay competition and the plays, the question of the literary expression of values would be given concrete form. Students would have yet another opportunity to confront, with the aid of the tutor, the distinction between various patterns of thought and action, particularly as these patterns of thought and action were directed at explicating and dealing with the meaning and implications of race and racism in America. The art instructors would guide their students to express the problem through different styles of painting and sculpture (their works would also be exhibited in the festival). The summer would conclude with a "creative graduation," with the appropriate pomp and ceremony invented by the students themselves. It would, we hoped, be a Happening in the most serious, yet joyful and meaningful sense of the term.

In short, we saw the structure of this new curriculum as being ideally suited to the task of mediating an educational community in which all members, students and adults alike, could increasingly come to know — and more importantly — *be* themselves. So, we would be an educational Utopia of sorts — a school intended to prepare all its students, both old and young, for the world as it might be, not as it was. But, we reasoned, only such an education might produce the leaders the "new world" seemed to require.

**Summer of '68: Results, Feedback, and
an Overview**

The totality of the Yale Summer High School was on the line from the very start in that summer of '68. Some of our brightest, most articulate, and most socially conscious students were more than ambivalent about their relationship to this "new intellectual bag." To many, books, the realm of ideas, and the written word were all the white man's preserve. Others would read, but only selectively, from among Cleaver, Fanon, Malcolm X, and Iceberg Slim. Behind it all was *the* issue, that of independence and personal integrity as it related to the possibility and the desirability of a coming together of the races. If indeed there was a mutuality of interests and concerns, how might it ever be realized, and at what price? As the summer wore on, black and white tensions surfaced fully on campus. They were not overlooked, nor was any attempt made to diffuse them. Rather, in the classrooms, in the tutor groups, and in hundreds of ad hoc discussions, a context was provided where all of us could have an opportunity to become self-critical on the issue. The school its people and its style engaged each other together with the tradition from which we were all alienated — and we learned.

There were Problems and Incidents

The bedsheet hanging outside the window on July 4th with the message boldly painted on it calling for a boycott of the honkie holiday and affirming that although independence had not yet come to Black America, it was near.

The mini-delegation of black students to my office to protest my invitation to Floyd McKissick to speak at the school . . . Much talk . . . "Sorry — thought he was from the NAACP."

The scenario played out near the parking lot of the Divinity School. Distinguished and greyed Divinity School Alumnus on encountering two of our students: "Lovely day, eh? You go to the Yale Summer High School — do you? Its a good thing that colored boys are now getting their chance. Perhaps you remember a boy named Levi Jackson who went here?" (Former "Yale-Great," black athlete, now an executive for Ford). Response: "He's not a boy; he's a man."

A southern white student considering the idea of going to an all-black high school to get a better education.

A student in a core class making connections between Kojeve, Marx, Faulkner and issues of Americanness and blackness.

The incident with the police. It was 1:30 A.M., a warm Saturday night in late July. The girls from a visiting Upward Bound program were boarding their buses for the trip home following a dance — but not without much kissing and hugging — when two campus policemen on their evening cruise arrived on the scene.
Evidently disturbed by what he saw, the officer at the wheel took to his speaker and blared a warning to disperse. Things tensed up perceptably, and several of the tutors and myself began walking around trying to relax the now explosive situation. Tonda (young, black woman) then walked over to me, and said: "Larry, let's blow his mind." She took me by the hand, walked me over directly in line with the patrol car's headlights, and gently kissed me on the cheek.
As the students dispersed, I spoke my mind to our "protectors," telling them that I felt they had acted thoughtlessly and that their actions could easily have provoked a serious incident. Pointing to the departing students, the officer replied: "We sent them on their way. Now you see what *they* understand."

The students, black and white, together, hastily arming themselves with chains, sticks, and pipes, and appointing sentries to patrol the quadrangle until the early hours of the morning to prevent another outside raid by a gang from Dixwell Avenue.

An early evening performance of the Yale Summer High School African Dance Troupe, organized and programed by the students themselves. It was a moving, exhilarating, and beautiful happening as was a program inspired by it — one of American Indian dances by our own Red Power contingent. It, too, was executed with the minimum amount of "outside" help. In both instances, the students created an artistic vehicle as an expression of faith and pride in their ethnic and racial heritage — and in themselves.

Genet's great ritual play of social revolution, *The Blacks*, produced by the Yale Summer High School Drama Workshop under the direction of German Wilson — after long hours of rehearsal of a most difficult and complex piece — capped by three flawless performances played to overflow audiences at the Ezra Stiles College Dining Hall: one for the students, staff, and friends of the school; a second for other members of the Yale community; and a third for the residents of New Haven and its inner city. One of the highlights of our summer.

One of the tutors wrote: "The first clear observation one could make was that the 1968 Yale Summer High School was not going to be a quiet community of scholars. The old ethos was not going to develop. The presence of disenchanted souls was going to make conflict and dissension part of the way of life there for the rest of the summer. In every real sense, the conflict at Yale Summer High School mirrored the conflict in the nation as a whole. But the devices which separate rich from poor, black from white, the ghetto, the suburbs, neighborhood schools, were removed, and students from nearly all sections of the social system were left free to confront one another. This confrontation was not always pleasant, but the fact that it did occur, and that the Yale Summer High School did not go up in flames, is reason to hope for American society."

There Were Studies

It was especially in the core seminar, and through the active mediation of the western intellectual tradition, that we hoped to structure meaningful interpersonal and interracial encounter. What in fact did happen – and its impact, if any, upon individual students – can be understood only in retrospect through the comments of staff and students.

Through the school and particularly the core course I found new dimensions of depth in myself that hitherto had remained uncovered. In the program I found myself questioning old ideas and opinions long held, and casting them away as worthless. I became more aware of Me as I became aware of the doubt I had as to my own authenticity.

Larry, how could I explain how a mere seven weeks could do so much and change me in such a way as a person? The goals of the program were in themself an experiment. Literature was arranged so as to bring about a confrontation of the students with their own prejudices and fears. This was done with the same fears and prejudices *present.* Miracle of all miracles, I felt that to a great extent this goal was successful.

Lucy – Atlanta, Georgia

Most people filter reality and see only what they wish to see, but now I see the naked, blinding truth. What brought about this change in my perception of life I know not. Maybe it was the confronting of people and ideas in Core class. Maybe it was there all along simply staring me in the face, and finally in my growing maturity I grasped it. The important thing is that I have changed. Seven short weeks ago a naive young man from a small southern city came to YALE UNIVERSITY; now he spells it Yale University, for he is no longer the captive of his illusions.

Seven weeks can be a long, long time; the awe is gone now. Am I a better man now? Only the future will tell but I'm tired now, its been a long seven weeks. I'll rest a month and then I'll be going to college. Just four short years and . . .

Sam — Laurinburg, North Carolina

But Most of All, There Were People

I get the loneliest feeling now when I think of the people I met. They were to me the realest people I ever met. By real people I mean they were themselves and at no time could you ever catch them off-guard. Maybe all of them also had the idea I had to let the real me shine through this time. This realness created a society of 118 young men and 28 young women. They were Black, White and Red Indians. Together we made up a society of people.

Irma — Chicago, Illinois

There are students. There is no generality to a Yale Summer High School student. He is unique and individual, each different in his own right. They are of different backgrounds, religions, and beliefs. Yet they are brought together in a community in which there's no caste system based on color, economy, or religion. They are members of an institution that is as diverse in its definition as in the character of the people who make it up. It is a semi-utopian institution in some cases, a community in some cases, and a school — unique and diverse in others. Its existence has been questioned at times, and the school has been said to be unrealistic, for our society is not like the Yale Summer High School. In a sense the Yale Summer High School can be called an existing dream in a real world.

Dempsey — Cleveland, Ohio

It was my second night at the Yale Summer High School and I was attending a tutor group meeting in my tutor's room. Everyone had arrived except for one person, and that was the person who was to share my room with me for the next seven weeks. Suddenly, at the end of the hall stood Super-Nigger, the Oakland Pimp. He was black, tall (6'4") and wore a green suit, one of his so-called pimping suits, and a wide-eyed blank expression, which I was soon to learn seldom changed. It was then that I first met Anthony, my roommate. Over the past seven weeks Anthony and I have grown closer together, letting our different backgrounds mingle into one common one here at the Yale Summer High School. Not only were our backgrounds mingled into one, but they were mixed up and re-apportioned in such a way that now I am part of Anthony and he is part of me.

It's surprising how much one person can learn from another just
by living with him. Basically, Anthony has taught me about Black
people and their Blackness, and white people and their whiteness.
To him Black is what's happening. That's the reason for his alias of
Super-Nigger, defender of the truth, justice and the Black way.
About the most important thing he has taught me about blackness
is his definition of a black man. But also, Anthony and I had several good discussions about how we blindly accepted the conditioning of our separate racist environments and societies.
I've learned many things here this summer, but Anthony has taught
me much more than all of my subjects combined, and while I might
forget Antigone I don't think I will ever, ever forget Anthony.

> Wayne — New Britain, Connecticut

During the two years I was participating in the Yale Summer High
School, I learned a lot of things about myself, other people, and
what a *real* school should operate like. I believe I worked as hard as
I could in the program, inside the program and outside, learning
about the world with my newly-awakened senses. I've received in-
finitely more out of the program than the program has received out
of me. You gave me a look at life, Larry, you gave me a look at
beautiful people, and most of all, I was given a look at myself.
Peace and love.

> Joe — New York City, New York

Just in case you were wondering, I'm still in existence and doing
quite well at that. My year so far has been full, thanks to the Yale
Summer High School and its staff. During this past summer I learned the real meaning of life and how to live it to the fullest degree.
This involves at least one hour's explanation, but I think you know
what I mean.

> O.J. — Eunice, Louisiana

Once I didn't think anyone could have the least bit of control over
his destiny, at least no one who did any thinking. I tried to become
a part of the great cosmos. But that seemed beyond me. I began to
feel pleasure in closing up like a clam. I derived pleasure from the
realization of my state of mind, because I felt there was no way
out; there was nothing to change myself to.
The Yale Summer High School changed that. I have learned,
through my close association with other young people with similar
problems, that awareness of these uncomfortable situations is not
enough and isn't my limit of action. I can do something about them
just as soon as I quit sitting down.
Of course this brings up the question, "Won't your teachers at
home be teed off if you come back, not a kid full of answers but of
questions?" Sure they will. But issues were raised this summer that

have given me invaluably deep insights into the politics of an educational community.

For this, and for showing me that I can be the shaper of my life, I
am very grateful to the people who had faith in me. Thanks for
showing me that tree branch that has been over my quicksand pit
all along

>   Jonah — Birmingham, Alabama

Summer of '68: The Aftermath

The purpose of the Yale Summer High School in 1968 was to help students,
staff, and above all ourselves, the administrators, to learn to endure the agony of
choice; to define our own goals, to make decisions for ourselves — in short, to
opt for being human. This required a fuller definition, awareness, and control of
self through a clarification of our relationships to one another, and our mutual
relations to ideas and authority. This is not a simple task for a school, but one
the times demanded. Our experience and study suggested that the root of the
racism which appears to be one of the major causes of contemporary poverty
and violence is the radical failure of the majority of American citizens to achieve
self-knowledge. Education for self-encounter, however, requires prior preparation and training of staff, together with the right kind of supportive structure
that both allows and encourages a turning inward.

Coming out of the summer, though, we understood that such goals stood
little chance of being realized within the space of a brief seven weeks, and thus
recommended that the Yale Summer High School, insofar as it was dedicated to
these ends, no longer be continued and be replaced by a full year-round experimental boarding school, representing both a higher level of commitment and an
opportunity to work intimately and intensively with students over a period of
several years. We concluded that anything less would border on the irresponsible.
We therefore proposed one more summer session, however, to serve as the planning stage for the full year effort, and made a number of specific recommendations, including the above purpose, together with specific structural changes in
the summer phase consistent with that purpose.

This was not to be, however, for the fall of that year brought with it the decision on the part of the Yale administration to alter the scope and direction of
the program. It also brought with it my dismissal as director of the Yale Summer
High School.

The faculty and staff of the Yale Summer High School took issue with the
decision and the shift in emphasis, and made the following statement to the *Yale
Daily News:*

> We, as a representative group of the faculty of the Yale Summer
> High School, protest the firing of the Director of the Yale Summer

High School and the destruction not only of the continuity of the program but of its very essence.

This past summer the Yale Summer High School created an exploratory community where students alienated by their society could confront an intellectual tradition they had come to think of as bankrupt.

Its only possibility of success lay in its commitment to the active appropriate involvement of its students and staff in the decisions affecting the structure and function of the school.

Without consulting the staff or students of the Summer High School, Yale dismissed its Director. Yale now announces its plan to restructure the school. This means that Yale's admissions policy will come to determine the shape of the school community.

This arbitrary use of power signifies, we believe, the abandonment of the idea of the Yale Summer High School as a participatory community.

Its transformation into an admissions-oriented institution eliminates the possibility of a free, self-critical institution where students can experiment with new ways of dealing with their own goals and values, thus making its genuine rebirth difficult if not impossible.

Yale has to do more than respond to political pressures with deliberately political programs. The University's responsibility to minority groups and to the American educational system is not only to increase black enrollment but to deal as well with the more basic problem of why talented students have become increasingly alienated from the educational system of which Yale is part and symbol.

Yale's administration can, if it chooses, create a program to tailor Black students to its academic style. We deny that this school replaces the kind of educational community that the Yale Summer High School represents.

We ask, moreover, that the University make a frank and public statement of why increasing Black enrollment in the College necessitates the abandonment of the ideas represented by the Yale Summer High School.

Such a statement was not forthcoming. The Yale Summer High School was transformed into a "college prep" school in 1969 and 1970. Shortly thereafter it expired completely.

*Analysis and Prospects: Implications of
the Experience*

There were difficulties and complications surrounding the operation of the Yale Summer High School. I believe, however, that both the real difficulties faced by the program and the imaginary difficulties some believe it faced resulted primarily from a single source: the fundamental lack of a genuine university commitment to solve the problems we sought to address. In addition, the Yale Summer High School has led us to become deeply involved in the problems surrounding the development and implementation of alternative educational settings. It is to both of these issues — the university, and the creation of educational alternatives — that we now direct our attention.

The University

The university, particularly its administration, has good reason to want to exercise significant control over experimental educational programs insofar as these programs have the potential to engage the attention of the public at large to a far greater degree than most other research projects at the university.

The university's reluctance to be associated with a "dangerous" program, "dangerous" students, and "dangerous" dialogue (i.e., ones it does not yet know how to handle) is understandable. For errors in handling such programs, such students, and such talk can have serious consequences both for those within the program and for the image of the university in the community-at-large. But the solution, of course, is not to exclude this student (or those who would work with him) from the university or its special education programs, but to give this student and the dilemma his plight points up the full attention it deserves. The type of student with whom we chose to work was not "typical Yale material," though we believed he was a student Yale should seek; and the experimental educational setting which we designed was one where students might come to define their own goals — which might or might not be those of their sponsor. For our primary aim was not getting more black students into Yale, but to discover what it was that was wrong with our schools and our society that made programs in contemporary education necessary.

Thus, the lack of a positive university response to the meaning of the Yale Summer High School was not accidental. Rather, it was the ultimate expression of an ethos at the university wherein the political has come to dominate all other considerations; an ethos which is intolerant of criticism received, and unwilling to engage independently in self-reflection, lest it disrupt the performance of the university's central function — the efficient production of knowledge and leaders. Thus we have another example of the paradox of the schools: employed as instruments for the equalization of opportunity but concurrently subverting that kind of education most desperately needed by our democracy in order that it might find itself.

*New Schools and Alternative Educational
Settings*

Our effort to create a new kind of Yale Summer High School was the concrete expression of our belief that the center of the political crisis which this nation now faces is in its educational institutions, and that the "revolution"
required is the generation of a new ethos in our schools and universities. In retrospect, the Yale Summer High School experience was only a primitive beginning
towards this end. However, we believe that we learned much from the planning,
implementation, and aftermath of those summers, especially about the kinds of
changes required in our schools and universities if they are to better serve their
students and the nation. Consequently, in the final pages of this chapter, let me
try to sketch out the form and content of an alternative educational setting
which could begin to address itself to the issues raised by the Yale Summer High
School experience. For purposes of description, let us call this new educational
setting, "School I."

School I's primary focus would be the increasingly large number of students,
ranging from black and/or poor ghetto youth to the sons and daughters of the
white middle class who have become alienated (at least in part) through their educational experiences. And while we would hope to help all types of youngsters
through School I, we would attach special significance to the existentially alienated — for it is their thirst for self-knowledge and control which would highlight
the self-reflective ethos of the school itself. School I would seek to address their
dissatisfaction and despair by direct confrontation and engagement with the
source of their alienation, "the system" itself. And through those young persons
presently least well served by our schools, we would strive to help our public educational institutions gain the necessary insights to become more responsive and
relevant to the interests and concerns of all its constituents. School I would thus
not only minister aid to the casualties of our schools and other social institutions,
but work actively towards helping influence and shape those institutions in a
more humane image.

Most importantly, School I would address those polarities which at the present time threaten to tear our nation apart — most especially that of black-white.
White racism, identified by the Kerner Report (1968) as one of the major causes
of poverty and violence, is still upon us. School I would be directly concerned
with the creation of new settings in which black and white might be brought together.

Most educators have for many years assumed that psychological integration
would naturally follow statistical balance, when in fact evidence has shown that
racial conflict is as likely to be the outcome of integration as racial harmony.
Yet they continue to give insufficient thought to the special nature of the setting
(and its requirements) in which constructive interaction between black and

white people can take place. Compensatory programs, for example, have not and will not do the job. The continuing flow of evidence indicates the failure of compensatory education and an accompanying disenchantment of its sponsors and early champions. While these programs have done some good for some kids, and have stimulated a new concern for the poor in local school systems, they have not addressed other pressing needs, and have created real problems.

The problems that need to be addressed require a full-time deployment of resources and personnel; yet most compensatory programs are part-time endeavors and possess merely the most peripheral of commitments on the part of their sponsoring institutions. The severely underachieving poverty student underachieves primarily because he lacks the sense that he can control his own fate. For this reason, this kind of student tends to react against highly politicized (and therefore manipulative) programs which are designed to get him where the government thinks he should go. For this reason, too, he reacts against the great majority of high school, prep school, and compensatory educational settings which embody the "we know what's best for you" ethos. These students do not perform better in "better" schools nor do they respond to "better" teaching, because the superiority of the schools and teaching methods tends to be judged in terms of the very criteria against which the student is reacting — in particular, in terms of the ability of these institutions to get students into "good" colleges whose quality is, in turn, measured by the ability of graduates to get the "best" jobs. The failure of schools and the compensatory programs to reach this student is extremely serious, because all indications are that he (or she) is the brightest and most creative student: this is the student *most* concerned to achieve control over his own destiny, the student most likely to ask *why* he is being asked to do what he is being asked to do in the school, and to refuse to do it until he gets a satisfactory answer. Few seem to understand that the sensitivities and concerns of such youths, whether expressed in our schools and universities or in the streets, stem less from their exclusion from existing institutions and opportunities than from their reaction to the subtle and insidious injustices, contradictions, and lack of meaning which they sense to inhere in the inner workings of the "system" itself. They do not in fact wish to be integrated into the system *as it is presently constituted.* They are troubled by significant value questions.

Compensatory programs tend to approach this student with greater relish, concern, and patience than the public schools; but the assumption which underlies all these efforts is that the major responsibility for the student's maladjustment rests primarily with him as victim of his social and economic circumstances rather than with the school. Accordingly, the job of the program is seen as getting him to "shape up" to the school's style and expectations. Yet in most instances, the source of the student's hurt or damage is that very institution to which he is asked to return and to adjust. More often than not, the school and the social and economic circumstances remain for the most part untouched. In short, though it is recognized that there is a critical need for new contexts to be developed in which those sectors at the farthest poles from one another (e.g., black-white, male-female, rich-poor, over 30-under 30) might learn to work, learn, and live together, compensatory programs for the most part focus upon the poor black and the poor white. There appears to be no awareness that the phenomenon of white racism is not susceptible through treatment of black people alone — or even poor whites.

The major problem which any new school must address is the plight of contemporary American youth in seeking ways to reconcile the contradictions which they sense are inherent in the larger society. They need support, encouragement, and a real working knowledge of the culture. The young have a sense of what might be, but they do not know whether to choose to begin — and if so, how or where. They require guidance and healthy and constructive adult relationships that will help them strike a balance between their own personal conflicts and those of the outside world. There is a felt need to interact with adults who, by example, might show how it is that one maintains ones integrity in the face of a continuous and ongoing onslaught that is the system itself. School I would take this need seriously.

Through our work in the public schools and at the Yale Summer High School we came to see that contemporary American education is driven by a discriminatory ethos — not solely racial in nature, though it did manifest itself most clearly in the manner in which it dealt with black student — but rather a discrimination against the questioning attitude, especially in the concerns of youth to establish their own identity. The establishment of identity is contingent upon being convinced of the possibility of controlling one's own fate with regard to the important dimensions of experience. Given this, racism, for example, can only be approached through the development of a structure which is sufficiently encouraging and supportive of its students' efforts to be human — learning to endure the agony of free, individual choice. For in helping the adolescent, black or white, to address his central concern (i.e., the liberation, affirmation, and acceptance of self), the school frees him of the need to define himself at the expense of another human being — what is more commonly known as racist behavior.

An educational setting characterized by confrontation, testing, and dialogue would allow students, both black and white, to explore the implications of their membership in a particular race and the possibility and desirability of working together. Thus, School I would directly address their concerns which center about the authenticity of human relationships, honesty, and the quality of interpersonal communication. It would provide a new way of dealing with adults both within the school and outside of it, and thus meet the adolescents' need to engage adults in dialogue in order to discover what a just social structure might be.

Simultaneously, School I would be employed as a vehicle for social change, thus helping students to honestly gauge the extent to which contemporary American ideals might serve as grounds for identity. It would have to directly confront the major areas of alienation among contemporary youth: (1) Education and school — books and the realm of the cognitive; (2) The interpersonal polarities — black and white, male and female, blue collar and professional, parents and children; and (3) The nation and the community.

As it moved into full operation, School I would also begin to develop its political dimension. Consistent with an ethos that would stress personal integration, the school would be characterized not by insularity, but by an active interaction with the world, the real world. An integral part of the student's education, for example, would be his involvement and training in the areas of social and human service. A range of opportunities in the helping professions (broadly defined) engaging him in direct community action would be one of the many educational options open to him.[b] Young people are for the most part excluded from the work world and the social world of the adult — sealed off by an educational process which holds them captive. The limited occasions for dealing with adults generally occur under the worst possible circumstances. As a result, there is very little opportunity for the gradual, paced learning of the world that will someday be theirs.

School I, however, would go much farther than gradually introducing students to the world by assigning them to apprentice-like positions in the community. It would strongly address the conviction of so many of our most talented young people (and adults) that there is nothing that any individual of group of individuals can do to influence the quality of life in this country. It would acknowledge the difficulty and complexity of effecting meaningful social change, but would itself, as a school, bear witness to the generation of a strengthened will and the development of a new body of social knowledge. It would reject the fatalistic vise which presently appears to have this country in its grip.

In Summary

There would perhaps be no more fitting way to conclude this chapter than with the last section of our ill-fated prospectus for the Yale Summer High School (1968), for it perfectly embodies a vision which we still hold:

This Prospectus represents the product of our total reassessment of the Yale Summer High School. We feel that the need exists for a national educational community where, in microcosm, our strength in diversity might be brought to bear on the critical area of American life.

---

[b] What was missing most from the Yale Summer High School was action — a sense of participation in something larger than the self-enclosed enclave on the Yale campus — an opportunity to move beyond ourselves.

Our point of departure is the widespread disaffection and estrangement felt by many members of the body politic towards the quality of American life; whether reflected in the Black-White polarization and the spasms of civil disorder that have shaken our cities, or in the apathy and despair of those who have chosen to 'turn-off'. For many of its most talented youth, as for many of its most gifted adults, America has ceased to inspire commitment. A functional concept of citizenship itself is in crisis; a crisis stemming from the gradual loss of common bases for action and common social goals. As educators, we feel compelled to address ourselves to this problem.

Our effort is directed primarily to those potentially creative youngsters who are in danger of being ignored and discounted by society. We would have them grow into responsible participants in our culture. We would nurture a valid commitment to American society via those young persons currently most at odds with it.

However, there exist few values, taken seriously, either universal or uniquely American, which might bind our citizens together. An effort must be made to structure contexts wherein such values might be rescued from our past; and new values generated so as to ground our common choices and imbue them with redeeming significance. We agree with Socrates that 'wisdom cannot be taught', yet feel that contexts can and should be structured where it might best be learned. Nowhere is the need more clearly felt than in the area of race relations; for it is only through the recreation of shared values that freedom will be possible for both Black and White.

Our school would be such a workshop, for young persons, in the problems and possibilities of modern America. It may appear that we are seeking students of heroic dimension, and exhorting them to a heroic task. Perhaps this is true; but we concur with Lerner (1962) that one of the saddest things that has happened to American education has been 'the squeezing out of the heroic'. Adding this necessary dimension is one of our goals as a model educational community." (YSHSP 1968, pp. 64^{N}-66)

References

Friedenberg, E. *The Vanishing Adolescent.* Boston: Beacon Press, 1959.

Harrington, M. *The Other America.* New York: Macmillan, 1962.

Lerner, M. *Education and a Radical Humanism.* Columbus; Ohio State Univ. Press, 1962.

U.S. National Advisory Commission on Civil Disorders. *Report of the National Advisory Commission on Civil Disorders.* New York: Bantam Books, 1968.

Yale Summer High School Proposal. New Haven, 1965.

Yale Summer High School Proposal. New Haven, 1968

5

Organizational Duplicity and Professional Ethics: A Tale of Two Settings

Alan P. Towbin
Private Practice

[Editor's Note] : *At the present time, Alan P. Towbin devotes a major portion of his professional time to the conduct of his private practice. Previously, however, he was a staff and research psychologist, first at a noted VA Hospital and later in a supposedly innovative educational project. Towbin's chapter deals essentially with the process through which one becomes acutely aware of the difference between a project's "public" goals and its "real" or underlying intentions. His analysis of this process, through a recapitulation of his experiences with a hospital-based self-care project and a learning center tied to the public educational system, focuses needed attention on the manner in which the helping professions can become a part of the scenario through which institutional needs take precedence over client or consumer needs. Towbin's chapter is a study in "consciousness-raising" or, as he puts it, an experience which highlights both the truth and implications of the fact that "we learn most about the world through its resistance to our wishes."*

This chapter describes two new settings; one in the mental illness field, the other in public education. Both were successes, but neither had any discernable impact on the larger system of which they were a part. Here I will describe my experiences and analyze the failure of these programs to have a wider impact. The analysis makes use of some elementary notions about organizations (especially the concept of *primary task*) and professions (professional commitment and ethics).

The origins of these new settings are to be found in the politics of the 1960s, when pressures developed on and funds became available to the mental illness field and public education to improve and extend their services. Indeed, there seemed to be a mandate to abandon old methods which were obviously ineffectual and try something new. In the mental illness field, the community mental health centers exemplify this trend. These centers were intended to supplant the practice of sweeping the lower-class victims of "mental illness" into the state hospital system where they become chronic inmates. Similarly, public education, confronted with its failure to help the nonwhite, non-middle class, and even large sections of the white middle-class population, produced an efflorescence of programs aimed at one or another specific shortcoming of the system. The new settings I describe illustrate the point that new programs do not necessarily lead to changes in traditional practices, even those practices they surpass in effectiveness. The operators of traditional institutions often appear uninterested in or opposed to consideration of the limitations of their practices, let alone willing to consider how they can be improved. New settings die, and leave a residue of perplexity and bitterness among the professionals who aimed at improving things.

In retrospect, and not by way of consolation, I want to point out that these are circumstances that permit a kind of learning not available to us when all goes according to our hopes. We learn most about the world from its resistance to our wishes. The circumstances I report here forced me to make explicit and examine my tacit assumptions and the unspoken premises of my professional activity. Perhaps by sharing this process with others, I may make it easier for them to participate in change productively.

The Self-Care Unit

Until 1966, the West Haven Veteran's Administration Hospital was the exclusive placement for first-year psychiatric residents in the Yale Medical School program, and for medical students' internship in psychiatry. It became one of several placements after 1966. The acute medical and surgical services of the hospital also served as a locale for the training of medical students from Yale, and for residents in the various specialities. The psychology service provided externships for graduate students in clinical, counseling, social, and experimental psychology, and hosted post-doctoral research associates as well. Relations between psychiatrists and psychologists were cordial and collegial; we all participated in the training of residents and there was little rivalry or contention between the two groups. The leadership of the two professional groups shared the assumption that the best organizational arrangement was one in which each staff member pursued his own interests, as if he were in business for himself. The Department of Psychiatry at Yale was the focus of many of our practical interests and concerns. The psychologists held joint appointments in the Department of Psychology as well. The atmosphere was that of a community of intellectuals where theoretical differences were accepted, and the dialogue lively. But it was a community somewhat removed from the main thoroughfare that was across town at the medical school.

My associates had their interests — their intellectual hobbies, and I had mine. Psychological testing occupied me for several years until I felt that I had developed a conceptualization of its practice in social psychological terms (Towbin 1960). I became concerned with the matter of a model for training in clinical work (Towbin 1961), and then with the problem of characterizing and explaining the behavior of the "deranged" in the same framework we use in understanding each other's everyday behavior (Towbin 1966). Several of my colleagues

(Rakusin and Fierman 1963; Laffal 1965) had operated the long-term wards, the ones with chronic psychiatric patients, and had developed a conception of these men which I came to share, especially after I became chief of such a ward. We saw the bizarre, deviant, chronic psychotics as essentially human, behaving purposefully, and found them responsive to human contact and respectful relations. Their minds, we assumed, were deviant neither in structure nor function: they were distinguished by their goal — to remain an inmate, at the price of the stigma of mental derangement. This viewpoint, we believed, made it possible to achieve gratifying success in influencing the behavior of these patients, in transforming the madhouse-like atmosphere of these wards into places where a "score-card" was needed to tell patients from others.

It seemed our success was based in large part on our being able to assure the patients that they would not be discharged unwillingly, and that it was therefore unnecessary to act "crazy" in order to convince us to keep them there. We had our clinical success at the price of an extremely stable population. Only if a patient found that the constraints of institutional living were interfering unpleasantly with his personal interest would we expect him to leave. Few did. We had reached a Mexican stand-off. Into this quiet, thoughtful, ivory tower the cold winds of change began to blow.

The publication of the report of the Joint Commission on Mental Health and Illness was the first cool draft. The concept of prompt local care for the mentally ill was soon embodied in a concrete plan for a mental health center in New Haven. This plan, when fully realized, would have the effect of breaking the monopoly and privileged position of the VA Hospital as a training facility for first-year residents in psychiatry. The anticipation of this change roused the critics of the VA facility in the Department of Psychiatry to higher levels of activity as much as it heightened the anxiety of the VA psychiatrists over their academic futures. This change in the balance of power set off a series of struggles in which the psychologists found themselves bystanders at first, bewildered and dismayed. We then turned anxiously away from the role of observers and commentators to an examination of our own professional roles, programs, plans, and identity.

In retrospect, several factors emerge as having fostered changes in our thinking and attitudes — changes which culminated in an abandonment of the premise that the chronic patients had to remain in their dependent relation to the hospital indefinitely. In 1964 we had decided to replace the residents who staffed the chronic wards with psychology trainees. The main reason for this was that we had tired of the struggle to get the resident's attention when his primary interest was in the program on the acute service to which he was also assigned. In addition, we wanted to teach our psychology trainees to carry out the kind of work we, their teachers, were doing. But soon it became clear that the existing long-term wards were not a suitable place to train a "well-rounded" clinical psychologist. The chiefs of psychiatry and psychology endorsed the idea of an end to segregated acute and chronic services; and we sought a training program in which psychology trainees and residents were integrated as well. This aroused the bitter and prolonged opposition of some of the psychiatric ward chiefs. But I began to tell my patients in the regular ward meetings that they should consider how they wanted to spend the rest of their lives, because they would not be able to stay on my service indefinitely. Perhaps they didn't believe me, but as I recall, there were no outbursts of hospital-stay-justifying behavior.

Stories and reports that the VA was going to change its funding practice began to circulate about this time. VA hospitals have largely fixed operating expenses, but funds were disbursed to them on the basis of bed-occupancy over the year. Thus, a large group of chronic patients is like money in the bank to a hospital manager. If the VA included a turnover factor in its funding formula, the premium on chronic patients would go down. There was also, I must acknowledge, a recognition that the nationwide shortage of hospital beds might be alleviated if other domiciles could be found for chronic patients who no longer required the regular attendance of physicians. The VA did initiate programs to facilitate the transfer of such inmates to other settings — nursing homes. However, we found these programs were of little help in moving our patients out of the hospital.

Note that none of the pressures for change came from the psychology staff's commitment to better patient care. The impact of changing circumstances and experiences upon our conception of *our interests,* primarily interests in training, prompted some of us to seek integrated patient care and an integrated training program. And, obviously, it was their anticipation of threat to *their* professional interest by other staff members that led some of the psychiatric ward chiefs to *oppose* the changes proposed by the chiefs of psychology and psychiatry.

The self-care unit (SCU) was begun in this atmosphere of unsettled change-in-the-air times. The program is described in detail elsewhere (Towbin 1969). It was a new setting operating in an old one. It provided a group of long-term patients with conditions of self-care, in the hope that if we reduced dependency gratification and gave them more autonomy in running their own affairs (e.g., passes were dispersed by the SCU group without staff review), they would leave the hospital within the year. I didn't expect the program to work because I still believed patients stayed because they were motivated to remain sheltered inmates.

It didn't work, but instead of abandoning the program, we changed it. I wonder now why we did one and not the other. I suspect it has something to do with the fact that we had earlier discharged one of the most psychotic younger (49 years old) patients on the ward in the face of strong family protest, and he was not only living independently and successfully in the community, but, he reported, was also happier there than he had been in the hospital.

But change the program we did. We set a rigid time limit (six months) to find a job and a place to live in the community or be transferred to another VA facility. The SCU members were responsible for helping each other develop plans for leaving, and for presenting these plans and weekly progress reports to the staff. It worked. The members of the unit left within the prescribed time and stayed out. When we applied the same format to the rest of the ward, it worked there, too. Of the fifteen patients whom we thought could have left the hospital if they preferred to do so, only five elected transfer to other VA facilities. The rest of the patients on this ward were either severely physically disabled, or were elderly and without families who would take them in. They were transferred to other VA facilities.

The phenomenon to which I wish to call attention here is not the development and execution of a highly successful clinical program, but that this program was essentially ignored. Patients whom generations of residents, trainees, and staff had psychotherapized and were regarded as veritable barnacles, dropped their "crazy" behavior and left the hospital without creating more than a ripple of interest among my psychoanalytic and nursing colleagues on the acute services, and without any apparent (to me) impact on practices and programs elsewhere on the psychiatry service, with the exception of the other two long-term wards administered by psychologists. I felt very sad about this, especially when I heard the scuttlebutt that on the acute services the word was true, those patients were out, but "weren't they still as sick as ever?"

By treating these men as mental patients and assuming that they would not engage in more independent living because they wanted to remain patients, we had doomed them to what might have become life-long institutional living. The departing inmates left vacancies on my service; I then spent time in the admitting office of the hospital and interviewed applicants for psychiatric admission. There I could see the process of producing chronic inmates begin. The applicant for admission seems to know that if he discredits himself sufficiently, the admitting physician will lend his authority to the admission. Once the medical expert has decided that the applicant "needs" hospitalization, the latter need feel no responsibility for entering the hospital. Self-discreditation is a demand characteristic of this situation, and it appeared to me as a self-degrading, humiliating situation for the applicant.

As the days and weeks went by, I noticed that I was becoming grumpily intolerant of practices and conceptualizations I had hitherto ignored, and criticized them to my colleagues and students. For example, I openly expressed the views I had long held that psychological testing contributed nothing to patient care or to the education of the resident, let alone that of the trainee who did the testing. More important, I supported trainees who voiced these ideas during supervision sessions, instead of trying to defend the practice. I shared my opinion with others that the weekly case conferences were obviously rituals fostering the illusions that hospital psychiatry was a medical practice and that psychiatry had accumulated scientific knowledge that would be helpful if passed on to the residents. Finally, I stopped attending these conferences.

A growing mood of agitation marked my days at work. Perhaps an episode from this period will convey the kind of experience I had been having. The change in social atmosphere on my ward during the new group program is exemplified by the change in Mr. James, a 39-year-old "chronic paranoid schizophrenic," who had been hospitalized for over ten years. Over the course of seven years of intensive individual psychotherapy, Mr. James had changed from a kind of wild man whose assaultiveness required that he be kept on a locked ward, to a neat, scholarly-looking man who managed his own affairs on an open service. He had earned an Associate in Arts degree from a local college during this period, and was almost always seen carrying a book. His manner was haughty and supercilious, as if he were royalty living in the era of the divine right of kings. I always addressed him as Mr. James; he called me Alan, as one might address the butler. His speech was often a mixture of puns and allusions which were, in a Joycean way, intriguing and charming, if confusing. Some would say it was typical schizophrenese." When angry, he became incomprehensible. Frequently he showed his annoyance by kicking or spitting at, or bopping some low-ranking hospital employee over the head with his ubiquitous book. Mr. James had been required to move out of his single room when the SCU was created and was upset about it. But he refused to apply for membership in that unit. He elected to leave the hospital. When his parents heard of this, they hurried to see me and urge me to keep him there. Their son didn't plan to live with them, but Mr. James' parents were dismayed at the idea of his being at large in the same city. They reminded me that their son had been legally committed to the VA. They might feel differently about his discharge, they indicated, if he would only do some work in the hospital.

I checked the records after they left, and confirmed Mr. James' court commitment. Discharging him would mean lifting his commitment: he could not be returned to the hospital against his will without another commitment. I drafted a note to his parents explaining that although I intended to proceed with caution, I did not believe their son should unwillingly spend the rest of his life in a hospital. If he found a place to live and wanted to go, I would release him on a temporary basis; if it worked out, he would be discharged. I kept Mr. James informed of the discussion I'd had with his parents and I invited him to read the letter I'd drafted. He did so with interest, put the paper down, and thanked me. From that moment on, I never heard him speak other than a lucid word. A psychiatric colleague examined Mr. James about this time, and declared him free of signs of psychosis. He left the hospital and soon thereafter got a job, as he proudly reported when he came back to visit the ward staff.

This kind of experience was pervasive during the final period of out-migration of this group of long-term inmates. It left me with the feeling that I had been doing harmful things to patients for years, albeit unwittingly, and that if I became involved with other psychiatric wards, as I must now that my own service was empty, I would be participating in a process whereby the institution created its own clientele. I felt that I didn't fit in any more. I was becoming a troublemaker, and my criticisms of the institution were, I feared, having a demoralizing effect on the students. The service would be better off without me. I decided to leave institutional psychiatry.

In May of 1968 I resigned, sadly leaving my many good friends who stayed, and cheerfully turned to what I hoped would be a new career in public education, an area in which I thought I might do good and no harm. I joined a Title III program called the Learning Center.

The Learning Center

The SCU, a setting created in the framework of an old one, had little impact on the operation of that larger setting, and its accomplishments seem to have been ignored and denied by the operators of the system. Perhaps more could be expected from a completely new setting, explicitly addressed to problem-solving with what appeared to be considerable organizational autonomy, and at the least, financial independence from the institutions whose clients it served — the public schools. These features of the Learning Center were not enough to prevent the failure of this program in the sense of a failure to have an impact on existing operations in the larger system or on the methods used by operators of that system. Probably no dispassionate report and analysis of the LC is possible, especially since the LC failed to survive as a setting. In this report and analysis, however, there emerges a framework of consideration that seems illuminating, retrospectively, on the fate of the SCU as well, and seems to generate some implications for the formulation of new programs and the preparation of psychologists.

The SCU was a new setting in the physical and organizational context of an old one, created by the managers of the old setting. The Learning Center was a new setting. Its location in a public school was not fortuitous; but it was organizationally separate from any single school system, and newly created by a group of people who came together for the purpose of initiating the new setting. The founders of the LC represented the school systems of six contiguous communities in central Connecticut, agencies of the state government, a regional, federally-funded educational agency, and the state mental health association.

The interested parties sought and obtained a grant from the U.S. Office of Education (under Title II of the Elementary and Secondary Education Act of 1965) to undertake an innovative project "to develop a multi-disciplinary, inter-community, intra-educational approach for the diagnosis and remediation of problems presented by children in kindergarten through grade three who have shown or develop behavioral or neurological dysfunctions; this is to be done through a comprehensive program of individual diagnosis, appropriate educational planning and training of personnel."

The impetus for this project came most directly from a state law (Public

Law 627) requiring every town in the state to identify children with "learning disabilities" and provide educational programming for them, much as they had been required to do earlier for children characterized as mentally retarded. The learning disability child was one of at least average intellectual potential, and thereby was distinguished from the retarded child. This law required that the administrators of the public schools of the state carry out its vague mandate and exposed them to lawsuits by parents if they did not do so. Of course, the law did not mandate additional funds to school budgets (though a state would reimburse a *town treasury* to the extent of two-thirds of the funds expended on such a program). The law could not create experts trained to identify and remediate such children; such trained individuals were and are in short supply; no generally accepted standards of accreditation of teachers in this area existed, and no college in the state had a program to train teachers for this work. The law, in a word, had shortcomings.

In June of 1967, the funds were approved for the first year of the program, with a commitment to continue funding for two additional years. The region served was expected to fund the program after the third year. Work began on the extensive remodeling of the old wing of an elementary school which was to be the site of the LC. An advisory board was created, the voting members represented the superintendents of the six school systems served. The board, as is customary, was expected to set policy and hire the staff who would implement the program. Obviously, the LC was not independent but a subordinate of these school systems.

A master teacher with extensive experience with the gamut of learning disabilities was the first staff person hired in September of 1967. A month later a director, and four months later a school social worker were hired. In May 1968 I went to work full time, replacing three psychologists who had been giving a day per week to the center. Part-time consultation by a psychiatrist (who also served as medical director) and a pediatrician, had been arranged by the director.

The staff was charged with achieving the following objectives:

1. Provide assessment and remediation procedures for students with learning disabilities due to neurological and behavioral dysfunction;
2. Develop new approaches for the education of children with specific learning disabilities. This approach was to be based on specific learning prescriptions for individual students rather than on diagnostic labeling;
3. Provide in-service training for teachers. The specially trained teachers will be available for assisting in filling the prescriptions of students throughout the area;
4. Serve as a Demonstration Center and provide follow-up research to determine the value and feasibility of its new approach;
5. Provide special education materials for use in the Center and in schools throughout the area;

6. Provide teacher training institutions, such as Central Connecticut State College in New Britain, an opportunity for developing a graduate level of training including internships in special education;
7. Bring together well-qualified educators and medical and psychological personnel for a global approach to the improvement of diagnostic and remediation services for students with learning disabilities; and,
8. Inform professional and lay communities about the activities of the Center and the problems of students referred to it. Inform the public about the special education opportunities needed by schools throughout the area.

During the first calendar year of the program, the training of "prescription teachers" (under objective 3) and the evaluation of and prescription for about fifty youngsters occupied the major part of the staff's time. From these fifty children, the staff selected those who would be the initial group in each of the two demonstration classes planned for the second year. The five classes intended by the originators of the program far exceeded the space and funds available. A teacher and teacher-aide were hired for each of the classes. After a basic experimental design was worked out during the summer, a research associate was hired to help me with the evaluation of the various programs.

This tiny group of professionals could not hope to meet the needs of the 8,000 or so children estimated to suffer from "learning disabilities" in the six-town area. All we could hope to do was try out these innovative methods, try to achieve the program objectives on a demonstration basis, and evaluate the phases of the program with respect to feasibility and effectiveness, as guides to decision-making when communities made commitments to full-scale locally-funded service programs. The staff shared this conception of our task, and had begun to carry it out many months before I arrived. The result of their efforts was a period of intense conflict between the director and the advisory board, or at least between a faction of the board and the director. The board appeared split, one faction representing three towns friendly to the director, the other a three-town faction antagonistic to him.

The conflict is worth examining both because it long diverted the staff from the basic issues in the situation, and because, in retrospect, it reveals the underlying structure of the relation of the program to the schools. This conflict expressed itself around several concrete issues, of which I will give several examples. One of these was the staff's conclusion that several features of the original proposal and other board initiated plans were not feasible. The first of these features was the model of an evaluation and prescription service, which seems to have been derived from certain medical-school affiliated centers. Hiring a pediatric neurologist, opthalmologist, etc., and having each child seen by all the associated experts in the LC was not only economically unfeasible, according to the medical director of the LC, but also would arouse antagonism in the local medical community.

The board's plan to locate the LC in the local state college, where it would have become part of the program for training teachers, was another feature of the original proposal which was eventually abandoned. The director had pointed out to the board that such a move would directly violate the stipulations of the law under which our grant was made, since it was not intended to fund formal teacher training. This view was accepted by the board, but it went down very hard with the representative from the college, a nonvoting member of the board. He had hoped that LC resources would be used in this college's new graduate program in special education. The reduction in the number of demonstration classes was, similarly, a blow to several school systems.

The members of the negative faction seemed to have particular difficulty with the matter of group boundaries. It took the intervention of a representative from the State Department of Education to elicit a formal agreement on the rights and obligations of the LC and those of each community, with respect to each program area. The board and superintendent of schools of each community endorsed this agreement.

Throughout the first program year the director's decisions had been criticized by one faction of our board and attempts to veto his decisions were frequent. The atmosphere became increasingly tense and the staff felt hampered in their ability to do their work by the antagonistic relations developing between the administration of three of these school systems on the one hand, and the director and staff of the LC on the other.

The staff developed the theory that the presence of a hostile faction on the board was our "problem." The prescription program had been operating only in the three school systems of the friendly faction. The other faction had won in a vote calling for the rejection of the experimental design to be used to evaluate the prescription program. Their objection to it may be inferred from their order to the director that he present a design which did *not* use a control group. Even though the design was modified to meet the objections of the negative faction, they referred no children for the evaluated phase of the prescription program in the second year. That was the reason we carried out the prescription program and its evaluation procedures in only three of the six communities during the second year.

Our evaluation of the program was informal, based on unsystematic observations. (The limited experimental evaluation the friendly faction accepted would not have been completed for another year.) We came to the conclusion that the prescription program was ineffectual, that the "demonstration" classes were wasteful, that they were harmful to some children and of small, though noticeable, benefit to others.

The prescription program assumed that the children referred weren't learning because they needed special pedagogical techniques, and that if visiting experts provided the classroom teacher with these techniques, this would influence the classroom experience of the referred, as well as of other children. The program was ineffectual because it had misidentified the problem; we found the problem to be the unresponsiveness of the classroom situation to the individual differences among children. Even if the program's definition of the problem had been correct, it is not likely that a group of experts, operating on a hit-and-run basis, would do much to influence the pedagogical methods of the classroom teacher.

The demonstration classes were wasteful in as much as they consumed about half of the resources of a program costing about $180,000 per year, for the benefit of nine children. The classes were created by bringing together a group of behaviorally disturbed or poorly socialized youngsters, representing the most serious problems to the administrators of their school systems. Often the entire staff, in addition to their teachers, was absorbed in the effort to manage the youngsters and create an atmosphere in which learning might occur. Our success in doing so does not diminish the dubiousness of the entire enterprise. For example, our star pupil pleaded with me several times during the year to send him back to his "regular" school; the promise that he could return to a regular classroom was his most powerful incentive to do academic work, even though he had been unhappy in the class he had left. As another child, a seven-year-old boy put it, all of his classmates were "crazy," the teacher was "crazy," and it was a "crazy school." I don't think clinicians want to operate settings that foster such negative self-concepts and stigmatization; the openness of these children made it clear we were doing just that. The harm done by this setting is, in principle, no different from that which arises from segregation by race.

Aside from our belief that this type of program does not have the desired effect on its target individuals, we came to appreciate that the problem of school failure was even more extensive than the initiators of the program had indicated. A program aimed at individual youngsters is simply not a feasible way of coming to grips with the problem. The overall operation of the schools was left untouched by our efforts. After the third program year we would fold our tents and slip away, with little to show for the half million dollars that would have been spent by then. We recommended that in the third year the staff concentrate on in-service training programs for the schools of those communities which remained in the program, and that special classes and the prescription program be abandoned. The board rejected our recommendations, knowing we planned to resign if they did so. They announced that the plan of the second year would be followed in the third. We did resign, and were vindicated when the advisory committee to the Commissioner of Education recommended against the refunding of the planned third program year.

What was this conflict all about, and why did things end the way they did? The program of the LC, PL 627, and the system called "special education" shared the premise that the failure of general education to teach the child effectively, reflects a problem having its *locus in the child*. We had come to regard the strategy which follows from this premise as a *segregative* one — get the child labeled deviant, and move him into a "special" setting, run by special (specially trained) educators. The staff had concluded that the premise was unjustified by our experience, that the strategy was often harmful and that it was simply economically unfeasible. Only the wealthiest communities could afford to employ this approach at a level that would be responsive to the actual failure of general education. We could see that this segregative strategy was the basis of the entire LC program. But what we did not appreciate was that the conflict with the unfriendly faction was simply the outcome of their efforts to implement this *same* strategy in their school systems in a form suited to their resources.

The unfriendly faction represented three "have not" communities, "have not" in the sense that special education and pupil personnel services were at a minimum in those systems. School social workers were not to be found in two of the three; psychological examination was contracted for by one, and available from part-time examiners in the other two. The educational specialists in speech and in the basic skill areas (e.g., remedial reading), were not to be found, or where present, were available in token numbers.

The "have" communities varied in the extent of their services, but all had departments of pupil personnel services with school socialworkers, full-time psychological examiners, remedial specialists, etc., as long standing features of their educational system. The fiscal resources of the "have not" communities were not necessarily inferior to those of the "haves," but their educational leadership had not moved in the direction of "special ed," and PL 627 caught them flat-footed. They were almost completely dependent on the resources of the LC to meet their responsibilities under PL 627, and therefore had a great stake in *controlling* those resources.

How had they managed the many youngsters in their schools with whom they failed? I believe our experience points to several methods, each line of defense to be held as long as possible, but when necessary, abandoned for the next:

1. Ignoring and denial (teacher blame).
2. Brush off and put down (parent blame).
3. Evaluation by outside experts, labeling as deviant, segregation in special settings (child blame).

When I tried to convince the principals of one of the "have not" systems of the feasibility of our research design for evaluating the prescription program, they pointed out the conflict between the research design and their own strategy. The research design and their own strategy. The research design called for a control-group of children, eligible for LC service, tested on two occasions a year apart, but in receipt of no special services from the LC or any other agency outside the school during that year. Everyone was prepared to admit that there were many times more children in "need" than the LC or the school system could hope to serve; the situation existed long before there was a LC. The principals had learned to manage this situation by not identifying the child in any official way as having a "need." Just as one becomes "deviant" only when officially labeled, the child has an immediate need for special education only when officially designated. If parents complained, these administrators reported that they would try to brush them off and/or temporize. But as one principal remarked, it wasn't working any more. Obviously, these school systems could not tolerate an independent agency scurrying about the schools, identifying specific children as failing to receive the services these administrators were obliged, by law, to provide. Only slightly less threatening was the figure of the director of the LC, fulfilling the objectives of our grant by addressing PTAs, parent groups, women's clubs, and the general public on radio and TV concerning the nature and extent of the *unmet need* for special services in the schools. In the light of their reliance on the tactics of ignoring and denial, the LC staff was a threat to the school administrator, especially those of the "have not" communities. The efforts of the administrators from the "have not" systems to subordinate the director and staff, and to dominate the day-to-day operation of the LC are understandable, as is their successful effort to quash the control-group design of the evaluation research.

We were familiar with the "parent put-down" as an administrative tactic, from our contacts with the parents of children referred to us, as well as others who sought us out. Since few families are without some conflict, and the school problems of children often arouse parental guilt feelings, parents are vulnerable to innuendoes and assertations that the child's difficulties in school are the expression of "home problems," and the parent should examine her soul before bringing any further complaints to the principal's door.

It is obvious that the tactic next in line was one for which the LC was meant to serve: evaluation by outside experts, labeling as deviant, and segregation. Dunn (1968) has discussed this strategy in special education for the "mildly retarded" and points out that the referral of children to "special education" and special educators' readiness to receive them, makes it unnecessary for general education to face up to the problem of individual differences among children. This line of defense was an essential, desperation measure for the "have-not" systems. They had hoped to find in the LC the epitome of expert evaluation, a collection of medical experts that would be required to discern the arcane anomalies of the children for whom they, as *general* educators, could not be expected to be qualified to provide an educational program. The original plan to have no less than five demonstration classes at the LC was transparently intended to provide locales for the "deviant" children of these systems. Certainly one or two classes are all that their alleged demonstration function required.

The "have-not" faction lost on most of the issues that were important to them. But their contentiousness, carping, and obstruction distracted the staff from the fact that *both* factions were adherents of the basic assumption that the child is the locus of difficulty, and of the strategy of segregation that follows from it. The "have" school systems only required of the LC that it supplement the existing apparatus that implemented the segregative strategy in their systems. The "have not" systems needed to have the LC function as a subordinate unit of their administration in order to implement the strategy *discretely* in their schools.

It seems, in retrospect, that both groups of towns had intended to use the resources of the LC not as a trial and demonstration project, but as the receptacle from which would be drawn the solutions to their particular administrative problems under PL 627. Title II was a mere form for funnelling federal money into local school systems to help them solve a new administrative problem, using old strategies and techniques. The segregative strategy was established nationally, was the standard practice in three of the towns, and was accepted as the goal of program development in the other three. There was no interest among the administrators in finding out whether the program was effective. Since it followed established nationwide practice of helping individual youngsters, how could it be harmful? (At the 1968 convention of APA, I had occasion to hear complaints about lack of interest in evaluation research from psychologists who had been employed as research consultants or as researchers to evaluate Title III programs. They were not getting any support from program directors for evaluation efforts. The atmosphere at this meeting was full of gloom and one psychologist told me privately that she had just resigned in despair of being able to do the evaluation job her position called for.)

The apparent duplicity of the board, their use of the program for purposes other than intended by the grantor, was *not* the basis of the continual conflict between the staff and the board. Nor was the negative faction-staff conflict the reef on which the LC finally floundered. That reef was a conflict between the premise of the program, its strategy, and the consequences of that strategy, on the one hand, and the professional ethics of the staff, on the other.

Let me summarize the conclusions to which this analysis leads. The LC, as an *innovative, demonstration* project, was a fake. Its originators and managers were not primarily interested in trying out a novel solution for educational problems, and assessing its feasability and effectiveness. Its actual primary task (the task an organization must carry out in order to survive) was the implementation of a standard, widely accepted strategy, so as to provide the administrators of these systems with a "cover story" — that they were fulfilling their responsibilities under PL 627. The staff were willing to serve the actual primary task of the LC (we were not troubled by the board's duplicity), until we experienced the fulfillment of the task as being in conflict with our professional commitment — to develop a feasible solution to the problem we confronted, and our professional ethic, to do no harm. We were all seriously troubled when we came to appreciate that the overall strategy was not a feasible method of coping with the failures of general education, that the resources of these systems could never reach the multitude of children in need of help, that we would be pursuing a policy not of demonstration but of tokenism. But, I think it was the experience of seeing youngsters develop self-concepts as "crazy" or "dummy" and seeing *them* upset about it that turned our objections into resolve to change the premise of the program or quit it.

It is striking, in retrospect, how well this analysis fits my experience at the VA. Teaching hospitals in the VA system are subject to organizational duplicity, too. The primary task of such settings is publicly trumpeted as service to veterans. In actuality, the primary task of these hospitals is training. At West Haven, termination of the training program for psychiatric residents would have led to the departure of the psychiatric staff. Full-time psychiatrists would have to be hired to run the treatment facilities. Indeed, the SCU came into being in response to the *training* interests of the staff. It had no impact on the psychiatric service because service, hence effectiveness of service, *was not the primary concern of the staff.* The success of the SCU had the effect, however, of laying bare the *conflict* between teaching and service — that is, the price to the client of the kind of teaching operation we conducted. By price I mean that in order to have minds on whom the residents and trainees could practice psychotherapy and learn the professional rituals of the mental illness system, there had to be bodies housing those minds in residence on the psychiatric service. The admission process required collusion by resident and veteran applicant. It resulted in the induction of the needy or troubled person into the patient role, his degradation and stigmatization, and fostered the development of a deviant identity (Scheff 1968). In a sense, the biggest problem of the mental illness system is not how to provide service for those troubled people it hasn't yet reached, but how to effect the reintegration into society of those it has reached, and upon whom its mark rests so heavily.

Ordinarily, perhaps, the mental health professional observes only that small segment of the system in which he tries to do his good works. But when one has occasion, as I have, to witness the entire and chronic services, to abandonment of the patient role and of the self-concept as mental cripple, one cannot ignore one's responsibility as part of the system, for the "doing" one subsequently demonstrates can indeed be undone. In my opinion, professional commitment and professional ethics demand that the mental hospital system be abandoned as a strategy for "helping" people, and for the management of deviance as well. It was clear to me for a long time why I had to leave the institution, but it did not become clear to me for a long time why the institutional psychiatrists had ignored my work. The contributions of other students of the problem, whose work has challenged existing conceptions of the mental health professions (e.g., Mendel 1966; Rothstein 1966), have been ignored by institutional psychiatry as well. Because I had been denying organizational duplicity, I couldn't understand the system's indifference to my discovery. Aside from its threat to their interests in teaching their "brand" of psychiatry, it seems plausible that an additional factor promoted the staff's ignoring my work. Appreciating that one's heartfelt professional endeavors do unwitting harm that outweighs whatever benefit it provides, is probably the most bitter pill a helping profession can swallow. Semmelweis had a very hard time of it when he tried to tell physicians they were killing their patients by infecting them with puerperal fever while attending them in childbirth. I don't think psychiatry takes any more kindly to the idea that not only is mental illness a myth, but the institutional system based on that myth does harm. No more will special educators take kindly to the idea that their well-intentioned effort to help children in the context of a segregative strategy does harm.

Conclusions

The following may be taken as hypothese about institutional change and the preparation of psychologists for practice, which have grown out of my experience.

1. Operators of a system introduce or accept changes to the extent and in a form that will reduce existing threat to their interests in pursuing the primary task of the enterprise they operate.
2. The management of any new program will aim at controlling and limiting its impact on the larger system of which it is a part.
3. Organizational duplicity will be expressed by paying lip-service to the goals of innovative or novel programs, while attempting to use the resources of these programs to pursue old strategies in the service of the primary task of the organization.
4. Organizational duplicity, however, will not be a source of conflict for professionals until they appreciate that there is a conflict between the actual primary task of the institution controlling their program, on the one hand, and the goals and ethics to which professionals are commited, on the other.

What are the implications of my experience in two settings for the preparation of psychologists? In reading the ethical standards of psychologists (American Psychological Association 1953), it seems to me that the dyadic helper-client relationship is the focus of traditional ethical concern. That is a misleading perspective for our times; the crucial contemporary ethics problems are triadic, encompassing the relation of helper-client-agency. Psychologists are trained in institutional settings — graduate schools, clinics, hospitals, mental health centers, and psychological service centers, and I hypothesize an inexplicit but effective aspect of that training is the *desensitization* of students to organizational duplicity and to the conflict between the tacit primary task of the organization and professional ethics. Graduate training of psychologists, or rather, those responsible for this training cannot or will not foster anything but an insensitivity to those matters unless or until they are willing to open the *settings of graduate training* to examination of its organizational purposes. For example, the actual primary task of graduate departments of psychology is usually to further the careers of their faculties (i.e., research, publish, consult, etc.), while the *ostensible* primary, but actual secondary or tertiary task, is the training of graduate students. Many other training settings have their version of this organizational duplicity. This situation is discussed only by *students*, wryly, as if it were the inevitable way of the world. Perhaps they can live this duplicity in silence. But if they do not, and their complaints about the effects of the actual primary task on their learning are treated as if they were not legitimate, students will rebel or become cynical. When the organization of graduate training is itself the subject of collaborative faculty and student study and discussion in graduate school, perhaps psychologists in their professional careers, will scrutinize the strategies and goals of *agencies* more critically, and be less available to do harm in innocence.

References

American Psychological Association, *Ethical Standards of Psychologists*. Washington, D.C.: American Psychological Association, 1953.

Dunn, L.M. "Special Education for the mildly retarded — is much of it justifiable?" *Exceptional Children* 35. (1968): 5-22.

Fierman, L.B. and Rakusin, J.M. Institutional Treatment of Chronic Psychotic Patients." *Psychiatry Digest* 26 (1965): 41-49.

Laffal, J. "The Therapeutic Attitude in Treatment and Management of Chronic Patients." *Psychotherapy, Theory, Research, and Practice*. 2 (1965): 28-30.

Mendel, W.M. "Effect of Length of Hospitalization on Rate and Quality of Remission from Acute Psychiatric Episodes." *Journal of Nervous and Mental Disease* 143 (1966): 226-233.

Rothstein, C. "Four-year Follow-up of a Non-traditional Treatment Program for Chronic Psychiatric Patients." *Journal of Nervous and Mental Disease* 142 (1966): 355-68.

Scheff, T.J. *Being Mentally Ill: A Sociological Theory*. Chicago: Aldine, 1966.

Towbin, A.P. "When Are Cookbooks Useful?" *American Psychologist* 15 (1960); 119-23.

_____. "The Way to Professional Maturity." *Journal of Clinical Psychology* 17 (1961): 115-19.

_____. "Understanding the Mentally Deranged." *Journal of Existentialism* 7 (1966): 63-68.

_____. "Self-care Unit: Some Lessions in Institutional Power." *Journal of Consulting and Clinical Psychology*. 33 (1969): 561-70.

6

Exit/No Exit

Irving H. Frank
Private Practice
and
Paul M. Quinlan
American International College

[Editor's Note] : *How does one experience, and then begin to negotiate, one's entrance into the community – particularly when one's past professional life has been devoted almost exclusively to working in traditional academic and mental health settings? What are the problems that must be anticipated; how must one begin to view the question of strategy; in what ways must we be prepared to deal quickly and decisively with issues that appear only tangentially related to the objectives we were led to believe covered our mandate? From 1967 through 1971, Irving H. Frank and Paul M. Quinlan were forced to deal with these issues as a part of their efforts to train paraprofessionals as mental health counselors in areas of the community where such services were either sparse or nonexistent. This chapter details the essence of those "port of entry" problems. In addition, it provides an overview of the often bewildering institutional and interagency dynamics that await mental health interventionists who stray into settings in which they have little prior experience or apparent leverage. It is important that we begin to understand the nature of these Catch 22-like situations, and the work of Frank and Quinlan represents an important step in that direction.*

Bombs have been falling a million times a day in our streets but they have not until recently been the bombs of rioters. Vehement protests have been waged and people's lives have been put on the line long before the Vietnam demonstrations or the civil rights sit-ins. A war has been waging for many years, right under our eyes, and for the most part we clinical psychologists have ignored it, at best studied detached and fragmented elements of it. No one understands what has been happening in the communities of the country. There are too

---

While the ideas presented here are the result of the close collaboration and mutual effort of both authors, in the interest of a coherent and focused presentation, it has been decided to formulated both our experience through the activities of the senior author. Dr. Quinlan has been associated with an integral to the para-psychiatric training program for the past two years.

many forces working, often beneath an obscure surface, for anyone to pretend to understand much more than some of the extent of his ignorance. In this chapter, we will attempt to describe some of the forces and the nature of the complexities which confront the community psychologist as he emerges from the shelter of the office into the streets of the community. We live partly in these streets because of the great challenge, stimulation, and gratification we have found there.

In the summer of 1968 a conjunction of circumstances occurred which lead me to reassess the state of clinical psychology as I had experienced it, and to reevaluate my own professional commitments and premises. After fifteen years of professional practice, both as a psychologist in a VA clinic and as a private therapist, I was invited to apply for the position of chief psychologist in a well-known child guidance clinic. The reflections which led to my decision to withdraw from consideration constituted a serious reformulation of my own professional orientation. Considering my education and training as a 1952 Ph.D. in clinical psychology, I was forced to confront the essentially restrictive nature of much of that which had once seemed so promising. As a student the mystical aura of projective testing and psychotherapy had fascinated me. The possibilities for application in the arena of human behavior and adjustment seemed, at that time, immense. The general atmosphere of VA facilities where I was trained was electric with the enthusiasm and high hopes of students and staff embarking together in new and great ventures to help and cure the emotionally disturbed with the arts of diagnosis and therapy — arts which took so many years to acquire and so many more to apply effectively. Gradually, I was forced to face the reality that the much vaunted diagnostic tests had in fact little relevant relation to the therapeutic situation. Test interpretations were seldom more than portentous cliches. Those that were specific and penetrating in their insight seemed barely related to the fashioning of a therapy plan. It seemed, basically, that the major reason for the continuance of diagnostic testing was that it served in functional terms to define for the psychologist and his clinical colleagues his sense of role and professional identity.

For me, as for many practicing clinicians, the heroic mantle had fallen from the shoulders of the testing expert to those of the psychotherapist long before 1960. To work therapeutically with both clinic and private patients, and, thereby, to develop a general expertise in therapy was an immensely inviting challenge. Many are the rewards that await the skilled practitioner. It is a rare and even ennobling experience to become immersed in the intimate relationship built up with each patient — a relationship conducted in an isolated and relaxed atmosphere which permits the establishment of confident and tender closeness without limitation of time. Such a relationship can grow and mature precisely because it is removed from the pressures of time, the press of bureaucratic interference, the clamor of social nicety, and the intrusiveness of countless busybodies waiting to pry into another's life. The agreements between the therapist and the patient are clear and each is aware that the patient will, in all probability, return again to pursue, alter, or rectify elements of the previous visit. The social prestige accorded the psychotherapist, further, is not to be gainsaid. He is a member of a rather exclusive and often exalted community. And, within the private sphere, the financial return for his efforts is considerable.

Surprisingly, then, the prospect of becoming chief psychologist in a well-known and highly respected child guidance clinic stimulated mainly oppressive reflections. In this clinic, insofar as I could judge, I would be given a free hand to recruit a large staff, rethink and remould existing treatment programs, and fabricate new programs that could be grossly nontraditional in conception and execution if I wished. Almost a year earlier I had resigned my VA position where my professional development was, it seemed to me, at a dead end. An increasing portion of VA patients were recidivists for whom the role of financially-compensated psychiatric casualty was an entrenched and unyielding way of life. And, increasingly, the veteran population appeared to me to be a tight and compact subculture of citizens tucked away from the mainstream of a society which served them as a total benefactor. The position which tentatively lay before me seemed an infinite improvement over my VA job. But less than a year after leaving the VA, changes in my professional outlook, of greater depth than I had previously sensed, had already taken place.

Easiest of all to recognize was the single, unadorned fact that I had had my fill of working as a staff psychologist in a psychiatric clinic. Over the years my working relationships with colleagues in the clinic setting were essentially cordial and satisfying to me. But professional rivalries did exist that were dissipative of energies more usefully expended in the care of patients. And, as I grew in confidence and enlarged my perspectives, the restrictiveness under which I labored chafed with increasing soreness. It became less and less tolerable to me to work alongside colleagues whose professional horizons, in my view, were perpetually contracted to serving principally at the shrine of established dogma and personal prerogative and less so in the temple of aid and comfort to those who suffered. Second-class citizenship within the professional nucleus of the clinic could not elicit my best efforts and my morale sagged. And I realized that what had kept me at my position over the last years was the liveliness and stimulation of working with graduate students whom I trained, I say unashamedly, as a labor of love. By 1968, however, any clinic operating within a traditional structure was suspect to me.

But other influences were at work also. The publication of the Joint Commission's report in 1961 opened up new and exciting vistas that I could only read about so long as I confined my professional work to the clinic and private practice. These vistas became concretized when, as a longtime official and eventual president of our state psychological association and its representative to the Council of Representatives of the APA, I felt myself plunged into a world that fairly dazzled and churned with ideas and hopes for rendering service to multitudes of people who were not living and often could not live effective lives. These ideas, however vague and sloppily hung together, often spoke for the immersion of treatment approaches *inside* the community itself, within its structure and its purposes, which, insofar as I could judge, could at least mean *outside* the ambience of traditional hospitals, clinics, agencies, and the like. Also, the center of attention in therapeutic work was opening wide to accommodate the view that social conditions could harm groups of people and that changing these conditions could be helpful — more so than seeking to resolve inner psychic conflicts. A powerful implication loomed ubiquitously in the background. To participate meaningfully in these developments psychologists would have to become vocal advocates of new treatment approaches and even of social change. Such prospects tugged hard at me.

What of the influence of my continuing and stratifying engagement with the practice of psychotherapy? For all the sense of value I felt as a therapist I had but few illusions concerning its efficacy and range of application. Foremost in my mind for years was the shadowy relationship in therapy between cause and effect. My powers of predicting which patients I could help after the exertion of often great effort were pitifully thin. Many are the psychotherapists, well-trained and knowledgeable professionals, who understand the dynamics of human behavior and the dynamics of therapeutic interactions. But their competence, like mine, can only be inferred from a body of nebulous information, extraordinarily difficult to demonstrate directly, about how the therapeutic process is *presumed* to proceed. How common it is for the therapist to be unable to state confidently, even on a clinical basis, whether or how he helped. How often does it seem that some symptoms, as it were, disappear of their own accord or in response to some environmental event over which the therapist had no influence. How often do we, as therapists, plod bravely on trying more of the same with a patient who has not yet responded adequately and bracing ourselves with the hope that more exposure to the assumed impact of the therapy hour will eventually make a difference. And, conversely, how often have we known the immense joy of witnessing dramatic improvement in a patient who senses in the innermost fiber of his being that what we have done has made the difference for him. Nevertheless, without a coherent body of cause and effect data about the results of psychotherapy, we must remain modest about its general utility and not seek to declare it a primary mode of psychological treatment merely because it came on the mental health scene many decades ago. If we cannot explain or predict its effects we must in honesty hold open the possibility, for each individual case, that improvement might have been achieved through other methods or that other methods were required in the first place.

Further limiting considerations were apparent to me. The psychotherapist, because of his self-conception and his social function, tends to see a certain kind of patient to the exclusion of others. By and large these tend to be functioning, middle-class neurotics with a variety of emotional problems. But the partial homogeneity of these patients creates an artificially delimited world for the therapist to function in. As a result he tends to think that other worlds cannot meaningfully exist for him in the professional sense. The very isolation of the therapeutic environment, its isolation from the world of the community, and the assurance of the duration of treatment become stultifying and restricting — the therapist's world contracts to that type of individual he meets in his inviolable office. As a result, his reactions as well as his horizons become narrowed. Insofar as this is true, he becomes a less effective therapist, although again it is impossible to measure or demonstrate the diminution of his effectiveness.

Finally, the very nature of psychotherapy in our environment precludes its mass effectiveness. Psychotherapy tends to be exclusive in terms of the socioeconomic classes which either can or will appeal to it, and perhaps as a result, it tends also to be restrictive in terms of the kinds of disorders it selects for treatment. But this very exclusiveness would seem to fly in the face of the statistics which show a declining ratio of therapists to disturbed people, and would seem particularly unrealistic in terms of the masses of people from other socioeconomic levels who have recently forced their very existence upon the consciousness of the entire community. It is fundamentally unrealistic to persist in a program of restricted and restrictive psychotherapy exclusively, especially at a time when it is evident that there are masses of people with emotional problems demanding help, and when professional manpower statistics indicate that the ratio of therapists to patients is diminishing rather than expanding. Finally, it is strikingly incongruous that this unrealism should obtain in a profession whose traditional concern has been to help the individual cope with the "real!" In sum, I was ripe to extend my professional efforts into the arena of the community and, providentially, such an opportunity came my way in the fall of 1966.

At that time I was contacted by a psychiatrist who desired my assistance in developing a training program in counseling for professional people who, while not specifically utilizing counseling skills in their work, could benefit greatly from developing such skills and the perspectives associated with them. Specifically, the program was geared up for school teachers, guidance counselors, welfare workers, public health nurses, etc. In return for the training to be offered them, they would serve for some portion of their time in the program as counselors for emotionally disturbed individuals otherwise unable to obtain any professional help whatsoever. We called our students paraprofessional counselors. With them we hoped to demonstrate an available source of mental health personnel who could be efficiently and expeditiously trained to provide mental health services that extended the scope and reach of therapeutic assistance far beyond the boundary of either the traditional clinic or the private office. The program was experimental and exploratory at first but proved to be so successful that we sought to enlarge it. In the fall of 1967, having just resigned from the VA, I was able to give much more time to the program now braced with more extensive funding. New students, who could be thought of as subprofessionals, were added.

These students consisted of some suburban housewives with a college education but no particular knowledge of or experience in mental health work. Mainly, however, they comprised a group of mothers, mostly black, who were on welfare and were seeking to find a career opportunity via the training they would obtain. Traditional training programs would ordinarily have considered these groups incompatible with each other and certainly as innappropriate candidates for such a course usually reserved for professional university preparation. Our aim was to take a further initiative, by reaching out into the community itself on a broad scale. We would train our counselors so that they could function in neighborhood centers, confident and capable of reaching masses of heretofore excluded patients with adequate therapy and counsel. We had ceased to think of ourselves as doctors in the usual sense. Rather we came to look upon our roles as those of mental health professionals whose responsibilities lay not solely with individuals, but with those individuals who make up a community; not with highly-selected individuals in isolation, but with a broad spectrum of individuals in the world in which they must live. What we learned *very* quickly was that a rigid schedule was impossible. Our students were committed to part-time work, and in many cases had families to care for. One could never be sure what portion of the class would be absent for reasons ranging from a sick child to having been arrested for assault the night before. But most students, intrigued by what they had begun to understand, attended as regularly as was physically possible.

In even conceiving such a program, a series of difficulties emerged from the nature of our own training and experience. In the first place, and perhaps most important, the philosophy of training for psychologists tends to be counter to the very premise which even such a rudimentary community program necessitates. And both the clinical and the private experience reenforce this initial premise. Most psychological training tends to produce individuals whose orientation is toward analytic thought rather than overt action, toward the grappling with a particular problem rather than with strenuous action in the face of the problem. We psychologists have been trained to conceive a problem and to devise valid experiments to explore it, often over a number of years, rather than to cope with the problem in its complicated and often contradictory context. The experience of the clinic clinician no less than that of the private therapist has tended to amplify this initial training, to encourage us to withdraw into the relative isolation of diagnostic testing and the therapeutic hour, rather than to proceed into the helter-skelter of the community. In short, we are habituated to our patients seeking us out, or at best being brought to us, rather than actively searching out individuals who are disturbed and convincing them that we can be of help. Further, a degree of professional snobbery has developed in the profession, which makes the training of paraprofessional mental health workers seem incongruous, a guildhall sense that only "initiates to the mysteries" are competent to treat them with the proper awe. This is a social as well as an educational snobbery, one which, unfortunately, is shared by those in the community as well as those in the profession. The mental health community has taken on the aura of a priesthood at whose services only the elect can be present, a priesthood whose members alone are capable of celebrating the holy mysteries in isolation. And as with most guilds, this attitude must be shared by the laity if it is to be efficacious in excluding interlopers. This double attitude was the first hurdle which we found that had to be surmounted.

In training a group of welfare mothers, we encountered individuals whose whole experience of any kind of governmental programs had tended to reenforce an attitude of hopelessness and a sense of personal inadequacy. In order that they would possess both the skills and the confidence in their own abilities to counsel persons of a wide variety of emotional problems, the first obstacle to be overcome was the situational one of the training sessions themselves. On our part, we found ourselves in a strange situation, one in which we tended to feel almost like outsiders, aliens, because we were forced to discuss highly technical subjects without the convenience of the shorthand of professional jargon. We confronted people in a professional situation, whom we would not ordinarily have considered as part of a professional community. And the women themselves regarded the program with more than a little suspicion, as they did all government-sponsored projects. The contextual situation was unique: professional mental health practitioners met with people who would normally be considered as totally outside the population likely to be engaged in a counseling situation in any capacity and where the professionals intended to train the nonprofessionals to be their colleagues. The complex of social taboos and expectations to be conquered on both sides was considerable. We found that only by being entirely open and honest with the women could we even hope to bridge the gap that initially stood between us, a breach that consisted of equal parts of suspicion, strangeness, vastly differing backgrounds, and perhaps most importantly, the women's lack of confidence in themselves as potentially competent in a professional endeavor.

Our plan in these classes was to relate the theoretical and experiential points through life situations, through ordinary interpersonal interactions with which these people, like most people, were familiar, if not particularly conscious. And, as far as possible, we attempted to reproduce the life situation in the classroom, stimulating the dynamics of the life-problem among the women who were being trained. Denied the safety of professional jargon, forced to translate the principles of intrapersonal and interpersonal interaction into ordinary language, we also found that we knew much more than we thought we did, for stripped of the semi-arcane aura of the professional language, we rediscovered for the first time since graduate school, and in a way that was much more immediate and concrete, the extent of our comprehension of human activity. What was theoretical became concrete, what was intuitive had to be communicated — in effect, what our jargon permitted us to hold at a distance as conceptually true became, through the necessity of speaking of it in a different language, humanely valid and specifically and concretely applicable.

The results of these classes were reassuringly successful, both in terms of the trainees personally, and in terms of their developing competence as counselors. In the first place, the program held out to individuals who had been accustomed to seeing themselves as lost in a bureaucratic maze, the possibility of their being able to perform valuable and rewarding functions well beyond their wildest imaginings. From conceiving of themselves as perpetual appendages of the welfare system, without goals or demands, either of themselves or of others, these women began to realize that they could indeed function in a professional fashion, rather like the doctors who command such exalted social prestige. From being passive recipients of welfare aid, they began to conceive of themselves as capable of both earning a wage, and earning that wage in a function that was not only socially valuable but, indeed, necessary to the functioning of the society. Not only were they entering into the community but the community itself needed them in their function. As far as their ability to perform was concerned, our informal but close evaluation persuaded us that they were competent and useful, given the supervision, advice, and general back up facilities that new counselors necessarily must have. And it was most heartwarming to realize that some of them had exceptional gifts of intuition that spoke for the possibility of their becoming superior mental health counselors in time.

Our first movements into the community at large introduced us to the real complexity of community work, to its frustrations and obstacles, not all of which ought properly to be unavoidable. In the first place, the attitude of the professional mental health community had been, as a whole, passively antagonistic. The project to train paraprofessional counselors affronted the very highly developed guild sense that one observes in professional therapists, and their attitude was, generally, one of waiting to watch as we made mistakes, until we erred ourselves out of existence. We were, after all, in the first wave of a future which violated their sense of exclusiveness and importance. A common attitude was, rather than train paraprofessionals to assume some of the functions of the professional therapist, we should devote our energies to raising money to increase the number of professional therapists trained in universities — an attitude whose defensive naiveté is belied by the statistics. Thus, with little support from the professional community, and indeed with a degree of tacit if passive opposition, we began two successive projects in the community: the first, a storefront facility in a sparsely populated lower-middle-class ghetto, staffed in the main by our paraprofessional trainees, and a further project in a large urban housing development. It cannot be said that either project was a success, but the fundamental reasons for the lack of success are illuminating and instructive. In the first place, we were working with people who had had little or no experience in seeking out professional assistance even from established and prestigious institutions. Even those who at one time or another appealed to a hospital for help did so under the authoritarian promptings of a doctor or a social worker. In the second place, we were unable to identify ourselves with the professional mystique, and hence were faced with the problem of both making our function clear, and of gaining the trust necessary to the performance of our function. Had we been able to appeal to the mystique of professional credentials, one major obstacle would have never occurred: our function would have been readily identified and our professional status obvious. Then too, the problems we were there to attempt to treat were intimately related to the conditioned sense of futility and suspicion which the inhabitants had been accustomed to; most were only too well acquainted with the bureaucratic structure of the urban hierarchy, and most had experienced only too often the frustration of attempting to secure aid through the procedures of delay and denial which often constitute the administrative channels of assistance. Lastly, the social conditions in which many of our clients were forced to live operated against the projects. Not uncommonly, we would canvas apartment buildings and homes and often begin a series of counseling sessions with a tenant. But these sessions were typically short-lived and we felt ourselves slowly but surely being pushed out the door. These clients, no matter the appalling way in which they lived or their oft seeming indifference to improving their lot, were terribly human — and terribly loathe to expose their profound sense of shame to an outsider. No matter how good our intentions, then, we failed in the most important preliminary task — we remained outsiders, representatives of an unresponsive hierarchy who would arrive in the morning and leave when the working day was over. Remaining outsiders in a subcommunity which has already experienced and become conscious of its division from the mainstream of community life, we failed to gain even the needed trust from the people we were there to help. We knew officials of the subcommunity, not the people; we were, in a sense, "alienists" — foreigners who immigrated for the day, and then returned to a distant and alien way of life.

The personal barriers we encountered in these projects were not our only difficulties. We learned that our trainees, however competent, were extremely insecure and easily shaken in situations where there could be no question, from our point of view, of their sensitivity and their ability. Their morale — so lone in getting established — proved to be very fragile. It was not unusual for us to stumble badly in our relationships with these women in the first few months. For example, one student so surprised us with her sensitive comments during a clinical case discussion that we nicknamed her "Doc." She, however, construed our admiration as implied criticism and mockery. Further, when our counselors found themselves immersed in a trying interview where they lost command of the situation their usual response was less to unravel what happened with a supervisor and more to declare themselves as basically unfit to be counselors. They were themselves, we had simply forgotten, products of long years of grinding frustration and anticipation of failure. For them to develop self-esteem was to become involved in a reorientation of their self-image that was in its way as frightening as it was earnestly desired. Back-up supervision and easy access to

supervisors became critical for our students to win their way through to a reasonably staunch view of themselves as effective and self-assertive human beings. The
favorable response of some of them was reflected as much in their improved personal appearance as in their ability to be counselors. They looked better, they
dressed better, and they walked with a more erect and proud carriage. But the
telltale marks of yesteryear's harshness can still be witnessed. None of them, as
yet, is truly comfortable and steady with her new self. It is all too clear that it
hurts not to be one's old self — even when the change is distinctly for the better.

Therefore, from the entire counstellation of these impressions grew our conviction that to advocate mental health in the community meant to become an
apostle for social change in the community at large. The true community mental
health professional, then, must deal with the health of the community as an entity, with its structures and functions, dislocations, and malfunctions. Insofar as
he *is* concerned with the entire complex of the community, he must seek to
bring about necessary changes in the structure of functions of the community in
order to alleviate abnormal conditions affecting part, and thus in a lesser way,
all, of the community. We move, then, from the politics of experience to the experience of politics — a field of endeavor foreign to the traditionally trained psychologist.

In the early fall of 1968 I willingly undertook on a voluntary basis a position (officially titled "Acting Area Director") to help develop and coordinate a
comprehensive program of mental health care in the same community in which
the training project was located. It, therefore, became possible for me to witness
mental health programing efforts from several vantage points — the one, as training director for the project; and, the other, essentially as an administrator who
would work with the community leaders, professional and otherwise, and would
be looked to by these leaders as one to direct and guide the assembling, fabrica-
tion, and initiation of badly needed mental health programs of various kinds.
And I have remained a private practitioner of psychotherapy — wherein my
bread doth lie. Working both in private therapy and in the arena of the community provides situations and ideas which stimulate the practice of private therapy,
and the close interpersonal relationship of the therapeutic office prevents the
community work from becoming merely impersonal manipulations. My professional life continues to be exciting, and I am the busiest, most uncertain psychologist I know. Each month brings new problems and new challenges which call for
skills that I may or may not have. Many are the times when I feel, as I survey all
in which I have become immersed, that my responsibilities are like those of a
builder who is setting about to build a house — lock, stock, and barrel — by himself and must, therefore, learn to be a plumber, electrician, roofer, carpenter,
etc. The mysteriously veined channels whereby communities are organized and
run must become familiar to me. The complex, interlocking relationships between departments of state and civic government must fall into place in my
mind. Rules and regulations couched in the appalling idiom of legalistic jargon

must make sense to me. And, underlying all, is the need to sense how to get people to work together effectively.

Perhaps a clear way to relate an important development in my operating philosophy as a community psychologist is by a vignette. More than half a year ago I was asked to review a study detailing the results of an inquiry into the mental health needs of a nearby, upper-middle-class suburban community. A questionnaire had been devised and the results beautifully tabulated. A principal recommendation of the study was to gather more data to test the reliability of the questionnaire and to validate the original results more definitely. But the obtained results were well within expectation. Badly needed were emergency psychiatric services, services for children and adolescents, and services for married couples experiencing marital disharmony. Feeling that I detected in the report the sure hand of a psychologist I remarked that effort would, under the circumstances, more usefully be directed toward effectuating some of these needed services. After several months of silence on the substance of the report, I at last saw some evidence that it had, however tenuously, come to official attention. A fellow professional asked me to look over a list of recommended services suggested by the study and arranged in *order of priority*. My inclination, however, was to array these services in the order of their *likelihood of accomplishment*. My emphasis was upon strategy but my colleague's was on conceptual symmetry. A scant two years ago would have found me in his corner.

In the broadest, meaningful sense of the phrase, a community mental health program may be defined as any nontraditional, innovative treatment or prevention-oriented program which visualizes problems basically in population or group terms and takes into account the valued participation of the community in serving its aims and goals. Such a definition is valid insofar as the program, if indeed structured in this way, must necessarily involve its administrators and professional and nonprofessional participants in a degree of political activity undreamed of in the private or traditional institutional situation. Any innovation or newly-conceived idea of providing services where they are needed immediately arouse the distrust, the resistance, and probably the opposition of the conservative professional community. Even so apparently simple a program as training mental health sides for a hospital ward or clinic involves a myriad of political considerations and machinations: *if* the project is funded, adequately staffed, and *if* competent recruits are found and are willing to enter the training program (all difficulties which depend on political acumen and action in the face of improbable odds), the problem still remains one of how to place these workers in the hospital clinic itself in such a way that the director of the hospital and the hospital boards are not unduly prejudiced against the trainees. These are the tasks of the master politician, certainly not those of the traditionally trained psychologist, whose education has predisposed him not to act until all the variables are known and understood, to think and analyze, run pilot projects and finally to act *only* when the outcome is as certain as possible. Were the traditional psychological philosophy applied in community work, we would be confined to collecting end-less data that might never lead to effective action. The variables are too great and are constantly changing. To wait for complete or even reasonable understanding may mean to wait forever, deep in well-intentioned but impotent thought. To wait for partial but consistent and non-contradicting data may mean to lose ir-retrievably an opportunity to act.

In passing from the world of the clinic or private practice into the world of the community at large, one moves from the finite, bounded universe whose principles are relatively well known and understood, into an infinite and expand-ing cosmos whose principles one must constantly rediscover and reevaluate. It is the movement from the closed Ptolemic universe into the exploding Einsteinian one, and like the emerging Renaissance man, we discover that this new cosmos is both electrically exciting in its possibilities, and frighteningly new in its opera-tion. In the clinical environment, plans have a well-defined beginning, middle, and end. The course of action is structured and orderly, whether one is speaking of the therapeutic situation or of the planning of a new clinic facility. Each step of the procedure is mapped out beforehand, and one does not proceed to a fu-ture step until the preceding steps have been accomplished. In both the clinic and in private practice, areas of responsibility are usually well delineated, each member of the team involved possesses a clear idea of his responsibilities and to whom he is responsible. The psychologist knows that he can depend upon the structure remaining intact, and he is certain of the precise identity and function of each element of the relationships involved. All contracts are clear — between the therapist and the patient, and between both of them and whomever else is connected with the treatment.

Thus, when the traditionally educated and experienced psychologist moves into the community, he is bewildered by the extent of his ignorance. How is the community organized? He must initially determine the structures and relation-ships between the lay and professional organizations. In setting up one program, he must be aware of the needs, capabilities, and sensitivities of the other care-giving organizations, of the channels of giving and support, of the individuals with financial, political, and communal influence and power. He must deal end-lessly with people of conflicting interests and personalities, within the context of a dozen different agencies, interest groups, and many more personalities. No wonder then, that this psychedelic impact of stimuli strikes the therapist, fresh from the serenity, quiet and isolation of the clinical situation as an unstructured welter of information, without form or sense. One's initial reaction tends to be one of either confusion or anger at one's own incompetence. But to marshall and utilize potential and existing resources, the community mental health pro-fessional must give form to these stimuli, must forge in the fire of necessity the rudiments of community organization. Overnight he must put on the mantles of Machiavelli, Levi-Strauss, and Keynes, and act in such a way that he takes best advantage of those elements he can recognize as advantageous — as I have noted.

Perhaps the most obvious result of the complexity of community work is an overwhelming feeling of frustration. Whole days may pass without one's being able to complete a single important telephone call which is critical to a step in the project. Successful communication, which one had supposed to be private, immediately becomes public (it is safe to assume in community mental health work as in politics that there is no private conversation). The very regulations seem, in their irrationality, to exist merely to make any action impossible; for instance, one statute empowers local mental health boards to collect funds but not to disburse them. Hence, to make these funds useful, to bring their force to bear upon those conditions which need remedy, some administrators have been forced to knowingly break the law, to use the funds scrupulously, though technically illegally, to produce results. Sometimes one merely needs to be aware of the legal difference that simple terminology makes; a rose by any other name may smell as sweet, but to governmental and administrative functions, too often a rose is a rose *is* simply a rose. In short, the private therapist soon finds that community work demands expediency from him — and often what is expediency in the community would seem like dishonesty in the clinical environment.

Most important in the community perhaps, and, unfortunately, most foreign to the traditional psychologist's mode of thought, is the necessity to *do*, to start a project before the future variables are known or foreseen. It is not at all unusual for community projects to be funded at six month intervals, even though they do not complete a cycle of operation for a year. To await certainty in this situation, as in many others, is never to begin. One must accustom oneself to getting a program off the ground, with the beginning, middle, and end still not coherent, perhaps without full legislative validation and without adequate funding. In addition, there are many groups operating at the community level, each confident that what it is doing is more right and necessary than what others are doing. This leads, naturally, to intense competition for the limited funds available, a condition that can easily produce a kind of defensive paranoia on the part of program administrators. Since in the community there is no immediate way of discerning which set of contradictory data is more reliable, one's humanitarian impulse must often yield to the expediency of partially informed politics. It appears that in the community a program which is operating can become self-justifying, whereas a program still being planned will remain a subject for debate. To exist and to continue to exist tends to justify one's claim for support in order to continue, and elicits support from both known and unknown sources. There is no opportunity here to run a pilot project; one either starts or he is never given the opportunity. Unfortunately, all of this involves qualities not ordinarily considered ideal in a psychologist — faith, "brass," and the courage to act. And often the community mental health professional finds himself engaged in practices which as a private therapist he would have regarded as unethical. For instance, it was with more than a bit of shock that I realized during the ghetto project described above that I was compelled to actively "sell" our services. In private practice such an attitude was unspeakable. But to be effective in the community we were forced to sell our services to people who felt no need for them and in fact tended to regard them as a threat to their pride.

Subjectively, the experience of community mental health work contrasts vividly with clinical work. In the first place, the physical wear and tear involved, the number of phone calls, private conversations, the number of times one gets into and out of his car are inconceivable in clinical practice and the university setting. The latter, with its clinics, offices, classrooms and laboratories was quiet, scholarly, comfortable, and ordered. Nothing could contrast more with the community, where it is impossible to escape from noise and confusion. In our paraprofessional project, we had borrowed the basement of a local church scheduled for demolition. The pipes rattled, the room was drafty and cold in winter and oppressively stuffy in summer, and complete strangers felt free to wander in and out at will while classes were in session. One is likely to be called upon to provide information with which he is not prepared, to think on his feet, to articulate that which is by its very nature vague, to be aggressive. Then too, one is impressed by the sense that everything one does possesses an element of the political: behind the person one is talking to lies an interlocking set of power structures, and what is said in a conversation will be reported, in varying degrees of reliability, publically. In clinical practice there is time to clear up misunderstanding. In the community a misunderstanding becomes public, and often irreversible. Thus, whereas the function of the clinician is to be sensitively honest, the community professional must be shrewdly honest, and he often finds himself speaking the most specious generalities, falling back upon cliches and truisms, to protect the point he must communicate. The traditional psychologist — a speccialist in human behavior and communication — finds that the community is so complex that he must relearn and discover what *is* in fact occurring. Instead of establishing a vertical program from inception to termination, he finds himself working with a half dozen equally important elements simultaneously, with no focal points of fixed responsibility. Thus, what finally emerges is likely to be the product of chance, accident, and circumstance, plus the community professional's ability to capitalize on fate.

From our experience there is little significant correlation between the conceptualization, logic, and procedures of the clinic environment and the community because the clinic is structured according to a homogeneous, linear order, whereas the community is composed of many simultaneous, interlocking, self-cancelling hierarchies. For example, if the chief psychologist of a large hospital attempts to initiate an emergency telephone service between his hospital and the community to help people during moments of acute crisis, his procedure is presupposed, and the progress of the innovation is always clear. He will first speak to his superior, often but not necessarily a psychiatrist, about his plan in such a way that the psychiatrist's professional sensibilities are not ruffled, that is, sensitively and tactfully. He must demonstrate sufficient knowledge of the community to indicate that he has determined where the telephones would be placed, how most efficiently to advertise their presence, and the nature of the personnel that would man the telephones at the hospital. Prolonged discussion between the psychologist and other members of the professional staff will probably be necessary to determine the precise details of the system's functioning. Even though funding might become a serious problem, it is likely to be measured in terms of man-hours that will be diverted from other, equally important hospital functions. No matter how well the psychologist has thought out his program, and no matter how tactfully and shrewdly he has sought its implementation, he may still fail, for reasons beyond either his control or foreknowledge. The community, for example, may recently have reacted unfavorably to the suicide of an outpatient under clinic care, or the program may fall victim to tensions and rivalries of the professional disciplines within the hospital and the community. And even with relatively little obstruction, the psychologist will have to work in terms of a maze of practical and emotional factors. But even so, it is obvious that the psychologist knows what his program objective is, can in all probability present a comprehensive statement of his plan, and understands most of the important steps he will have to take in order to initiate consultation on his program and succeed in its actualization. No doubt many frustrations will arise, but these can still be conceptualized within the overall structure of the environment and its logic operation.

Complicated as is the task of the hospital psychologist in initiating a new, possibly controversial but potentially valuable function, it is remarkably well structured compared with even the most elementary proposal in the community. Since my appointment as acting area director, I have been using my own private office and facilities, for there appeared to be none other in the area. The relatively simple question arose as to who would be responsible for the telephone expenses incurred, expenses which were quite low but which were necessary to the function of the position. An area director cannot begin to function without a telephone. A local state agency – in this case a perenially under-funded clinic – would have been the first place to appeal to for office space and telephone facilities. But this request would have been an intolerable imposition on their already inadequate finances, since the state funds salaries of personnel only and provides nothing for their overhead. Another possible source of assistance would have been a private hospital which had donated land for a new mental health center. But there seemed no logical reason why the hospital *should* provide office space and facilities for a state appointee. The Community Chest was closed, since it cannot support any but civic nonprofit institutions, and private funds were unavailable because there was no evidence of available, long-term funding from other sources. The regional office of the Department of Mental Health had no regulations permitting funding for such purposes, and while the Area Board might have obtained funds, it was restricted by law from disbursing them. Finally, the local Mental Health Association verbally agreed to supply the required funds, but in practice found it necessary to refer back to department regulations (or the lack of such regulations) which made such expenditure impossible in fact, if not in theory. In short, nearly a year after assuming the office of Acting Area Mental Health Director, and having exhausted the regular channels, I am still using my private office and facilities. While I am now convinced that had I acted more aggressively, manipulated a bit more shrewdly, applied the right pressure at the right time in the right place I might have secured the funds, it remains true that the various structures made it difficult if not impossible to work out of an office with communication facilities except at my own expense. Mercifully, recent regulations permit payment of telephone expenses, *but* nothing else. The procedures of appeal in the community, for even so elementary a problem as the procurement of office facilities are diffuse, circular, and sometimes futile. The community worker must become accustomed to traveling through a strange country whose highways are laid out according to no discernable pattern, without map or compass, and finally to arriving back where he started.

Recently, the Commissioner of Mental Health invited to a luncheon in a private dining room of a nearby restaurant the local Area Board presidents and the acting area directors to discuss with himself and several assistant commissioners how his office could be used more efficiently to implement and accommodate local programs. He expressed his sincere desire to do whatever was possible to further the progress that was reported in the several areas of the state. Toward the end of the meeting one board president, after detailing the legal confusions and contradictions which impede substantial and meaningful progress in the area of Community Mental Health, pointed to a door over which hung the sign, "Exit." Beneath it hung a cardboard sign, "No Exit." We all laughed; we knew exactly why he had called our attention to this exit which was not an exit, a world in which we knew only that the doors existed. Our function is to open the doors, though we might not know whether they lead out or in. The stairways on the other side may lead upward to substantial successes, or they may lead downward. But even if they descend, we must open the doors to begin building at the bottom — this is "The Way Down and Out" into a new light and a new atmosphere for the community as well as for the individuals that comprise it.

7 Requiem for a Dream: The Job Corps on Trial

Harold I. Lewack
U.S. Department of Labor

[Editor's Note] : *To its everlasting credit or damnation, the War on Poverty – perhaps more than any other domestic program undertaken within the last thirty years – served to heighten the expectations of the poor and powerless. It also succeeded in attracting to its ranks many professionals who, long before the advent of OEO, were hard at work trying to alter the existing balance of power and opportunity between our society's "haves" and "have nots." Harold I. Lewack was such a man. In this chapter, he traces the conflicts and contradictions that surrounded the development and implementation of one of the War on Poverty's most heralded and earliest casualties, the Job Corps. In this chapter, Lewack analyzes, through a recapitulation of his own involvement in a particular Job Corps Center, the conditions under which, as he puts it, "a shining jewel lost its luster." But even more importantly, his chapter includes an attempt to define, however preliminarily, a set of concrete working principles regarding the problems associated with social action and institutional change.*

Prologue

Unlike many other contributors to this volume, I am not a mental health professional. I was a high school dropout, and, although I hold an undergraduate degree in economics and a graduate degree in adult education, I have never worked at either trade, except peripherally. On the other hand, I have spent eight years working with the "helping professions" and have probably been contaminated to some degree. Surveying my credentials, first as union organizer and labor negotiator, and then as a manpower expert, I must conclude that the common denominator in all of this is that I am probably what sociologists call a "change agent," heaven help me. As I view it, the other contributors started out knowing who they were and arrived at the same confused state unintentionally, whereas I am an old hand at this sort of thing.

There does not appear to be any single path that one can follow to become a professional change agent, such as choosing a particular major in college. In my own case, my university training was less important than my avocational interests. I spent a number of years in youth and student organizations, serving in various leadership capacities. My first real job was as a writer, although I did not view myself as especially talented in this regard. I spent more than a dozen years in the labor movement, holding various paid staff positions. My principal function was negotiating contracts, a skill I had to learn the hard way. During this period, I spend a great deal of time representing and observing social workers and fund raisers, two groups of skilled professional practitioners who sometimes fancy themselves as change agents. It was also during these years that I began to question both the uses to which philanthropic resources were being put and the structures which had evolved to serve them.

Suddenly, in the mid-1960s, a new agency emerged on the scene, with money supplied by Uncle Sam and a new kind of mandate to serve the poor. This agency, the Office of Economic Opportunity (OEO), in developing and implementing the programs it defined as consistent with its "mission," gave birth to the Job Corps. A chance advertisement for a "Community Relations Director" in a Job Corps Center being established in New England gave me my chance to join the late-lamented War on Poverty

Time Frame

In the Spring of 1969, the Job Corps component of the War on Poverty was fighting for its life. In the election campaign of the preceding fall, the Republican candidate for president had publically denounced the Job Corps as an extravagance. Speculation concerning the new president's intentions following his inauguration ranged from a total beheading of the patient to the number of limbs to be sheared off. Without revealing his true intent, President Richard M. Nixon asked his new Secretary of Labor, George P. Shultz, to consider the problem of incorporating the Job Corps into an overall attack on the problem of youth unemployment. Back came the answer, and shortly thereafter it was announced that the Job Corps would be absorbed into the Department of Labor. For some unexplained reason, the effective date was delayed for several months. On the heels of the first announcement came word that nearly half the camps would be closed before the end of the fiscal year, thus reducing the overall program budget by one-third. Supporters of the Job Corps attempted to delay its transfer to the Labor Department in the hopes of avoiding these closings, but without any significant success. Most observers concluded that the Job Corps might be granted a reprieve, but that it had not gained immunity from further prosecution. Others saw its curtailment as the first stage in a total dismanteling of the Office of Economic Opportunity and, as things have turned out, their predictions came true.

The question posed by the Job Corps experience is clear: can an idea be divorced from its antecedents? For all its rhetoric, the Job Corps was not conceived of as a program to meet the needs of young people. Its roots were set in three separate but related responses to the potential unrest posed by disadvantaged youth in the 1960s: *nostalgia* (it worked in the thirties, when it was known as the Civilian Conservation Corps, so why not now?); *fear* (get the troublemakers out of town); and *greed* (the cost-plus-fixed-fee contracts negotiated with industry, and the expectation on the part of some conservationists that the corpsmen would become a source of cheap labor for back-logged projects).

The story told in this chapter is about a men's urban center located in New England, how it got started, the kinds of people who were attracted to it, and why it failed. It attempts to make the point that new programs do not necessarily imply new ways of confronting problems, and that unless a serious attempt is made to understand assumptions and define objectives, and to relate these to theories of behavioral change, we are merely "tinkering" with our future and are not likely to make much headway in effecting real change. It also makes the point that the "solutions" have to be developed in the old settings, otherwise we find that we arrive at the gate with nothing but the old ways to "get us through the winter."

The Setting: Unfertile Ground

At the tip of Clark's Point, a peninsula which juts into Buzzards Bay, Massachusetts, stands deserted Fort Taber, a granite monument to the Civil War, built in anticipation of a Confederate naval assault which never came. In due time, its cannons were spiked and hauled away. During World Wars I and II, the gun emplacements went underground. But again the preparations for war were not needed. Suddenly this quiet, nearly abandoned military post became the battleground of a real war. Not one that was fought with bullets, but a war nonetheless.

The stage had been set earlier, when Congress approved the Economic Opportunity Act of 1964, whose declared purpose was the elimination of poverty in America. The symbols of this new kind of war were classrooms. Along with the other reminders of past wars, these classrooms are now deserted. The wind whistles through the old fort, past a new gymnasium and dining hall, past refurbished dormitory buildings and classrooms-in-the-round. Clearly, a battle was lost here.

The casualties of this war were our youth. Other battles followed with the same outcome. Apparently those who managed these new settings were not very adept at defending themselves. The reasons for their predicament are not hard to understand. This is the saga of one such setting, which cost the taxpayers nearly $15 million. Through it, we may perhaps comprehend why the outcome in these battles is always so predictable.

Our tale begins in the spring of 1965, when the sound of hammering could be heard in a dozen reopened military bases. Job Corps officials across the country were preparing to transport thousands of underprivileged youth from the inner city and rural areas to these new centers of learning. Many saw in these new centers of learning. Many saw in these new camps a revival of the successful Civilian Conservation Corps experience of the 1930s. Others saw a new partnership with industry being forged, one destined to have an impact on public education.

All of this speculation receded into the background when the first corpsmen arrived. One of the points of destination was Rodman, the picturesque site of Fort Taber, now renamed, and designated as an urban center for male high school dropouts who wanted to study data processing and office skills. The new Job Corps Center was located on the edge of the old whaling city of New Bedford, with its largely immigrant working class population of 100,000. A preliminary survey had indicated a desire on the part of this community for the new business this venture would bring, and the presence of a large nonwhite population seemed to insure a tolerance for newcomers, a majority of whom would be nonwhite. The sponsorship of this center was also impressive. Science Research Associates had acquired a reputation as an innovative publisher of educational texts and testing materials, and had only recently been acquired by the giant IBM corporation. What better teacher of data processing could one ask for, than this desirable combination? Or so the Jobs Corps reasoned.

The idea of moving young men and women out of poverty by physically removing them from the environment of poverty is not a new one. Our landscape is dotted with institutions of various kinds, from children's reformatories to halfway houses to YMCAs. Unlike the others, however, the Job Corps would offer training and, hopefully, a job tied to this training.

Each center was expected to experiment with different techniques for accomplishing this objective. For example, the Kilmer Job Corps Center, which was operated by the International Telephone and Telegraph Corporation, tried sensitivity training (it wasn't called that, but it worked the same way). The Lincoln, Nebraska, Job Corps, operated by Northern Systems Corporation, divided itself into small "campuses" built around the skills being taught at the center. In addition, corpsmen who did well were rewarded with extra privileges and improved living quarters. Rodman also adopted the campus concept, except it referred to the four groups of 120 enrollees as "teams." Each was concerned with a single stage of training (e.g., orientation, remedial and prevocational education, skill training, and work experience and graduation). In addition, the Rodman formula was based on the use of recent college graduates as role models, together with a high staff-to-student ratio, and daily meetings of all staff as a form of sensitivity training, but without the focus on the "self." Like most industry training systems, neither the corpsmen nor the community were involved in the design of any of these centers.

The Jobs Corps assumed that the contractor, Science Research Associates, knew what it was doing when it awarded a contract to train dropouts in data processing. SRA assumed that dropouts could be trained by the same methods that had worked successfully in the past with industrial workers. The staff of the Job

Corps center assumed that enthusiasm and motivation could overcome deficiencies in training and experience on the part of those working with disadvantaged
youngsters. Finally, the community of New Bedford assumed that it could have
federal money, without making any effort to see that the money would remain
in the community. Assumption upon assumption. But, then again, in 1965 assumptions were the stuff out of which realities were expected to spring.

One of the lessons that sociology has taught us is that social institutions cannot be transplanted from one environment to another without considering the
impact of the new environment on that institution. It seems characteristic of reformers that they assume the reverse — it will be the new environment and not
they themselves who will change.

New Bedford, like many New England towns, had seen better times and
looked its age. Its tallest buildings were not offices but an aging hotel, two department stores, and the home of the city's only daily newspaper. Along the
waterfront stood a row of nearly abandoned textile plants, left over from another era. Some are now occupied by garment manufacturers and small electron-
ic firms. New Bedford also has its street of fine old stately mansions, and its ex-
clusionist Wamsetta Club, which caters to the few remaining Yankee bluebloods,
now vastly outnumbered by an assortment of immigrants who are the true legacy of the textile era. The latter live in less elegant surroundings (i.e., three-story
wooden tenements which are characteristics of New England towns). Chief
among this immigrant population are the Portuguese, followed by the Acadians
(descendants of the French-speaking settlers of Nova Scotia, who were driven
out by the British), a large Cape Verdian contingent (a people of dark complex-
ion who speak Portuguese, from two groups of islands to the west of Africa),
and the English settlers of the past few years. In New Bedford, the Irish are the
power brokers, with an interest in catering to this separation.

The eyes of the citizens of New Bedford were turned inward toward a romanticized past that served to obliterate the drab reality of the present. That present, a result of the city having been repeatedly bypassed by wartime prosperity,
finally caught up with it during the Korean War. Twice it had been visited by severe hurricanes which had left much damage in their wake. Before the city could
think about doing something about its high unemployment rate (thrice the national average) it first had to obtain federal help in building a hurricane dyke, a
wall of granite boulders that stretched across the mouth of the Achusnet River,
interrupted only by a small sea gate. After the sea wall came a small industrial
park. Outside the city limits there arose a new university, Southeastern Massachusetts Technical Institute. The new four-year institution combined two former
community colleges and was to be housed in a striking campus complex designed by the world famous architect Paul Rudolph. The resulting furor over the design of the buildings was overshadowed only by the announcement of the coming of the Job Corps.

Into this closed society there now came a new breed of city slicker — some were graduates of Ivy League schools, others came from small midwestern colleges where they had been recruited into the Peace Corps, and still others were graduates of the streets of major cities. They shared one thing in common: in time, they would explain to their new neighbors how things ought really to be done. In the meantime, there was much happening at the center.

Understandably, the staff's first concern was with the inadequacy of the facilities. An engineering survey team had recommended against the site, because it lacked sufficient space to feed and house the number that was required to run a center efficiently. While the dormitories were adequate, none of the other buildings were large enough for a dining hall; only a few of the smaller buildings were suitable for classrooms, and there were no facilities for recreation. A year was to go by while center officials pleaded with the Job Corps for these facilities. Eventually, they were provided at a cost of $3 million. Rodman became the only Job Corps camp with buildings specifically designed for its use. With the ocean on three sides, it could now qualify as one of the brightest jewels in the Job Corps constellation.

Dazzled by the beauty of their surroundings, heady with the realization that they now had freedom to apply their ideas, and preoccupied with the problem of how to provide leisure time activity for fifty-five hours per week (which had been overlooked by the planners), the staff could hardly be blamed for ignoring the warning signs. In their first meeting with community people they were amused by their neighbors' total preoccupation with security arrangements, a subject which the center directors had hardly begun to discuss among themselves. In almost every community in America there are contending forces that achieve a kind of equilibrium, until something intervenes to upset the balance. In a large city, people tend to take sides even before the event. Not so in the small town. Fear of taking unpopular positions caused those who were opposed to the Job Corps to take an indirect route. They played on the fears of the immediate neighbors. They wrote stories in the newspapers that exaggerated minor incidents. The more venal among them sought to profit personally by the presence of the Job Corps, either through business dealings, or by achieving notoriety through unfounded attacks which could not be answered in kind, and then exploiting this for political gain. How does one begin to mount a defense against this kind of thing?

As was true in other towns near Job Corps centers, a majority of the whaling city's residents remained aloof. Just before the Center was officially dedicated, an effort to establish a community relations council came to no avail, primarily because the city's leading citizens saw no need for one. The Center officialdom was equally unconcerned, as evidenced by the fact that the top brass stayed away from this first significant encounter with the people who had it in their power to make the corpsmen feel welcome in a strange community.

Relations with the community was part of my responsibility during the first few months of the Center's existence. I had only limited experience in this area, yet I had been hired because the Center director felt uncomfortable with company public relations types. I had hopes of breaking down the community's reserve by involving various organizations in the Center's programs. Accordingly, I pressed for a posture of openness and consistency in the Center's dealings with the community. But preoccupation with internal problems drew my attention and the rest of the staff's away from thoughts of the community to what was happening with the Corpsmen.

Enter the Private Sector

What had brought dropouts and company men together? The genesis of the decision to involve American business is described by the former Deputy Director of the Job Corps, Christopher Weeks, in his book, *Job Corps: Dollars and Dropouts* (1967):

> Suddenly and unexpectedly, something happened which radically changed the situation. A letter arrived on Shriver's desk from Robert Chasen, president of the Federal Electric Corporation in Paramus, New Jersey . . . This letter was not based on any hasty decision by Federal Electric; for eight months earlier, Chasen had called together a special study group of top corporation staff. Their mission — figure out where the corporation could expand its business for profit over the next five years in the face of well known predictions that the Defense Budget had reached a peak, and would level off or even fall. Their specific target — diversify operations from their present total reliance on Defense contract to a position where at least half their income came from non-Defense sources. Federal Electric was not alone in facing this problem . . . The corporation might move into the regular commercial market, or it could look for ways of tapping others areas of governmental spending where major increases in activity seemed imminent . . . Appropriations for aid to education . . . were skyrocketing and Labor Department training programs also looked like a good bet for major increases. So the call went out to the Washington office to collect all available material on federal government training programs . . . As a result, corporate management made a decision — try for a piece of the Job Corps business, and be prepared to commit whatever company resources were necessary to carry out a Job Corps contract. The first step to implement that decision was the leter . . .

Since Job Corps contracts were cost-plus-fixed-fee arrangements (which meant that the contractor would be reimbursed after he had spent his own money), very few small companies or universities were in a position to quickly assemble a detailed proposal and begin operations with full confidence that any expenditure disallowed by the Job Corps would be absorbed by the parent company. Of course, one of the primary considerations in using private contractors was the hope that they would persuade other private companies to hire their graduates. As a hedge against the possibility that this would not occur, the Job Corps contracted with the various State Employment Services to place returning Job Corpsmen.

One Job Corps Center, Gary, in San Marcos, Texas, distinguished itself in this regard. Located away from major population centers, with a staff that lived on the grounds, Gary's success caused it to become the largest men's center in the nation, with some 3,000 corpsmen in residence. With the full support of the governor and the president, a conference of industry representatives had been convened to discuss how industry could help the new center. It was agreed that each group of employers would loan the Job Corps key executives to help design its training program. In addition, each industry accepted a quota of graduates that would be hired upon completion of training. By way of contrast, company recruitment at most other Job Corps centers was accomplished by visiting teams of interviewers (usually the same ones who did college recruiting), with the predictable result that only a handful of the best corpsmen and women were selected for jobs.

Because of its preeminence in data processing, a skill which was looked upon as a high paying option for the disadvantaged, the Job Corps asked IBM to submit a proposal. The initial proposal was actually drafted by IBM's educational subsidiary, Science Research Associates, whose experience up to that point had been confined to publishing testing materials and educational texts. However, SRA found that writing and implementing a proposal were two entirely different matters. SRA soon realized that it would have to recruit noncompany men to run the center's educational programs. Only in the area of general administration was SRA able to utilize borrowed IBM personnel who were already knowledgeable in these matters.

On paper, the mixture worked well. For example, the company men supplied engineering skills that enabled the physical rehabilitation to go forward on schedule. A second asset supplied by the corporation was administrative skills that cut through the myriad of regulations pouring forth weekly from the Washington based "contract specialists" spoke each others' languages, since both had been trained by and in the aerospace and defense industries. These regulations provided the basis for a large on-board staff of administrative people, almost equal in size to the teaching and counseling staff.

Along with their preference for the familiar, the corporate men brought with them a tendency to view education as a form of balance sheet, wherein each dollar of expenditure was expected to yield comparable value, despite the fact that the product they were dealing with here (i.e., corpsmen) was not uniform. Having had no experience in working with the disadvantaged, these executives favored the lock-step method of teaching, with individuals being paced by the group and the blame being on the student if he falls behind. These attitudes were reinforced by the influx of retired military officers, whose "second income" made it possible to undercut civilians competing for the same jobs.

The existence of these two diverse groups did make for some tension, but at Rodman it was held in check by the personality of the Center director. Many of the company men thoroughly enjoyed their Job Corps experience, which proved to be a welcome diversion from the business of selling computers. Others counted the months until rotation would return them to the corporate womb. With a few exceptions, the educational reformers and the company men never grew close, because their jobs did not bring them into daily contact with each other, as mine did.

It is not IBM's fault that those who might be most qualified for this type of assignment, by virtue of their experience as teachers and educational administrators, could not be pried loose from their regular positions with job offers that had no future. Some of those who did leave regular jobs did so through leaves of absence. Just at the point when they had learned their lessons and were beginning to apply them, the year was over and they were gone. The company took advantage of existing vacancies to place its own men in key positions, on the theory that it could rely on their seasoned judgment. However, for a brief period they achieved a false sense of security, until the next wave of public criticism forced them to reevaluate the situation.

Training and Education

Given this history, it is understandable that the content of the training turned out to be largely traditional vocational education, with some basic education thrown in. This was to be expected, since contracts were awarded on the basis of reputation and not on the uniqueness of the training methodology (the Job Corps is not alone among agencies in its use of such criteria). Thus, in effect, the effort to retrain the disadvantaged was entrusted to the same professionals who had failed with them in the first instance. The result was a higher than expected dropout rate, a problem which continued to plague the Job Corps in its first months of existence. But the failuire to understand the world of the dropout went deeper than mere statistics. The following story of IBM's experience in teaching data processing to the disadvantaged is revealing.

IBM is a corporation that believes in the value of training, and its record of support for that belief is unmatched by any other company. At the same time, IBM's policy is to select only those scoring highest in aptitude and achievement tests and to screen out all the rest. When SRA announced its intention of training dropouts in data processing, IBM was less than enthusiastic. Now data processing, as the term is used by laymen, covers both punched cards and computer operation. When Tom Watson, Jr., Chairman of the Board, gave his reluctant consent to the project, it was with the understanding that the training would be confined to the accounting machines and would not cover computers. As a result, the young men who came to Rodman expecting to learn about computers had to go away disappointed. Moreover, these same IBM representatives were telling them that the punched card was already obsolete. The teaching staff was understandably unhappy with this decision and they finally succeeded in getting the limitation on training removed. It was agreed that an initial group of twenty-five would begin training as programmers at a nearby facility, using rented time. At the same time, OEO was asked to authorize rental of a computer to be installed at the center.

IBM had agreed to waive the requirement that only those in the ninetieth percentile on the Programmer Aptitude Test were eligible for training (only one corpsman met this requirement). Having come this far, IBM balked at the next step. Although IBM is the leading exponent of Computer Assisted Instruction, which implied individually paced learning, it continued to train its own employees by the traditional lecture method. Using this system in its first class of Job Corpsmen proved to be a disaster, since only five in a class of twenty-five completed the course.

The IBM 1401 Computer, which had been ordered earlier, arrived before the first class graduated. The Center now felt committed to conducting a second class and, in due course, it was held with the same predictable results. Like many of today's public school teachers, IBM concluded that it was the student and not IBM's teaching methods that were at fault, and that its original perceptions had been correct. Rather than admit to its failure publically, the computer was put to use scheduling students. One cannot avoid asking why systems analysis was not used here to devise an appropriate teaching methodology. Obviously, the program did not enjoy a high enough priority to warrant such an investment of company resources.

The contrast between hardware and weapons system development, and the intuitive methods of education were nowhere more apparent than in this area. This was certainly true in 1963, when the California Youth Authority opened a youth work camp for dropouts as a precursor of the Job Corps. Their experience indicated that, due to the costs involved, more needed to be known about the type of youngster who is best suited for residential training and whether alternative arrangements were available, before further federal or state investment was justified. Some of the questions that arose were:

> Are residential centers aimed at rehabilitating hard core youth who are alienated from society, or will it be selective in that it will appeal to the most talented among the poor? If rehabilitation is the objective, how alienated can a youth be before he becomes ineligible? Do we accept the fact of his misconduct, or do we inquire into its causes? If we inquire into its causes, what weight do we assign to

an unhealthy life, and how much to weakness of character (which will *not* be materially affected by a short stay at a camp)? How do we obtain information about family experiences, without appearing to intrude into personal matters which society has no business investigating? (Testimony of April 25, 1969, before the Subcommittee on Employment, Manpower and Poverty, of the Senate Labor and Public Welfare Committee, p. 5).

With the wisdom of hindsight, we now know that the dropout is not a uniform type, and that costs cannot be held constant since needs will differ. The real issue then, is not man-year costs, but how do we match the right individual with the right program?

The original Job Corps cost projections had only been rough estimates of what was needed, since there were no models to follow. Some contractors did exceed these estimates and were reimbursed by the Job Corps for these added costs, although their fee remained constant. IBM was an exception. It decided quite early that staying within the cost limitations would impress the Job Corps more than results with youngsters.

It is no wonder that the Job Corps avoided asking embarrassing questions of its contractors in the beginning, since to do so would have set back the timetable and probably also added to the cost. Not only were the remedies offered from old bottles, but in their haste to become operational, they skipped from the blueprint to full production without pausing to field test a prototype. This explains, in part, why there were so many rejects in those early years.

Because of this haste, one of the issues that failed to receive consideration was that of near vs. far relocation of youngsters. While most women's centers were in urban communities, the great majority of men's centers were far removed from cities. Furthermore, most of the women residents were not from the communities where the centers were located. The Job Corps managers defended this practice on the grounds that a poor home life and bad companions go hand-in-hand. They also asserted that a "controlled environment" could achieve quicker results. The contrary argument was that the Job Corps wasn't reaching those who needed it most, and that whatever success had been achieved was due to "self-selection." The controlled environment turned out to be ye olde institution, which required reentry conditioning when it was over. The Job Corps relented a bit when, at mid-point, it began making assignment of youngsters to camps by region. But the debate continued until it was resolved by the Job Corps being absorbed into the Department of Labor.

"By Your Thoughts Alone . . ."

It is only fitting that a new setting should attract to it men and women who believe that a fresh start is better than trying to change established institutions.

Jerome M. Ziegler and R. Barry Fisher were representative of the best of this breed. As director and deputy director of the Rodman Job Corps Center, they generated a degree of enthusiasm and a zest for new ideas that became the inspiration for a host of young men and women with the same sense of commitment. From the college campuses and the Peace Corps they came. Each one was made to feel that he had something to contribute. This feeling was further reinforced by seminar-type staff training sessions presided over by the top brass. This "atmosphere of openness" continued even after the corpsmen's arrival.

Ziegler had headed a successful consulting firm before accepting SRA's bid to manage the Center. Previously he had worked with Dr. Robert Havinghurst on a study of the Chicago School System. Some of those who had worked with him in Chicago were attracted to the Job Corps, along with a majority of newcomers to the education game. R. Barry Fisher, formerly SRA's personnel director, became deputy director. The proposal had been his handiwork. In his youth, he had dropped out of school to become a fisherman, from whence he rose to the command of his own ship. His decision to return to school resulted in a master's degree from Harvard's Graduate School of Education, and finally to a position with SRA. Subsequently, he resigned to become the director of another Job Corps center. Both men were eventually retired, in feeble attempts to placate local public opinion.

The fate of these founding fathers concerns us less than that of their handiwork. The frail structure they had erected depended too greatly on the force of personality. Everywhere there was a resistance to the systematic analysis of problems. The Center director had made a virtue out of lack of credentials, and as a consequence, compassion was seen as the answer to every problem. One of the evaluators spotted the consequences of this policy:

> Although progress had been made in defining a curriculum in each
> of several instructional areas, more effort in this direction is called
> for. Discussions with Instructors, Tutor-Counselors, and students
> leave an impression of little consensus, and no little confusion, as
> to where they are going and how in general they will get there.

It now seems clear that highly sophisticated teaching methodologies, such as team teaching, core curriculum, and programmed learning, require trained practitioners to implement them. In their absence, there appeared to be no alternative but to fall back on traditional methods that at least work 70 percent of the time, militant slogans notwithstanding. That there is no substitute for know-how and experience is still sound advice.

Reference had also been made to the worsening relations with the community. While important, it was of lesser consequence than the story of how the "education gap" failed to become an issue. We had expected that our trainees would need lots of help in achieving a level of proficiency acceptable to employers. We did not suspect that we might not be equal to the task. The first indication that something was wrong with our training design came in the form of test scores from the graduates who took the National Business Entrance Examination. Our poor showing resulted in the scraping of plans to administer the Federal Civil Service Clerks Examination to all graduates. The second warning resulted from an accidental discovery.

IBM had commissioned a New York film producer to do a film about the Center. The star of this $80,000 effort was a Puerto Rican youngster from New York's East Harlem who had spent eleven months in the Job Corps and had married a local girl. He was accidently discovered working as a janitor in the New Bedford school system. Further inquiry revealed that he had never attended classes, since this was permissable. His counselor excused himself by saying that youngsters need time to find themselves. It was this young man's misfortune that time ran out when a new directive arrived indicating the maximum stay at Rodman would henceforth be only one year. A new job was quickly found for him, and a later film version deemphasized the permissive nature of the program.

One serious effort was made at reform from within. It came about in an indirect way, due to the belated discovery that those who elected to come to Rodman were somewhat older (average age 19) and had on the average earned more than the minimum wage before enrolling in the Job Corps. Unfortunately, most office jobs are held by women who either live with their families or are married and supplement their husband's income. Anyone coming right out of school was expected to start at the minimum wage, until they had some practical experience (most commercial high schools are strong on skills and weak on what goes into an actual job). Apparently, the planners had failed to take this into account, and the first group of graduates was dismayed at finding that they were expected to start at the then minimum wage of $1.25 per hour, which was less than they had earned previous to their joining the program. The Center could provide no answer, short of channeling all graduates to companies which paid more than the minimum.

Since my own interests were in the area of manpower planning, I asked and was given time off to prepare a report on the pathways to advancement within the average business office. I found that the same functions often carried different titles in different industries; and that wage rates were usually unequal, even though the same work was being performed.

As a result of my inquiry, I recommended that the Center change its focus from entry level jobs within the general office to training for the second or third step of the job ladder in particular industries that paid decent wages. Unfortunately, there was a shortage of teachers who knew how to train for jobs in this fashion. The individual who was responsible for developing the vocational curriculum was not in agreement that such a "drastic" change was called for, and my suggestion was never implemented. Fortunately, my second idea received a more enthusiastic reception.

During its first year, the Job Corps center had developed a unique concept of student-run enterprises, which trained corpsmen in business skills, while enabling them to earn additional income. These included a general story, a snack bar, a laundry, and a student-run bank. This arrangement allowed the Center to provide a limited form of on-the-job training. The next step occurred when the Center persuaded a nearby Air Force base (Otis, on Cape Cod) to take a group of corpsmen for a period of several weeks and allow them to work at real tasks. Some of these assignments were unrelated to the training at Rodman.

To maximize its value, I proposed that work experience be offered at the end of the training, and that it serve a dual function; that of providing the center with an evaluation of a corpsman's readiness to graduate, and the missing ingredient of realism, which I had earlier tried and failed to introduce into the curriculum. The new approach to on-the-job training was tried, first at the Newport Naval Base, and later in Boston with both the state government and private employers. The latter required the establishment of a "halfway house" in the Boston YMCA, because the distance from New Bedford made it impractical to commute on a daily basis. The success of these two programs resulted in making such work experience a prerequisite for graduation.

It was perhaps fitting that the departure of Messrs. Ziegler and Fisher was preceded by an incident that both characterized their personal style of leadership and the great distance between the national administration of the Job Corps and the constituency it served. During the period when the Job Corps officialdom in Washington became greatly concerned over newspaper disclosures that some centers had convicted felons on their staffs, Ziegler received a notice to fire a young black instructor who was greatly admired by the corpsmen. Ziegler had known of his prison record, and had nevertheless employed him as a model for corpsmen who also had served time and now wanted assurances that society would give them a second chance. After a long and bitter exchange of words, the Job Corps relented and the instructor was returned to duty at the Center.

After Ziegler's and Fisher's departure, a mood of complacency took hold among the remaining staff members. While proficiency testing was discontinued, enrollees continued to be tested for academic achievement, since it was now a Job Corps requirement. But no one paid much attention to the results, until a Senate sub-committee began looking into the matter. In comparing all men's Job Corps Centers, Rodman ranked at the bottom on both reading and math gains. To be more specific, Rodman had scored a zero gain on reading and a 1.1 grade level loss in computational skill. How was this possible? The Center claimed that the entering and leaving scores should not be compared since they involved different corpsmen. Since it had never been acknowledged that there was an "education gap," such questions could not be adequately answered. The scene now shifted to the community relations front, where the mood was anything but complacent.

The Community, the Corporation and
the Corpsmen

When the newspapers first began featuring stories about the criminal behavior of a small minority of corpsmen, the top brass of the corporation began making their appearance at the Center with increasing frequency. The Center officials would point with pride to various accomplishments, but the real concern of these corporation officials was the growing number of news stories that were unfavorable.

A minor incident involving a score of corpsmen and some town rowdies over the dating of local girls provided the spark that brought smoldering community resentments to a head. Within forty-eight hours, the City Counsil wired Sargent Shriver requesting that the Center be closed. The congressman representing the district, Hastings Keith, who up until then had been ambivalent, joined the chorus of opposition. In desperation, the major empanneled a "blue ribbon" committee to review the facts and make recommendations. Caught between a Republican congressman, a Democratic mayor, and a divided City Council, the committee chose not to examine the wisdom of the council's action, or the causes of disquiet within the community, which the head of the local NAACP had labeled as "racist." Instead, it confined itself to the real and imagined grievances of local residents, which it attributed to the lack of channels of communication.

Shortly before the City Council acted, the parent company moved to gain effective control over the situation — first by putting its own man in charge of community relations, and later by filling key vacancies with company men or retired military officers. Money for public relations now became available (previously it had been starved for funds). Soon there was a proliferation of committees, and people were now "talking to one another." The tragedy of Rodman was that, as the end drew near, each side believed that it was indeed moving closer to the other.

The story of the sewerage treatment plan illustrates the degree of "closeness" that was achieved. Shortly after the Center had "cleaned up" its image, it received a request from the mayor for permission to construct a sewerage treatment plant in the middle of the campus. The Center was delighted to acquiese in the city's request to the General Services Administration, which fortunately turned it down. While the community had found a property owner who would not fight back, the company's public relations expert hailed this agreement as an example of center-community cooperation.

But Rodman had clearly become a problem child to IBM. As the months passed, it became clear that nothing fundamental had changed. The company's "solution" to this problem was to delete "IBM" from the Center's name. Henceforth, the contractor was to be known as the "Rodman Training Corporation."

Slowly, inevitably, the Center grew increasingly isolated, first within the community, secondly from the parent company, and finally from the corpsmen themselves, when they sensed that something was wrong, and showed it in the only way left to them — by acting up. The drop out and "kick out" rates soared, as the new Center director sought to live up to his nickname: "Sundown Nelson." The latter referred to the fact that the last flight of the day left New Bedford's airport at dusk, and a corpsman who broke the rules in the morning might well find himself on his way back home by sundown.

The Center had made every concession to the community save one: it continued to maintain that an individualized approach was needed. However, as class size grew, the inevitable lock-step method of teaching returned. It was inevitable that the experiment would be formally pronounced dead when, at a conference of educators, it was announced that the Center had seen the wisdom of having a more "structured setting." Clearly, the community had made its influence felt. Now all that remained was for a belated economy drive to cut off its life support, some three years after it had opened its doors.

Reflections and Analysis

Settings which are designed to deal with problems and not people are self-defeating, and end up expending all of their energy in perpetuating themselves. This is equally true of settings dedicated to particular "mechanisms." Only those settings whose objectives are defined in terms of "results to be achieved" will ultimately survive.

Peter Drucker (1969), the noted management sage, uses the example of a shoe factory to make this point:

> Anyone who has ever tried to answer the question, 'What is our business?' has found it a difficult, controversial and elusive task. 'We make shoes' may seem obvious and simple. But it is a useless answer (because) it does not tell anyone what to do. Nor, equally important, does it tell anyone what not to do.

Neither is "making money" an adequate answer, since this is equally true of other forms of endeavor. Drucker concludes from this example that "what we actually do depends much less on the vehicle than the specific satisfaction it is meant to convey (i.e., protection for the feet, with comfort and style) and the specific contribution for which the business expects to get paid (i.e., acceptable product at a reasonable price)." In the conflict over efficiency vs. effectiveness, Drucker leans heavily towards the latter.

Nor does it follow that the solution is contained in the statement of the problem. An example of this was cited by Christopher Weeks (1969): "The kid is told when he joins that this is a last ditch attempt to salvage him. So on his first day he is beaten up; his stuff is swiped on the second day; after 10 days he goes home. The Job Corps has reinforced a failure." Weeks concluded from this that large centers are too visible. But how large is too large? In answering one question, Weeks raises others.

Returning again to our case study, we found that the results of testing were never fed back into the system and used to improve the program. Corpsmen were only asked if they were satisfied with the education they were receiving *after* they had left the program. In response, the Job Corps hastens to add that they have a Corpsmen Advisory System, and so they do. But it does not say that the corpsmen will be consulted about curriculum, or camp structure, or how staff is to be selected. These questions are not meant to imply that the camps should be turned over to the enrollees, but rather that the key issue is the effectiveness of the training and counseling.

Secondly, everyone seemed to assume that because what was being done was different, therefore it had to be better, else why bother to change? Certainly, the Job Corps was a new organizational form. Yet it failed to define it objectives in terms of incremental behavioral change.

Finally, let us try to be more concrete about defining the change agent. In the same way that a psychologist looks at behavior as an index of personality, a change agent looks at institutions as a network of interlocking public and private satisfactions and unmet needs. Before the change agent undertakes to propose changes in existing institutions or the creation of new ones, he attempts to ascertain which needs are being met and who in the institution is contributing to the meeting of these needs, and likewise who and what is responsible for institutional dysfunctionalism. To the extent that past events condition current responses, he attempts to relate the original objectives to current achievements, in order to ascertain the extent to which they have been and/or are being met. Unlike the sociologist, he is less interested in documenting the process of evolution, and more concerned with using such intelligence to devise a successful strategy for change, after it has been established in what direction such change should occur.

Obviously, the change agent is not a service professional who deals with individuals and therefore can attribute a client's improved position to some intervention on his part. Instead, he belongs to that group of professions which seek to exert their influence through others. Not only is the latter task more difficult in terms of being able to effect changes in "treatment" when they are not themselves responsible for such treatment, but equally frustrating is the fact that they are rarely able to document their impact. The case study included here provides some documentation. It also underscores the ambiguous role of the change agent, who is often suspect and therefore not entrusted with real power.

In closing this chapter, I think it important that we try to list, however briefly, some of the principles that seem to emerge from this case study of the New Bedford Job Corps Center. For if, as I should like to believe, there was some meaning in our efforts, this legacy must not be allowed to evaporate, thereby leaving those who follow us in the typical position of having to re-invent the wheel. Consequently, I have outlined below what I believe to be some of the principles that are involved in the problems of institutional change and/or the creation of alternative helping settings.

1. Piecemeal change should be related to some overall plan (i.e., it should be based on an underlying concept and interdependence with other systems). Programs based on questionable assumptions should be clearly labled as experimental and not as service programs, since to do otherwise is to invite comparisons which may be inappropriate;

2. In the absence of a plan, new institutions follow the "anti-principle"; that is to say, they are designed to replace something which they are clear about needing replacement, but are not clear about the exact nature of the replacement or even what it might look like. Because they lack a clear vision of where they are going, they tend not to wander too far from their initial point of departure;

3. New institutions are self-conscious about their lack of genuine traditions to uphold, and hasten to develop these at every opportunity. These they cling to more tenaciously than would have been the case in an older agency with a rich store of history to draw upon. Moreover, the more these new forms resemble the old order, the more likely that minor differences will be hailed as major innovations and precursors of a new order;

4. An institution that does not control both its input and output is in no position to either claim credit or accept the blame for any success or failure, except insofar as they occur while the enrollees are in the care of that institution. On the other hand, such limitations have their advantages, in that institutions in this position can reap the benefits of "guilt by association" when it is in their interest to do so; and

5. Institutional rigidity is directly proportional to the atmosphere of "openness" in communication (i.e., informal vs. formal channels of communication) which, in turn, is a factor of social distance. In other words, the more informal the socializing process between layers and compartments, the greater the overall institutional flexibility.

Epilogue

Little has been said here of the corpsmen and women, and their needs and desires. They have a point of view. The following poem, written by one of the corpsmen whom the author was privileged to know, sums up their view better than any words of mine. It appeared in the August, 1966 issue of *New Voices,* a student publication of the Rodman Job Corps Center.

> You say you're trying to help us
> How? In what way?
> You misguided oaf, you would destroy us
> by your thoughts alone.
> By what power would you defend us?
> No! we say to you, to belong with us
> is NOT enough.
> For, if you are to succeed, you must
> first understand yourself past and present.
> If you do not, your endeavors shall
> only end in further harm to us.
> Harken to our words for you are one
> and we are many.
> In order to fight, you must first fully
> comprehend the cause of the battle.
> To take, you must learn to receive.
> To demand, you must submit to demands.
> To order, you must first have orders.
> Heed this warning or you shall
> force us to destroy you in the interest of
> self-preservation.
> And, if we must destroy you, we shall
> not come as a mass.
> For then your death would be the death
> of a martyr.
> Nor, shall we come as organized individuals.
> Thus, you will die without honor,
> disgraced even in death.
> Remember this:
> "There is no honor in exploitation."

References

Drucker, Peter. *The Age of Discontinuity.* New York: Harper & Row, 1969.

Weeks, Christopher. *Job Corps: Dollars and Dropouts.* Boston: Little, Brown & Company, 1967.

8

To Age with Dignity: Developing Self-Determination Among the Elderly

Benjamin S. Hersey
*Massachusetts Association of Older
Americans, Inc.*

[Editor's Note] : *In a very real sense, this chapter deals with ourselves. As
Benjamin S. Hersey, so correctly notes: "While we may all never be Black,
or American Indians, or Chicanos, we will all someday be old." Thus,
the problems described in this chapter link us all, independent of our
current status, affiliations, or circumstances. The process of aging – the
inexorable and irreversible passage of time – will overtake us all: its
triumph is assured. What is really at stake, therefore, is the issue of what
this triumph will mean in terms of the conditions under which we are
required to live out the remaining days of our lives. Hersey does not offer
us all of the answers, but he paints a vivid and convincing picture of the
problem. It is not a very pretty picture but, then again, the subject
matter of his work has not been chosen for inclusion in this volume
because of its aesthetic appeal. In addition, as a social worker, Hersey
utilizes this analysis of his attempts to develop the Boston Center for
Older Americans (BCOA) as the fulcrum around which to raise some very
important questions concerning the education and training of social
workers. Most particularly, he focuses attention on the ideological and
practical limitations of casework and, consequently, the needs of his
profession to broaden its perspectives if it is to both "get it together"
and really begin to fulfill its commitments to its clients.*

I agreed to write this chapter for several distinct but related reasons, and I
think it important that the reader be aware of these reasons before reviewing my
contribution to this volume. The first has to do with the plight of older Americans in our society. Like so many other oppressed minorities in our society (e.g.,
blacks, Indians, Chicanos, etc.), they are either excluded from or short-changed
with respect to both participating in the decisions that directly affect their lives,
and/or controlling (or having unencumbered access to) the resources needed to
shape that life in ways that are personally meaningful. However, unlike their disenfranchised brethren, the elderly have neither been able (or, perhaps, willing)
to do the kinds of things that would focus public attention on their alienation,
nor have they evolved the kind of leadership, charismatic or other, that would

129

place them in a more favorable bargaining position from which they could deal with the rest of society. Thus, they remain a particularly mute and powerless group among other disaffiliated minorities.

It would, of course, also be important for us to realize that while we may all never be blacks, or American Indians, or Chicanos, we will *all* someday be old. Thus, the people dealt with in this chapter are ultimately ourselves.

The second reason has to do with my own profession, the field of social work, and the relationship between the "helping practices" developed by that profession and the needs of those it seeks to help. More specifically, this chapter will deal with the problems that result from an orientation that stresses direct individual services as opposed to efforts aimed at increasing the efficacy and political skills of whole groups seeking self-determination. Put another way, the field of social work, independent of its rhetoric or token-symbolic changes, essentially remains wedded to a casework approach to the problems of its clients. This chapter presents an alternative model — a community organization model — to problems, but should be read with the understanding that those of us committed to a community organization approach have had to learn those skills on our own. They have never been, nor are they now, a central or even serious focus of training, even though the limitations of the "casework ethos" have long been recognized, and roundly condemned. Consequently, our hope is that this chapter will serve to support on-going efforts to change both the ideological orientation and training practices of the field as a whole.

The final reason, certainly related to the previous one, has to do with our belief that mental health interventionists, independent of particular professional affiliation, have to become more acutely aware of the manner in which their own agencies or institutions can, either wittingly or unwittingly, impede social progress. It is axiomatic that individual practitioners can change their practices and orientations more rapidly and completely than the agencies of which they are a part, and to which they look for financial and personal support. The agencies and funding sources themselves are more cautious and self-conscious about their "public stance." And, while this may be an understandable fact of life, it does not diminish the harm that such caution can result in, particularly when it is self-serving in nature. Consequently, it becomes important that we begin to appreciate more fully the dynamics of our own sources of institutional and professional support. Without such an appreciation — and the subsequent development of viable intervention strategies — we may be dooming ourselves either to useless personal heroics or fruitless expenditures of energy.

The Elderly in a Youth and Work Oriented Society: A Social Conspiracy

Victims of the very society they had worked so hard to build, the elderly of the 1960s faced increasingly severe problems. Of the twenty million persons over sixty-five, nearly 25 percent had incomes below the poverty level. Another 25 percent had incomes barely above the poverty line, but still too low to allow for a decent standard of living

For all too many, decent housing was impossible to afford. Rents were high and still rising. Public housing construction lagged far behind the demand. Acceptable health care was becoming more and more expensive and, until the advent of Medicare, was far beyond the reach of millions of elderly people living on fixed incomes. Food, too, was often too expensive, and many subsisted on cat or dog food during the period of time between Social Security or Old Age Assistance checks.

As if lack of income were not enough, for many, the emotional necessities of life (e.g., companionship, friendship, and interaction with other people) were equally unavailable. Many became isolated in both rural and urban areas. Friends and family had either died or moved away, and there was little opportunity to make new friends. In the city, elderly people were afraid to leave the safety of their apartments. They became captives in their own homes.

Why was it that so many elderly people faced such severe problems? The answers are obviously varied and complex, but they are ultimately embedded in the very fabric of our society's evolution as a powerful and aggressive force in the world. Thus, while it would be impossible to isolate all of the variables in the equation, it is important that we try to provide at least some perspective on the problem. It is to this perspective that we now turn.

Colonial America, much like the rest of the world at the time, was an agrarian and rural society. The land was rugged and hard to farm. In order for each person to survive, every able-bodied person, from the youngest to the oldest, both men and women, had to work long hours at a variety of tasks. Punishment, both social and often physical, awaited the idle person. Work was indeed a functional part of the Puritan Ethic.

During this period of time, the elderly had a role in the family, in the church, and in the community. The men continued to work the fields until they were no longer able to — and then their sons took over. The women performed the household tasks and raised the young — until their sons' wives or their own daughters took over for them. The old were the cultural and historical link to the past, and both related and interpreted this past to the young, the children.

There was also a demand for skilled work in early America. The elderly were artisans and masters of their field, whether it was cabinetmaking, wagonmaking, blacksmithing, or something else, the older person was in demand to both teach and perform his trade. He could do it best.

When finally the older person could no longer function, he or she was cared for by the family until death.

With the development of the technological, industrial, urban society changes came, at first slowly, but at a persistent and increasing rate. By the early part of this century the country was already a vastly different society. The move to the cities ended the viability of the extended family as a funcational unit. The elderly person had no function in the household. Work was done in factories far from peoples' residences, and children were no longer educated at home and by the family. Finally, it became less expensive to live as a smaller nuclear family, for salaries could support little more than one's most immediate dependents.

The Industrial Revolution brought with it a possibility unprecedented in the history of man. It was no longer necessary for everyone to work in order to support life. It became possible for a smaller and smaller percentage of the people to produce the goods needed by the rest of the society. The technological advances that made this possible also resulted in the gradual disappearance of the skilled artisan. He was being replaced by machines and assembly lines. In addition, rapid developments in technology brought continuing changes in modes of production. Constant re-education of skilled and unskilled workers became necessary. No longer could a person learn a skill, use it, and improve upon it for the rest of his life. Older workers rapidly became obsolete as younger people became more available and brought with them sophisticated knowledge. Age no longer became a correlate of skills. Since, then, the percentage of workers needed for production was dropping, and the young could do many jobs better and faster than the elderly, businesses began developing policies of forced retirement, generally at sixty-five years of age. Thought of as a marvelous luxury for the society, for a great many it was (and still is) the first step toward oblivion.

The results, particularly for the elderly, were catastrophic. The work ethic had not changed. Work was still the way to obtain money. But the elderly were now being told they could not work. Work was still the way to maintain status. But the elderly were now being kept out of the process through which such status could be maintained.

In short, in a country that deified youth and work, the elderly had neither. They had lost their youth; they had been deprived of their vocation; they had been separated from their families; they had been denied access to status. The older American was alone. His condemnation to the "nursing home" was only a family request or a court order away.

It should also be pointed out that a society heavily committed to achieving and perpetuating its own "manifest destiny" generally has little time for those of its citizens who have outlived their *usefulness.* Thus, few efforts were made to prepare people, either formally or informally, for the years of enforced idelness that awaited those approaching the "Golden Years." And, all this at a time when medical science was extending their life expectancy. Thus, while we had developed the phenomenon of forced retirement (for both economic and political reasons), we had not yet learned either how to support it or how to prepare people for it.

In 1935, Social Security became law. Since that time it has seen many changes. Although it provided some income to all who had worked, it often did not provide for a *decent* standard of living. It provided a "floor" for everyone, but it had to be supplemented by other income from savings, pensions, or insurance in order to be viable.

In theory the idea was fine, but the gaps were many. For some, savings were either insufficient or quickly spent on health or other problems. Some, of course, had no savings. For others, pensions did not materialize or were inadequate. For all, the cost of living simply outstripped income. Similarly, services were either totally lacking or inadequate. Public housing, nutrition, and home health programs were always underfunded, mired in bureaucratic intrigue, or tacked onto other programs (e.g., programs for youth) in ways that guaranteed that the elderly would always be competing with the young for whatever limited resources were available — and the elderly usually would lose out in this competition.

In 1965, the Older Americans Act became law, and for the first time monies were appropriated exclusively for services to the elderly, and the aging had their own administration within the Department of Health, Education and Welfare. It was from this act that the money came for the project to be discussed in this chapter.

In summary, we have seen that in the sixties the problems facing our nation's elderly were extreme. As a result of changes in society, many of the elderly found themselves poor, destitute, without status, and physically and emotionally starved in the midst of plenty. Most importantly, however, others were making decisions for them, and they saw little chance of changing that fact.

The Setting and Its People

Just to the west and south of the center of Boston is a section known as the Back Bay. It is a mixture of old Boston and new Boston, old people and young people. At one time the area actually was a bay, but during the nineteenth century, it was filled in, in order to accommodate the expansion of the city. Hundreds upon hundreds of red brick row houses were built, along with some of the most beautiful mansions in Boston. Some still remain as a reminder of Boston's cultural heyday.

During the past century, the brick row houses began to deteriorate, and the mansions, now too large to serve as single family homes, were made into apartment houses, dormitories or other forms of multiple dwelling units. Many of the magnificent mansions were turned into cheap rooming houses and residential hotels. Much of the property became owned by absentee landlords, and the process of deterioration, already begun, progressed more rapidly.

During the late fifties and sixties, Boston went through a large urban renewal program. Much of the Back Bay was rebuilt during this period of time. Public agencies joined with private interest groups to tear down hundreds of deteriorated buildings, in order to create the new Prudential Center, the Christian Science Church development project, and the John Hancock tower. It was also during this time that the Massachusetts Turnpike cut through the area, taking with it several hundred more dwelling units. All of these modern structures now look a little out of place among the "Victorian Ladies" (e.g., Symphony Hall, Horticultural Hall, Public Library, and the Museum of Fine Arts) that remain from the bygone era.

The target area for the project to be discussed comprises about one-quarter of the entire Back Bay section. It contains hundreds of apartment houses, a few residential hotels, and a number of rooming houses. At one end of the area the rents are moderately high and the buildings well kept. At the opposite end, one finds the cheapest rooming houses, all poorly maintained and deteriorating. Most of the apartments in this area were at one time moderately low in rent, and many were owned by absentee landlords who showed minimal concern for their upkeep.

Several institutions dot the area. Most prominent and influential are a large private university and the Mother Church of the Christian Science religion.

The main thoroughfares were once lined with a variety of stores that provided convenient shopping for nearby residents. A number of cafeterias and restaurants were scattered throughout the area. The stores, the restaurants, and the streets were populated by large numbers of elderly persons, reflecting the fact that nearly one-half of the people in the area were over sixty-five.

Of the nearly 3,000 elderly who once lived in the area, most had moved there during their later years. The vast majority were women (75 percent) and most were single and living alone. Generally, they liked the area because of its proximity to downtown Boston, nearby hospitals, and convenient shopping. A few were wealthy, but most were poor and lived in or close to poverty.

Examples of poverty were everywhere. Near the end of each month, one could easily find many older people who were attempting to live for days on one cup of coffee and a roll or by rummaging through garbage cans. Or, one recalls a woman of seventy-five, dressed well (but in obviously dated clothing), pleading with a clerk in a cafeteria for a bit of pudding that cost a nickel more than she had. She had four days to wait until her next Social Security check.

The Project: The Boston Center for Older Americans (BCOA)

The United Community Services of Metropolitan Boston (UCS) is a community council whose board is primarily composed of representatives from industry and business throughout the Greater Boston Area. Each year the United Fund gives a certain amount of its money to UCS for further distribution to UCS's member agencies. However, it is not uncommon to find interlocking board members between UCS and the boards of its member agencies. UCS is not itself a direct service organization, although it does operate an information and referral system. Rather, its primary function is to consider funding applications from its member agencies who, upon receipt of such funds, supposedly provide whatever direct services are needed.

UCS itself is composed of various departments which work to plan programs and directions for the greater Boston community. Each department has a professional staff and a lay committee that sets policy. Thus, for example, there are committees on Health, Social Services, Research, and Special Services. The project described in this chapter evolved out of the Special Services department through what was called its Special Committee on Aging.

Our project, the Boston Center for Older Americans (BCOA), funded in 1966, was the child of several different parents. The initial proposal was developed within the Special Committee on Aging. After being ratified by the members of that committee, it was submitted to – and subsequently signed-off on by – the head of UCS's department of Special Services. From there, now as a grant application, it went to the soon-to-be retiring president of UCS for final agency approval. In approving the grant, the agency committed itself to financially supporting the project even though, as we shall later point out, this meant that UCS would be becoming involved in the direct provision of services. UCS alone, however, could not assume the total financial responsibility for the project. Additional resources were needed, and for this UCS turned to the Commonwealth of Massachusetts' Commission on the Elderly.

The Commission on the Elderly was, at this point in time, a very small state agency which, because of the passage of the Older Americans Act, found itself for the first time with a budget with which to work. It was attempting, often frantically, to gear itself up in order to meet the expected demand for services. However, as is the case with many state agencies, its orientation was fairly conservative and its director was continually the subject of considerable political pressure. Nevertheless, it quickly funded its share of the project and a marriage between UCS and the Commission on the Elderly was easily affected. In retrospect, the match seems to have been an appropriate one, for the agencies were quite well-suited to one another: both were old, tradition-oriented, and conservative in their approach to problems.

The BCOA was funded as a three-year demonstration project whose main purpose was to be the provision of a variety of services to the elderly. The goals of the project, as stated in the original proposal, were as follows:

1. To locate and identify the elderly residing in the target area, to determine their specific needs and interest, and to maintain contact with them in order to facilitate continuous, comprehensive, and coordinated services;
2. To foster the independence of the older individual by providing opportunities for him to take an active part in his community life;
3. To educate the aged in how best they may protect their own interests, obtain their rights, maintain their health, and care for themselves in their own homes;

4.   To develop an information and referral service that will make useful information available to the older individual and refer him to appropriate resources as necessary; and

5.   To serve as a focal point around which neighborhood planning for the elderly on a self-help basis could be carried out.

As a social worker with both experience in the Boston area and a knowledge of existing local agencies, I was hired as the director of the nonexistent Boston Center for Older Americans — and mandated to carry out its contractual goals.

The Early Days: Small Victories and a
Growing Concern

As is so often the case with newly-funded projects, there was as yet no facility to physically house the BCOA. Consequently, we had the opportunity to "hit the streets" and use the project's early months as a way of both informing the elderly about the embryonic BCOA and involving them as directly as possible in its development. We held a host of meetings in the target area, and through these meetings and a door-to-door canvassing operation we were able to begin to meet our "clients" and find out from them the kinds of concerns and priorities that dominated peoples' thinking. It soon became clear that housing and all the problems associated with one's physical dwelling were uppermost in the minds of the elderly.

Absentee landlords were raising rents to unprecedented levels because of the increasing demand for housing by students. A minimum amount of public and/ or moderate-income housing had been scheduled in the area to replace the dwellings being torn down. The Christian Science Church's relocation office was offering little or no assistance in helping people move or find acceptable new housing. As one despairing eighty-five-year-old man put it: "There . . . there just ain't no place to go."

Given this pressing situation, coupled with the lack of a physical facility out of which the BCOA could develop its so-called services, we felt we had to move rather quickly — to establish our credibility with the people we were funded to serve. But with limited resources and a small staff, in what direction does one begin to move in order to address the problem? To merely develop "services," and through such services be able to assist a few folks would have been to ignore the major problems facing the elderly as a whole. To try to organize people quickly in the hope that they could successfully confront those institutions and agencies primarily responsible for either creating or exacerbating their housing problems would certainly produce strong (and anticipated negative) reactions from the sponsoring and funding agencies. To embark on a long-range and time-consuming process of developing "communication links" between the elderly and those they identified as their "enemies" would, even if successful, likely result in many old people losing their apartments somewhere along the way. To do nothing would, in today's terms, be totally inoperative.

In part, our decision – to help people organize themselves immediately – was dictated by the "hands off" policy suddenly adopted by UCS, the sponsoring agency. UCS, while certainly not supportive of a community organization approach, was equally concerned lest the BCOA effectively drag the agency into the business of direct services, a role it neither wanted, felt itself capable of carrying out, nor saw as in keeping with its traditional "mission." Thus, it soon became clear that, at least for the time being, UCS would do little to either encourage or impede *any* direction for the program. Indeed, UCS even suggested that the BCOA develop its own Board of Directors as soon as possible.

The decision to "go the community organization route" was a calculated one, a decision made with the full realization that there were risks involved, and that not the least of these was the risk of eventually jeopardizing the program as a whole. Nevertheless, with clear client support, the decision was made to help the people organize themselves around the issue of housing. We also hoped, however, to buy enough time (by both emphasizing the BCOA's ultimate commitment to standard services and by actually developing some of these services) to enable a strong organization to be built up – the kind of organization that could ultimately survive disapproval from both the funding and sponsoring agencies. Thus, certain services were begun. A drop-in lounge was developed along with an information and referral program. In addition, a variety of recreational activities were started and a visiting program was initiated. Community people were hired and trained to run these programs and one of our staff members assumed the responsibility for the overall development of the BCOA's direct services. The rest of us began organizing the elderly.

The first group to be formed was the Housing Committee. Very quickly, the Housing Committee decided to approach the Christian Science Church and begin to deal with their portion of the renewal program. The requests made were clear and simple: that the Christian Science Church include in its renewal plan more moderate and low-income housing. To the delight of the people on the Housing Committee (not to mention the BCOA staff) the reception of the church was excellent. They would make alterations in their plans so as to increase the amount of affordable rents. They even volunteered to donate a portion of their land to another developer (if one could be found) for construction of a building for the elderly. (Another developer was found, and the Christian Science Church – good to its word – made its donation.)

The Housing Committee then turned to the Church's relocation policy, pointing out that the Christian Science Church did not have the capability for effectively relocating people, and that its past performance in that area left much to be desired. Again, the Church agreed, and quickly accepted the suggestion that it solicit help from the Boston Redevelopment Authority in all matters pertaining to relocation.

With the "sweet smell of success" still fresh in its memory, the Housing Committee decided to monitor and watch the overall direction of redevelopment in the area. At one point they asked that a particular area (where many of their homes used to be) not be turned into a parking lot. The request was turned down and, wonder of wonders, the elderly took to the streets with placards and protest signs. They also protested against the building of a stadium in the area, and although their protests were in vain, they received widespread TV coverage and managed a successful press conference.

Thus, there were some very concrete early successes and failures. More importantly, however, the people, the elderly as a whole, seemed to be growing, becoming more sure of themselves, more convinced that their cause was just and that they were indeed capable of standing up to (and confronting) the very same agencies from which they had so quickly shrunk in the past. In addition, the year being 1966, protest had become fashionable, and I think many found "something sexy" about the elderly – the "Wheel-chair Brigade," as they were called – rising up to demand recognition, their rights, and perhaps most importantly, respect. Thus, the group drew some immediate and anticipated support from politicians and businessmen; community activities were acceptable to a broad part of the population.

But there was also a growing concern, particularly at UCS and the state's Commission on the Elderly. Neither agency or its representatives had ever visited the program site, and although for purposes of public consumption each agency pointed to the program with pride, it was clear that the more visible the elderly were becoming, the more interested the agencies were getting in the development and implementation of more direct services. Discussions, memoranda, and inquiries "from above" made clear this need for services, and meetings between the BCOA staff and agency representatives began focusing more and more attention on these service expectations.

The Turning Point: Two Critical Incidents

Because of the BCOA's increasing visibility and growing constituency (a direct result of the efforts of the Housing Committee), it became a regular practice of the Boston Redevelopment Authority (BRA) to discuss with the BCOA whatever relocation and renewal efforts were being planned for the area. At one point, money became available to develop a playground in the community. Since the community was now made up primarily of elderly people and unmarried young people, BRA staff members asked the BCOA for suggestions concerning the kind of playground it might construct. Naturally, the BCOA suggested that a typical playground was inappropriate for the community, but that an outdoor recreation facility for the elderly would certainly enhance the quality of life for a significant part of the population.

These suggestions were ignored and a few months later, the traditional playground now built, a huge grand opening ceremony was held. While five young children cavorted in the sprawling new playground complex, and with the TV cameras of Boston's three major stations happily clicking away, the elderly demonstrated once again. Having decided to seize the occasion as an opportunity to reemphasize their housing and recreational needs, the elderly made signs and marched up to the BRA director who was both on-hand for the ceremonies and clearly on TV at the time. Eyebrows were raised, and while little was said, there was a distinctly different tone noticeable among those at both UCS and the state Commission on the Elderly most concerned with the BCOA program and its directions.

A second critical incident came shortly thereafter. As the BCOA's organizing activities gained momentum, we became acutely aware that problems concerning income were quickly assuming a position of central import in the lives and thoughts of the elderly. Rises in the costs of living, particularly in the areas of health care and transportation, were threatening the elderly, most of whom had to exist on fixed or near-fixed incomes. Legislation was needed to increase the total amount allowable under Old Age Assistance. Similarly, legislation was needed to reduce public transportation fares for those over sixty-five.

As each of these related needs surfaced, needs that could only be met through legislative action, it became clearer and clearer that only by gaining access to and influence on the political and legislative process, could the elderly begin to exert continuing leverage on the decisions and forces that controlled their lives. The people recognized, however, that in order to influence legislation on the state level, a much broader constituency had to be organized. They realized that unless they could begin to develop a strong and coordinated base of voting power — their only real power — any and all programs designed and implemented to solve their problems would be of the token variety. Further, they felt that whatever services or amounts of money became available, they would never be adequate until the elderly had a strong voice in determining what they should be.

In addition, strong voices were growing within the BCOA itself. During this, the program's second year of operation, vigorous leadership was emerging from among the elderly who had participated in the Center's development and its early skirmishes with the BRA and the Christian Science Church. One such man, a retired labor organizer and veteran of the struggles of the thirties, began to assume more and more responsibility for defining the Center's goals and organizing its constituents. His ideas and vision concerning the BCOA's mandate extended far beyond the immediate neighborhood, beyond any particular issue currently under debate. For him, the elderly could only begin to effectively seek a redress of their grievances by being organized throughout the state. His plan, linked to the people's growing awareness of the importance of legislative impact, was to begin to inform and organize the elderly both within and outside of the target area around the variety of bills and proposals that could conceivably affect their lives and were, or soon would be, before the state legislature. As a vehicle for this organizing effort, he created the Legislative Action Group and sought, through meetings with and presentations to a variety of Senior Citizens Clubs throughout the Boston area, to develop a solid, forceful and action-oriented constituency.

The idea quickly caught on, and senior citizens, now finally brought together, were beginning to speak and act in unison. Relationships were quickly formed and they began working together to develop strategies through which they might increase their impact and influence on pending legislation. The organizing activities, now largely in the hands of the elderly themselves, proceeded fairly rapidly and efficiently.[a]

Eventually, the Legislative Action Group, determined to have its voice on pending legislation heard in clear and unmistakable ways, organized what could be described as an assault on the State House. On a mild early spring day in 1968, 75 to 100 delegates of the elderly from the Greater Boston Area ascended the steps of the State Capitol, collared their senators and representatives in offices and hallways, and subjected the historic gold-domed building (and all its inhabitants) to the opening "barrage" of a "suddenly" organized and highly impatient constituency. For many of the elected representatives, it was the first time they had seen, let alone heard, their previously invisible elderly electorate. For others, there was surprise at the sight of older people scurrying back and forth from office to office and floor to floor. But for all, the initial "humor" of the situation was quickly replaced by a sense of the seriousness of the people, their demands, and their obvious persistence.

This activity — this symbolic storming of the barricades, as it were — established the Legislative Action Group as an organization to be listened to. It also marked the beginning of the end of all such activities by the BCOA.

The Finale: BCOA Changes But the
Legislative Action Group Remains

Within two or three weeks following the events at the State House, UCS reprimanded the BCOA staff in general, and me as its director in particular, for the "poor program at the Center." Demands were made that we spend the next months "getting things straightened out, getting the programs in order." No spe-

---

[a] Throughout the period of time during which the elderly, particularly the retired ex-union organizer, were involved in the development of the Legislative Action Group, the BCOA staff, while remaining in the background, was available to help and often offered technical assistance. We did not wish to control the direction of the organizing effort, nor did we feel it appropriate that we continue to run the show. The "clients" were taking over and that, we felt, was as it should be. Rather, our role now became one of "covering" for the organizing activities of the clients; that is to say, trying to keep sponsoring and funding-agency attention away from these non-service-oriented aspects of the program.

cific mention or reference was ever made to the BCOA's organizing activities. Rather, attention was always focused on the service programs that were either nonexistent or occupying "far too little of the Center's energies." Like UCS, the State Commission on the Elderly now also began raising concerns regarding the program's direction. More specifically, the Commission was worried about whether or not the BCOA was running the kinds of programs that would lead senators and representatives to increase the size of the state appropriation to the Commission on the Elderly.

Finally, after several months of inter- and intra-agency hassling, UCS was seeking to subcontact the BCOA's "service programs" to another agency (The Age Center of New England), an agency it felt was more committed to the development of "needed services." The writing was clearly on the wall, and so, in the ensuing months, most of our time was spent trying to help the Legislative Action Group establish itself as an independent and incorporated organization.[b] With this task well underway, I and other BCOA staff members resigned. Our work was done.

Service vs. Systemic Change: The Need to Reassess

While this chapter has attempted to increase the readers' awareness of the multitude of problems that confront the elderly, it has, I hope, also raised some issues relevant to the future of my own profession — the field of social work. The purpose of this final section is to focus attention on those issues. Broadly speaking, they have to do with the appropriateness of both service delivery *and* systems change orientations as co-equal partners in the practice (and education for practice) of social workers. Our aim, therefore, is not to condemn the profession for its past; nor do we wish to "pit" any of its "sub-group adherents" (e.g., caseworkers, groupworkers, or community organizers) against each other, for these divisions oftentimes stem from poorly defined differences concerning the meaning of social problems.

Individual (or small group) service is a legitimate and valuable goal, and those who view themselves as traditionalists need not apologize for their efforts. Over the years they have assisted untold individuals in coping more effectively with very real and difficult problems. But service, by its very nature, is predicated on the assumption that society usually runs both smoothly and equitably, and therefore, that the individual in need of service is caught up in problems that are both unique and idiosyncratic to himself. We know, of course, that this is not always or even most often the case. Systems malfunction, and frequently what ap-

---

[b] During this period of time the Legislative Action Group was transformed into the Legislative Council for Older Americans. The Massachusetts Association of Older Americans, the agency with which the author is now affiliated, works closely with the Legislative Council. The Legislative Council now represents 40,000 elderly people throughout the Commonwealth of Massachusetts.

pears to be an individual problem may well, upon closer examination, prove to be an appropriate response to a single or even a series of critical events from which there is *no* escape. In such cases, the provision of services alone may only serve to contain the problem (i.e., keep it at a low level of public visibility) or make life a little less uncomfortable for the person experiencing the pain. Thus, when performing exclusively in this manner, the profession of social work not only fails to serve its constituency to the fullest extent possible, but also puts itself in the position of being scapegoated when the direct institutional origins of many "individual" problems become a part of the public's consciousness. Service, then, is a legitimate and valuable function only under certain conditions. These are: first, when it is relatively clear that a particular problem is, indeed, individual in nature; second, when the service intervention does not preclude or prevent a reassessment of the problem in systemic terms; and finally, when the provision of service does not dilute action for systemic change when such action is called for.

A second issue. The field of social work, like many of the other helping professions, has traditionally adopted what could be called an essentially crisis oriented approach to problems. Consequently, it has tended to be a *reactive* profession; that is to say, a field whose energies have been expended in *responding* to problems once those problems have become visible in the form of individually experienced pain or discomfort. Only rarely has the field used its not inconsiderable resources to deal with problems in a preventive manner (i.e., by seeking out the sources of difficulty in ways that would decrease the probability of their escalation into problems requiring remedial types of intervention). Instead, the profession has floundered in a sea of rhetoric, trying desperately to insure its place and status among the other helping professions (e.g., psychiatry, psychology, etc.) against which it has always suffered by comparison. This search for a derived or reflected identity has consumed far too much of the field's energies. It seems appropriate therefore, especially at this point in history, that the field finally strike out on its own, become initiation rather than reaction oriented, and use this new stance as the basis for a professional identity that is truly unique unto itself. Thus, for example, it could use the elimination (rather than perpetuation) of service as its guiding, if apparently unreachable, goal. Such a stance would bring a decidedly new perspective to the problems surrounding the provision of service.

At the present time, however, there still need not be an artificial cleavage between the direct service aspects of the practice of social work and its commitment to community organization as a vehicle for social change. Carefully developed analyses of social problems, taking into account *both* individual and systemic malfunctioning — and the development of appropriate interventions stemming from such analyses — could go a long way toward helping the profession "get it together." And the field of social work desperately needs to get itself together, for intra-professional jealousies, fear of the new, and an unthinking adherence to tradition currently threaten to tear it apart at the seams.

A vigorous reassessment of social work education and training is also in order. The traditional casework and groupwork approaches must, if only to insure their own ongoing viability, move from center stage and begin to encourage new partnerships with other, less individually oriented approaches. In the face of our current and ever-growing level of awareness, we can no longer automatically assume that good will and responsiveness typify the workings of those social institutions (e.g., the educational, employment, and welfare systems) that so profoundly affect the circumstances under which people try to survive. Nor can we automatically look toward individual weakness, pathology, or maladjustment as the most parsimonious explanation for existing problems. In a very real way, the project described in this chapter is an excellent example of how our own training as social workers failed us all, both those of us at the BCOA and our brethren social workers at UCS. Had both of us, for example, been able to develop the kind of dialogue required, and had we been able through this dialogue to define issues in clear and mutually understood terms, it is quite conceivable that we might have arrived at a conception of the problems confronting the elderly that would have enabled us all to commit ourselves to a much more flexible and coordinated approach — an approach which would have minimized interagency conflict and increased the amount of time, energy and resources that could (and should) have been at the disposal of the elderly. As it was, we (the social workers at the BCOA) went it alone. But even here there were problems. How effective were we as community organizers when, as was certainly the case, none of us had ever received concrete training in this area during our years in social work school? How much more quickly or effectively might we have helped the elderly become organized if our own training had taught us such skills as the dynamics of power, the politics of confrontation, the uses (and mis-uses) of protest and civil disobedience, and yes, even how to run an effective neighborhood meeting? In many instances, given our own limited preparation and training, we were either "re-inventing the wheel" or frantically rushing about seeking someone, anyone, who could help us learn the kinds of techniques that would be useful to our constituents. Clearly, this is no way to do business. Schools of social work need to begin to educate and train future practitioners in ways that we were not. At the very least, this means preparing people and providing them with the skills to become the initiators of action, advocates who neither wait for problems to be brought to them nor remain passive in the face of problems.

The approach described above implies that the field of social work must cease its striving to become another institutionalized practice through which society can reduce its guilt by alleviating individual suffering. Rather, it must become a field capable of raising that guilt to new levels of consciousness; a field willing to enter into the arena of problem oriented political and social alliances; in short, the profession of social work must become as committed to changing itself as it is now committed to helping its clients change.

We Bombed in Mountville: Lessons Learned in Consultation to a Correctional Facility for Adolescent Offenders

N. Dickon Reppucci, Brian P.V. Sarata,[a]
J. Terry Saunders, A. Verne McArthur,[b]
and Linda M. Michlin
Yale University

[Editor's Note] : *Unlike the situation with respect to other areas of long-standing social concern, we currently appear to be in an era of reform with respect to the workings of our juvenile justice system and its attendant institutions. Programs to significantly alter (and, in some instances, completely do away with) existing correctional facilities for adjudicated youthful offenders are now dominating the thinking and actions of citizens as a whole, and helping professionals in particular. This chapter describes an early attempt by a group of university-based faculty and students to facilitate the development of a model rehabilitative setting for incarcerated adolescents. The authors label their efforts a "failure", but their report offers important insights into the role problems and political realities that encompass the consultation experience. As they point out, "we had very little to guide us in our endeavors." Hopefully, the appearance of this article will help to equip others in ways the authors were not.*

The publication of this paper at this time presents the authors with a dilemma. It was written with all due candor in 1969 following the first experience that we had in a consultation situation in the area of corrections. This experience was exceptionally valuable to all of us and was the initial impetus which caused the first four authors to pursue careers in community psychology and corrections. However, we are now even more aware of its deficiencies than we were then. For those readers with consultation experience, it may be dated as well as naive; on the other hand, for students and others with good intentions but little experience it may be useful. Thus we, in conjuction with the editor of this volume, have decided that the chapter should be published as originally planned, mindful of the fact that candor has exposed our early naiveties.

Names of any specific individuals or institutions connected with the State Department of Corrections have been changed for the sake of confidentiality. We wish to thank Seymour B. Sarason for reading and commenting upon this manuscript during its various drafts, as well as for his support during the intervention period itself. His suggestions have been most helpful and appreciated. Both the Director of Programming and Planning and the Commissioner of the State Department of Corrections made this intervention possible and were supportive throughout. Finally, Miss Anita Miller deserves our gratitude for being not only our secretary, but also our trusted confident.

[a] Now at the University of Nebraska.

[b] Now at Boston University

Several historical traditions within the social sciences have militated against behavioral scientists becoming effective agents of social change (Fairweather 1967). Academia has long been isolated from the institutions of the larger community. This isolation has been social and frequently geographic. In addition, it has been nurtured by the tendency of academic institutions to think in terms of a number of bifurcations which have often been inappropriately pitted in battle, one against the other: "pure" versus "applied" research; theory versus practice; inquiry versus action. Within the field of psychology, the battle has raged between academic psychology and professional psychology. Academic psychology has traditionally put a premium on pure or basic research; research concerned with theory and method without regard to its applicability to immediate problems of man or society. Academia in general, and academic psychology in particular, have not emphasized either the solution of important social problems or the social responsibility of the scientist-practitioner.

Moreover, social science, in modeling itself after certain aspects of the physical sciences, has become more concerned with precise measurement and methodology than with the study of significant complex human problems (Fairweather 1967). In particular, students of psychology have too often been taught by the system of rewards and punishments meted out by their academic institutions that research methodology is more important than the nature of the problem under investigation. The behavioral scientist who wishes to address complex social problems finds that he must concern himself with devising new methods, because no methodology exists which is adequate to their study or their solution (Sanford 1965).

There are also a number of specific intellectual traditions which hinder the effectiveness of psychologists and other social scientists as social change agents. Among these are: (1) the habit of social scientists (who "study" society rather than "engineer" it) to react rather than to act, to cure rather than prevent; (2) the tendency to train students in one or another narrowly defined subject area such as psychology, sociology, or political science, rather than in a multidisciplinary approach which is necessary to cope with most significant human problems; and (3) for psychologists, theory is largely pervaded by the "psychology of the individual" which neglects conceptualization of the social setting within which the individual operates (Fairweather 1967). All of these biases tend to take their toll when the professional finds himself confronted with the task of working within a community setting as an institutional change agent.

The reality and potency of these influences became vividly apparent to us during our experiences as consultants to a correctional facility for adolescent offenders. This was our first venture as psychological consultants whose aim was that of institutional rather than individual change. By adopting this role, we encountered a number of situations for which our graduate training programs in clinical psychology not only had not prepared us, but also, at times actually hampered our functioning. In retrospect, some of these considerations seem obvious and should have been expected; however, on first encounter they were anything but obvious and expected. Our goal in this chapter will be to describe briefly some of our experiences and then to discuss how these have altered our conceptual framework.

The chapter is divided into two major sections: (1) a case study of a consultation including the pre-history, initial, and action phases of our involvement, and some of our reflections as a group at the time; and (2) a discussion of some alterations in our thinking which have developed as a result of this consultation. The chapter, for the most part, is written in the first person in order to emphasize the personal nature of the experience.

Case Study of a Consultation

We had very little to guide us in our endeavors. There is a scarcity of literature describing consultation in most community setting (Sarason, Levine, Goldenberg, Cherlin, and Bennett 1966); in regard to correctional settings there is a virtual void. In 1968, as far as we could determine, there were only three articles which had discussed consultation in such settings (Berline 1960; Loomis 1966; Shapiro 1968); none of these provided any information as to the kinds of problems that we were likely to encounter. Of some help were our colleagues at the Yale Psycho-Educational Clinic who had been involved in community consultation for many years; however, even among this group of people there was no one who had consulted in a correctional setting. Ira Goldenberg and his associates had been involved with the establishment of facilities for dealing with delinquents (Goldenberg 1971), but they had created their own settings, thereby having relatively complete control over their operations, personnel, and programs. Thus, we entered into the consultancy with little past experience to guide us.

The following discussion is intended to be a highly selective and truncated version of our consultation involvement in a correctional facility, covering about an eight-month period. Its purpose is to illustrate the issues with which we were confronted. It is hoped that the reader will gain some feeling for the kind of situation in which we found ourselves. The amount of time spent by the authors varied from a total of about 30 man-hours per week during the initial phases to over 60 man-hours per week during the action phase.

Pre-history of the Consultation[c]

My position in the fall of 1968 was assistant professor of clinical psychology in the Department of Psychology at Yale University. I had accepted this position

---

[c] This section will be written from the point of view of the senior author as the initial decision to become involved with the State Correctional System was his.

primarily because of the Psycho-Educational Clinic which is an integral part of the Yale Clinical Psychology graduate training program (Sarason and Levine 1970). Community consultation is the major activity of the Clinic. During the course of my graduate training I had become disillusioned with the traditional activities of the clinical psychologist — diagnostic testing and psychotherapy — as these activities seemed to me to offer little aid in the search for solutions to pressing social problems. My hope was to find a way to apply what knowledge and skills I had to problems in the larger community. Of special concern to me was the etiology and treatment of deviant behavior among adolescents.

About a month after my arrival at Yale, the newly appointed State Commissioner of Corrections discussed with the staff of the Clinic a series of innovative ideas which he hoped to put into effect in the Connecticut correctional system.[d] He emphasized the need for a productive collaboration between the state and the university in improving the correctional system and his hope that some academics would become involved with him. I decided to inquire further about the possibilities of involvement and he introduced me to Dr. Samuel Smith, the director of Programming and Planning for the Corrections Department. Dr. Smith, a sociologist, was enthusiastic about discussing the matter with me.

We met about ten days later. Dr. Smith discussed the need for change throughout the entire correctional system, but emphasized the desire for assistance at two facilities, a local correctional facility[e] and a new youth camp for the adolescent offender which was located in Mountville, a town about 45 miles from the Clinic. Dr. Smith was quite agreeable to my involving graduate students in any endeavor. We decided that before making a commitment, I should see the facilities. We set a date for touring both facilities the following week.

Four interested graduate students and I toured the two facilities and the visits were decisive regarding our involvement. The jail turned out to be a dismal, entirely custody-oriented facility which offered little hope for meaningful change. It was outdated (built in 1857), seriously overcrowded (over 330 inmates in accommodations for 180), dangerously understaffed, no professional staff at all, and constituted some of the most deplorable living conditions imaginable. Its daily existence focused on little more than survival for both inmates and staff and we felt that any intervention could be nothing more than a stopgap measure with little likelihood of even limited success.

---

[d] During the 1967 legislative session, a bill was passed which provided for the establishment of a corrections department which would be headed by a Commissioner of Corrections who would bring all of the state's correctional facilities under centralized authority, and who would have wide latitude to implement change. Until this time, each prison and each jail was an entity unto itself. The new commissioner assumed this position on July 1, 1968.

[e] In recent years, the term "correctional facility" has been substituted for the terms "jail" and "prison." For convenience, and because in everything but official documents the terms "jail" and "prison" are still used, we will henceforth refer to the local correctional facility as the jail.

In comparison, the Mountville Conservation and Corrections Camp appeared quite attractive. It was a recently opened, minimum security facility for adolescent boys, and its stated goal was treatment not punishment. At the time, there were only six inmates and about a dozen staff: three counselors, one medic, eight correctional officers, and an inmate cook. There were plans to expand to accommodate forty inmates in the near future. Finally, it seemed clear that Dr. Smith, and presumably the commissioner, wanted us to become involved with institutional programming and development, and, as such, would be supportive of our endeavors. The obvious disadvantages were the camp's distance from Yale, its physical location, and its lack of a permanent director. The camp's distance meant a two-hour round trip drive which eliminated the possibility of short, unplanned, frequent visits. The camp's location was an old Nike missile base located on top of a mountain in the middle of a forest, five miles from the nearest house. This location violated the one principle of which we were convinced, i.e., that institutions should be located within the communities which they serve (Goldenberg 1971). Finally, the lack of a permanent director meant that we would have no one in authority to work directly with at the camp. Nevertheless, our group decided to become involved with the camp beginning the next week.

Initial Phases

During the early history of our involvement at the camp we explicitly declined to define our role in order to assess what roles would be mutually most beneficial (Sarason et al. 1966). For example, we rejected an offer by the head counselor that we each see one of the boys in a therapeutic situation, explaining that we neither wanted to commit ourselves to providing traditional psychological services nor did we want to usurp any of the counselors' functions. Rather we wanted to acquaint ourselves with the characteristics of correctional settings in general, and the unique qualities and needs of the camp in particular, before committing ourselves to a role. Thus, we chatted informally with staff and inmates, individually and in groups, in offices, day room or dormitory, over coffee, dinner or a game of ping pong.

Our reluctance to play an active role, e.g., to teach, direct activity, or solve problems, had a number of sources. First and foremost, our previous training had taught us that a consultant's role was to consult, suggest, or interpret. Moreover, we did not want the staff to become unduly impressed with "professional" knowledge and skills since we wanted to reinforce their independent efforts and to build up confidence in their own abilities (Levine 1967). We attempted to disclaim the magical aura professionals often either intentionally or unintentionally carry with them. We communicated that we had no more easy answers than they had, meanwhile couching our assumptions and ideas in the garb of alternative suggestions and hoping they would adopt some of them as their own. What did not occur to us at this time was that the staff had never had any experience with consultants before and that they had no idea how to incorporate suggestions into their own repertoire and then to act upon them. Their past experience had taught them that specific guidelines from people in authority would determine their functioning. Thus our suggestions regarding program development were not offered in a usable form.

Our first major input involved the camp's leadership, the history of which is of critical importance in the development of our story. The first two temporary directors were tenured correctional officers who were placed in the position as figureheads only until they could be removed to innocuous jobs elsewhere in the correctional system. By the time the second man was removed (approximately six weeks after our arrival), the permanent director had already been selected and was expected to arrive at the camp within a few weeks, as soon as a replacement could be found to fill his old position as parole officer. At the suggestion of the senior author, the chief counselor became acting director. Although our group stressed the critical need for a permanent director at the earliest possible moment because of the rapidly emerging structures and relationships, he did not arrive for three months. The chief counselor, both because of his personality and the temporariness of his position, was reluctant to take strong leadership at the camp. In addition, he had to answer to three immediate superiors, the head of the jail administration, the deputy commissioner for community services, and the director of programming and planning. The communication network between these three men was less than perfect, and it was not atypical for contradictory messages to be sent to the director.

Although we developed a relatively coherent picture of the setting within a few weeks, we decided that it was important to gather information in a more systematic fashion. We devised a structured interview to survey the staff's attitudes regarding delinquency, correctional settings, and, in particular, their feelings and expectations about the camp as it was then and as they envisioned its development. All staff members were interviewed, including the still absent, newly appointed director. One primary goal was collecting data which would aid us in understanding the setting and in facilitating change. As a secondary aim, we intended to relate the findings of the interviews to the staff, thereby stimulating discussion and activity which presumably would lead to "growth" within the setting.

The results of the interviews clearly indicated the staff's lack of ideas as to how to develop a rehabilitation program for the camp. Most staff felt that the camp would be successful if they were sent "the right kind of boy" and if guidelines were spelled out. However, there was no one on the staff including the new director, who had any ideas as to what the guidelines should be. There was univeral optimism that whatever problems there were — mainly pervasive feelings of insecurity (and fear), impotence, and incompetence — would be alleviated when the permanent director arrived. Waiting for their "Godot," the camp stood in virtual limbo, without direction, staff meetings, or an organized program for the inmates.

Another result of the interviews was that we became aware that the staff had begun to perceive us as irrelevant to their needs since we were not filling the leadership hiatus or directly developing a program for them. Since the interviewing did not produce immediate visible changes, it only reinforced their view that we were irrelevant. Even so, they did not easily abandon the fantasy that we had the necessary clinical magic, if only we would use it, to solve their problems. Our discomfort was exacerbated as a result of a meeting that the senior author had with the permanent director, the chief counselor, and two of the three men in the commissioner's office responsible for the camp. The meeting had been asked for by the senior author in order to ascertain the camp's guiding philosophy and major program ideas. To our surprise, the only philosophy and idea in this group was that the camp should be a "new and different" setting (different from the notorious State Reformatory where the boys would be incarcerated if they were not at the camp), which would "rehabilitate boys by means of fresh air, good food, a minimum security facility, and working for the forestry service for 25¢ a day." The unreality of this idea as a working program model did not seem to bother anyone but our group.

About a month later the incompatability of the structural arrangement that existed between the state forestry department and the corrections department and the goal of establishing a treatment facility was brought to the fore. We had known from the beginning that the boys were expected to work with the forestry service, but we had thought that this was in accordance with an idea that strenuous outdoor work would be rehabilitative. However, we had not been aware of the fact that this service was a requirement regardless of what treatment program was developed. We were jolted into awareness of this crucial arrangement one day when we found the inmate population tripled (to about thirty boys) from a few days before. We had emphasized with the central office administrators the importance of keeping the inmate population small (e.g., no more than ten or twelve boys) until a workable program could be developed and instituted. There had been agreement on this point by all parties. So how had the massive influx of boys occurred? The answer was to be found in the initial arrangement between the two state departments. The forestry commissioner had demanded more boys at the camp because the forestry crews needed more manpower. Thus, the corrections commissioner immediately ordered twenty boys shipped to the camp from the state reformatory. The camp staff had been given only a few hours notice of this irrevocable decision.

At this point, it is important to comment on an aspect of the correctional system in general, which we first became aware of during these early months: an emphasis on courting good public relations through favorable press, radio, and TV releases while at the same time neglecting staff morale. This is vividly illustrated by the events which occurred at the Mountville Camp. During the

early months of its existence, stories about the camp, emphasizing its being
"a new and experimental attempt toward rehabilitation of youthful offenders,"
were frequent. These press releases were climaxed by an article with pictures in
the Sunday supplement of the most widely read newspaper in the state. At first,
staff morale was brightened by these stories, but with the massive influx of boys,
no corresponding increase in staff, and the lack of a director to lay down guidelines, staff morale declined. An air of cynicism developed as expressed in comments such as "if they care about this place why don't they get a director down
here," or "you'd think from this story that everyone from the central office is
here everyday." The reality was that individuals from the central office seldom
came unless they had something to complain about. Nevertheless, while the press
releases lasted, the staff clung to the idea that the camp was a focal part of the
larger system, even though the lack of concern and coordination by the central
office became glaringly more obvious with each passing day. As we became
aware of the moral decline, we urged the central office to send a representative
out to talk with the staff to demonstrate concern and interest, but our suggestion was never acted upon.

Six months later, the largest single administrative input in the history of the
camp occurred at approximately 1:00 A.M. in early June 1969. The commissioner, the two deputy commissioners, the jail administration head, and the director
of programming and planning arrived on the scene. However, this input was in
no way concerned with the construction of an effective rehabilitative program,
but rather was a response to a "walk-off" by two inmates.

We continued to visit the camp and to consult, principally with the acting
director, in what might be termed an attempt at maintenance or "supportive
counselling." We now came to view the arrival of the new director as the appropriate point for us to begin to "actively intervene." We felt that it was imperative that the permanent director be intimately involved in the formulation of
camp policy and that he, not us, take a strong, active leadership. We saw this as a
necessity if the camp was to have any hope of functioning as a rehabilitation-
oriented setting within the security-oriented department of corrections. We were
not immediately aware of how this approach nurtured the staff's already existing fantasies that his arrival would solve the camp's problems and also may have
encouraged their reluctance to take initiative and search for solutions. During
the three months before the permanent director arrived, unplanned structures
and relationships, which would be hard to change, were rigidifying, including our
relatively nonactive role.

Hence, throughout the initial phase, we consistently opted for the role of
relatively passive advisor or consultant, rather than leader or active participant,
despite, as hindsight makes very clear, strong indications of the need for a much
more active role. We should again emphasize, however, that the role we took was
quite consistent with our psychological training.

Active Phases

We did finally conceptualize our intervention and formally presented it to the staff a few days after the permanent director's arrival. The program had three major foci. First, two members of the group were to become involved with improving the cooperation and communication between the camp and the community, i.e., both the inmate's family and other agencies with which he would have contact. Our group's efforts in this direction were envisioned as increasing this crucial but neglected activity and as aiding the counselors to gain confidence and competence in this type of endeavor. This program had an encouraging beginning, but had to be deemphasized when one of our group developed mononucleosis and withdrew from the consultation effort.

Second, we introduced a battery of psychological inventories and scholastic achievement tests to be given to entering inmates aimed at providing the counselors with scholastic and psychological profiles of the inmates; they would also provide a store of data for future research. However, we were most heavily invested in the other aspects of our intervention and the counseling staff seemed ill at ease even in administering the scales. These factors and the counselors' preoccupation with other daily concerns contributed to the testing program becoming just another chore than had to be done.

Our third and major focus reflected our belief that it was important for the camp staff as a whole to develop and then to implement a rehabilitative program and that our major function was to facilitate communication between all levels of staff to achieve this goal. We had noted an increasing polarization between the counselors and security staff which was rooted in their traditionally different roles. Communication both between and within these groups was almost nonexistent and hostility continued to grow. We felt that it would be useful to provide each group with a vehicle for examining and discussing their specific difficulties and developing a conceptualization of the role they might play in this new setting. We instituted a series of separate weekly group meetings for the counselors and for the security staff. Each group was to meet separately for eight weeks and to discuss its unique problems and responsibilities. Afterwards, there would be general staff meetings at which members from both groups would be present. The goal was to develop understanding within each group and then to focus on the problems between the groups. Meanwhile the senior psychologist would consult with the director, who was not included in either group meeting, to help him deal openly and in an assertive but reasonable manner with both his staff and the central office.

Each group quickly developed its own cohesiveness. The hostilities which each group felt toward the other quickly and repeatedly surfaced and obscured the differences within each group. The security staff wanted a full staff meeting immediately. This desire stemmed in part from the belief that only through a confrontation with the director present, could they, the low status group, gain a consideration of their needs, and from the fact that they did not want to deal with their own miscommunications. It also became apparent that the anxiety stemming from our attempts to get the staff to formulate their own roles was feeding their hostility toward the director, as well as toward us. Conditioned by experience to anticipate being told what to do, they felt at a loss to help define their own program and roles. They dealt with this threatening situation by expressing hostility toward the two elements which they perceived as being capable of and responsible for "organizing the camp" — our group and the director.

The first full staff meeting occurred about three weeks before the end of the projected eight week period of group meetings. This and the subsequent staff meetings probably represent the crucial turning point in the camp's development and our relationship with it. The Commissioner of Corrections had sent a memo proclaiming that a weekly meeting of the entire staff was appropriate at each correctional setting. The director responded to this edict and to the staff's desire for such a meeting by immediately scheduling one. At this point we reemphasized to the director that a staff meeting should allow open communication, both positive and critical, among staff members, and that he should strive to develop an atmosphere of shared decision-making regarding the creation of the program in order to upgrade morale (Leavitt 1965).

For the three days immediately preceding the first staff meeting, the inmate population staged a series of "sit-downs" and "sleep-ins." Explicitly they were reacting to the fact that they were not receiving the 25¢ a day stipend which they were promised for their work with the Department of Forestry. It was apparent, however, that the strike was mainly a reaction to the lack of structure and program within the camp. The inmates resented the treatment which was often inequitable and almost always inconsistent. There were no procedures for dealing with inmate misconduct — indeed, "appropriate conduct" had not been defined, and security and counseling staff members would often disregard an action taken by the other. The inmates seemed to be testing limits, especially in regard to the new director, whom they perceived as ineffective and, by choice, closeted away in his office.

The director reacted with a show of force. The security force was beefed up and a number of inmates were sent back to the state reformatory. The director, however, claimed that this action was unrelated to the strike. Immediately preceding the first staff meeting, the director, in conjuction with the chief counselor and the chief security officer, both wearing dark glasses, met with the inmates. The director informed the inmates that the "nonsense" would stop and that they were to treat staff members and each other with "respect." "Respect," he explained, "is the basis upon which society is built." He also retracted a number of privileges and countermanded other statements which he had made to the inmates at other meetings during the preceding three days.

Upon entering the staff room for the staff meeting, the director moved a table from its place against the wall and seated himself behind it, thus gaining a command of the room. He then ordered the chief counselor and the chief correctional officer to sit at his left and right, respectively. Both men, having become accustomed to the more informal atmosphere of the previous meetings initiated by our group, quietly declined; but the director insisted. During the meeting he informed the staff that he had, during the preceding five weeks, been observing the "lay of the land" and that now the period of observation was over. He stated that the staff would together mold a program and that, in order to do so, they must be free to communicate openly.

When personal differences were alluded to, however, the director managed to avoid them. When issues requiring decisions were raised, he noted them as topics for discussion at future meetings. During this and several subsequent meetings, staff members continued to articulate their concerns; the director continued in the same manner not to deal with these concerns, and the staff participation diminished. Moreover, he did not provide them with any ideas upon which to begin developing a program, although by this time we were making direct suggestions to him. Soon, the meetings consisted of the staff's hearing the problems the director was having with getting equipment and materials for the physical plant. In short, these meetings became "closed" and unproductive, neither aiding in the development of a program nor providing a forum for open communication among the staff.

It became clear that the director's behavior was motivated by more than an inability to deal with interpersonal and other tensions. He had adopted our model of a cooperative creation of programs and procedures, not because he understood and accepted the assumptions upon which it was based, but because he had little, if any, notion about how to proceed. He thus perceived the lack of organization as stemming from the staff's reluctance to develop and articulate a program. The staff, of course, felt incapable of the task and had thrived on the expectation that the director could and would provide leadership. The director, however, needed and wanted guidelines as much as they did. The only guidelines he seemed capable of following were those suggested by memo from the central office, and since these had to do only with technical matters, no program developed. The long hours spent with him seemed to have been completely for naught.

The staff had entertained similar expectations about our group. The anticipation that we *would* aid them had been slowly dissipated. We had, for some time, been viewed as "Monday morning quarterbacks." When we did present a tangible program, the staff did not perceive the program as pertinent to their chief concerns. The counselor wanted to know how to counsel and what a rehabilitative program might look like. The guards wondered how to guard at a camp without cells and what the guidelines were. They perceived us as offering community contacts and testing, things in which they were not particularly interested. We provided meetings in which they could talk with members of their

own staff subgroup, but these meetings were viewed as further isolating themselves from those with whom they perceived conflict and difficulty in communication. We continually resisted supplying answers about how to run the camp.
The perception that we *could* do anything appears, in retrospect, to have also
perished; but it died more slowly. It seems to have been in the context of the
staff meetings that their perceptions of us as potent dissolved completely. We
would often raise issues similar to those raised by the staff, and tactfully would
raise objections to action of the director. But we were consciously trying to
build rather than destroy the director's leadership, and our attempts were no
more successful than those of the staff.

Some Reflections on Our Own Group

If the turning point in our influence at the camp came during the staff meetings, the turning point in our awareness of our relationship to that setting and
our feelings toward it came at a later and very specific time.

A few months after the director arrived, the head counselor spent a week
visiting the well-known Highfields Project (McCorkle and Boxby 1958). He came
back with some ideas for a program he was quite excited about adapting for the
camp — one which seemed to evoke some interest among other staff members.
Basically, it involved organizing the inmates into three groups for their work,
counseling, and living experiences. Appropriate behavior would be encouraged
utilizing group competition for privileges and group social influence through the
counseling and living experience.

We quickly seized on this as a potentially effecting focus for some of our interventions. The kind of plan was one on which we felt we could bring our professional competence to bear, it was an idea originating from the staff, it was one
which required extensive staff cooperation and, hence, it might be a vehicle to
bring the staff closer together.

After the idea had "cooked" for a few weeks, a meeting was set up to plan
and decide the specifics of the program. Present were the counseling staff and
one of our group, but despite our strong urging, the director was not present nor
had any representatives of the guard staff been invited. Nevertheless, a fairly acceptable program was designed (with a considerable amount of contribution by
our representative) and everyone emerged quite enthusiastic.

However, we arrived the following week to find the program a shambles —
worse than anything suggested before. We soon discovered that in presenting this
plan to the director, the guard staff, and the inmates, each group had had strong
objections reflecting real and perceived requirements of their own functioning
and had insisted on some very basic changes which violated many of the principles essential to the program's effectiveness. Indeed, the resulting program would
be more likely to increase dissension among staff and between staff and inmates

than to alleviate it. The counselors did not understand the basic principles and thus saw no reason not to incorporate these changes or "compromises." They were determined to go ahead with it.

Needless to say, we felt quite frustrated, angry, and discouraged. This episode precipitated a series of meetings of our own group. We first responded by decrying the incompetence and stupidity of the camp staff, by bemoaning our lack of power, and by arguing over various drastic alternatives courses of action to assert our influence. We then realized that at this point we really had very little leverage from which to operate. We were no longer running our groups, the staff meetings were useless and we had no control over them. Finally, most of the staff saw us as irrelevant and unhelpful.

Our deepening discouragement led us to reflect over our involvement and to begin to identify a number of the characteristics of our relationship to the camp. We began to see how inappropriate our approach had been to the particular needs and style of the setting. Our initial resistance to respond at all to immediate staff expectations (for direct work with inmates and for specific programmatic guidelines) had created a staff perception that we, as the experts, knew how to work with residents but did not want to and would not tell them how to. Our relatively passive "kitchen consulting" style conflicted with the authoritarian norms and traditions of a correctional setting and was experienced as sporadic and disconnected advice from "Monday morning quarterbacks." Our later more explicit interventions had been either irrelevant (community contacts; psychological testing) to the immediate concerns for an internal program or structurally inappropriate (unfocused group meetings), and these had sealed the issue. The staff had learned to relate to us as if we were people from the central office. They were polite, they compromised with us, and they didn't pay too much attention to us when we were not physically present.

We became most impressed with the notion that early relationships are resistent to change. In retrospect, it became clear that our initial inappropriate relationship had very quickly led to the conviction that we were *going to be* irrelevant and unhelpful. The belief that we *could* act effectively died later, but the sense that we *would* act effectively died very early. Our later attempts to gradually become more specific and directed simply reaffirmed in the staff's eyes their initial impressions. While we saw our interventions upon the director's arrival as significant changes in our relationship, the staff did not. In addition to their continued, though somewhat lessened, inappropriateness of style and content, we now felt that they were probably doomed to failure anyway because of the previous fostered assumptions of irrelevance and unhelpfulness with which the staff approached them. We became convinced that our potential influence had been seriously undermined very early in the game and that a much earlier and more drastic shift in approach would have been required to reassert our effectiveness.

Part of the problem very clearly was our own failure to examine and modify our own initial expectations: that we would work not with individual inmates but with program development and that staff would be receptive and motivated by the opportunity to share in program development. Our rigid adherence to these expectations blinded us to repeated evidence that they needed reevaluation and modification. We tended to interpret our frustrations in terms of staff inability to alter their ways of thinking about program content and structure and of perceiving and reacting to us — rather than actively questioning and modifying *our* expectations.

It is, of course, difficult to know the extent to which our failure was really due to the staff's inability to modify thinking and functioning to create a truly rehabilitative program and the extent to which it was a result of not adapting our expectations to the specific setting. The basic point here is that the initial relationship established with the setting was crucial in creating attitudes and expectations on both sides which were resistent to change and seriously hampered subsequent attempts to change. Our conviction is that consultants to community settings must be acutely aware of the nature of initial relationships and must be ready to act quickly and decisively to control them in productive ways. The institutional change agent should realize that during the period when he is defining his role and strategy, the destiny of the intervention is being partially determined.

At this point in the consultation we again contemplated possibilities for changing our relationship based on our new understanding, but decided against it. Something quite drastic would clearly be required. We simply weren't up to it and were also convinced that it was probably too late anyway. We wrote a paper discussing principles essential to a rehabilitation program (a slightly revised version of this document was later published [Saunders and Reppucci 1972]) and circulated it among the staff, but it was treated as another esoteric discussion which was not pertinent to their reality. For awhile, we continued the community and testing program and attended staff meetings, but we essentially abandoned our broader goals and spent less and less time at the camp.

Alterations in Our Thinking

Our goal in this section is to highlight a few of the more salient issues which we became aware of as a result of our consultation experience at the Mountville Youth Camp and which have affected our functioning in subsequent community interventions. These issues are especially germane to consulting in correctional settings; however, to varying degrees, they are issues which should be considered in any community intervention. Finally, we have included a brief discussion of training issues.

Consultation Issues

A crucial decision was made very early with few qualms and little hesitation. This decision was to become involved with the Mountville Camp rather than the local jail. What dictated this decision was surely the result of an emotional reaction of revulsion toward the jail and a sense of being overwhelmed by its size and its problems. In comparison, we experienced a reaction of hope for the smaller and newer camp. However, the important question here is "Why did we have such hope for the camp and was it justified?" Our hope stemmed from the newness of the facility, the age and number of its inmate population, its designation as a "rehabilitation-oriented," minimal security institution and its physical appearance. We were optimistic that these factors, in conjunction with our perception of central office concern, would enable us to help develop a truly rehabilitative facility. What we failed to give adequate weight to was the pre-history regarding the establishment of the camp. In retrospect, three factors seem most crucial: (1) the guiding philosophy, (2) the "political reality," and (3) the lack of understanding and communication both within and between different levels of organization.

The change from a philosophy of punishing criminals to one of rehabilitating them may be seen historically as an outgrowth of humanitarian concerns. Unfortunately, rehabilitation and humanitarianism are often fused in the minds of those who honestly seek reform within penal systems. Granting that any effort at rehabilitation ought to contain a good measure of concern for one's fellow man, one nevertheless must consider any information or evaluation of rehabilitative programs by a set of standards which are largely independent of philanthropic sentiments. The guiding philosophy at the camp was indeed a humanitarian one, i.e., provide good food, fresh air, outdoor work, and most importantly, remove the boys from an environment (the State Reformatory) that had a scandalous reputation. However, it was not a rehabilitative philosophy, i.e., there was no commitment to establishing a program aimed at *changing* inmate behavior. The assumption was that providing a humanitarian environment would magically provide a rehabilitation program. Furthermore, because of the fusion between these two concepts in the minds of those responsible for the establishment of the camp, there was no understanding as to the type of persons who should be recruited to staff a rehabilitative facility nor to the fact that structural arrangements, such as the isolated physical location and the contract between the Corrections Department and the Forestry Service could have disastrous negative effects on developing a rehabilitative program. Finally, those charged with developing the rehabilitation facility were never open to education regarding these matters because they, in fact, had established a program that fulfilled their ideas regarding "rehabilitation."

Factor two, which we have labeled "the political reality," is one which we were relatively ignorant of before this consultation, but which now plays a significant role in all of our community interventions. By political reality we mean the central role that political considerations play in regard to what decisions are made and what actions are taken. Corrections departments and the larger criminal justice system are probably the most vulnerable of all systems to these considerations. Whatever happens in these systems is news. For example, the "walk-off" at the camp of two relatively harmless boys brought all of the top officials from central office out at 1:00 A.M., not because there was any imminent danger or realistic need for such behavior, but rather because the incident in all probability would be reported in the newspapers and on the radio and TV news programs. Thus, there would be a need to calm the fears of the public by showing that the top men were concerned and on the scene.

Favorable press coverage is crucial for a number of reasons. Any corrections department or facility needs as much positive publicity as possible since it is predictable that negative news coverage will occur sooner or later, e.g., an escape. Good public relations are necessary to counteract the adverse effects of such negative publicity. Moreover, the major officials are always on the firing line and their jobs are at stake. When a good reputation has been established, these officials enjoy political influence which can result in increased budgets from the legislature for their programs. However, too much adverse publicity, even when there is nothing that could have been done to prevent it, can result in the loss of influence or job.

Given the importance of "the political reality," we can begin to understand the Mountville Camp from another perspective. The multitude of initial press releases about the camp were a definite asset to the newly established State Corrections Department which could not count on opening other "innovative" facilities very rapidly. What was initially perceived by both the camp's staff and ourselves as sustained and energetic commitment was in reality more a political necessity than a commitment to innovative rehabilitation. The energy and commitment could only be maintained as long as other problems did not take precedence. This is not to imply that the commissioner and the other officials in the central office did not want the camp to be as fine a place as possible,[f] but rather to recognize the predominance of the political concerns in the central office and the fact that the Mountville Camp was but a very small part of a much larger system with manifold problems that constantly need attention. Combining these considerations with factor one, the guiding philosophy, we can now understand more clearly why certain relatively irrevocable forces had been set into motion long before the camp had even opened its doors.

---

[f] To emphasize this point, it is our opinion that the commissioner, the Director of Programming and Planning, and some of the other officials are probably as outstanding a group of individuals in this field as one is likely to find anywhere.

In our experience, the importance of the political reality in dealing with all aspects of the criminal justice system has been repeatedly reinforced. As such, we cannot overemphasize the importance of being aware of and attempting initially to calculate accurately where this reality is likely to help or hinder intervention plans and programs.

The final factor involves the lack of communication and understanding between all levels of staff both within the target institution (the camp) and the parent organization (the central office), and between these two organizations. Poor communication and understanding often results in low employee morale and little dedication to one's job. This factor is not specific to corrections systems; however, in the particular case being discussed, it was exaggerated. The most blatant example is explicit in the history of the camp directorship. There was no understanding on the part of the central office that by not recruiting a director before opening the camp, they were being insensitive to the needs of the camp staff for on-site leadership. Many problems of communication between the guards and the counselors at the camp probably could have been alleviated by a competent director who would have organized the camp initially. The lack of communication between officials in the central office was made excruciatingly clear by the issuing of well-intentioned but often contradictory directives to the acting director, and thereby contributing to his inability to function adequately. Finally, the appointment of a totally untrained person as the permanent director destroyed any real hope of salvaging the camp as a rehabilitative facility. The lack of understanding and empathy by the men in the central office for the camp staff was highlighted by these actions.

To emphasize the interrelationship of these three factors, let us take the following example. We became aware of the disintegrating staff morale at the camp very early in our consultation. In an effort to change this, we suggested on numerous occasions that someone from the central office should visit the camp regularly as a show of interest and support. This suggestion was never acted upon. And why should it have been? Since from the perspective of the central office, the camp was fulfilling the guiding philosophy and there was little communication and no empathy for the problems of the camp staff, such action seemed like an unnecessary frill. Moreover, given the political reality and the crisis situations which were continually arising in other parts of the larger system, to spend time visiting the camp did not seem justifiable. In the crisis world of the central office, time is seldom allotted for preventative measures, especially since they seem to be so little understood and tend to have so little visible payoff.

Had we paid adequate attention to the pre-history of the camp, we probably would have been less optimistic about the possibility of developing a meaningful treatment center. In addition, vastly different interventions, many of them outside the camp setting, would have been indicated. However, nothing we have said invalidates our initial position that to have chosen to intervene in the jail would have been a thankless task. What it does drive home for us is that our hope for the camp was not justified on the basis of the criteria we had used to make our decision.

Training Issues

In this final section, we wish to return to statements made in the introduction regarding traditions which militate against psychologists becoming effective agents of social change. For the most part, training in psychology emphasizes the study and diagnosis of the individual from a purely psychological frame of reference with little more than "lip service" paid to the importance of the social context and its influence. Seldom, if ever, is knowledge from the other social sciences discussed or utilized. Yet, such a background ill prepares an individual for functioning as a change agent within community settings.

Our tendency to react rather than act was readily apparent in our stance regarding the leadership situation at the camp. Within a few weeks we were aware that the leadership hiatus had to be filled. We analyzed, discussed, and interpreted this situation. However, we absolutely refused to attempt to fill the void ourselves. Given the situation, it would have been very difficult to accomplish this but the fact is that this alternative never really entered our heads as a serious possibility. If it had, it might have been possible to work out some sort of satisfactory arrangement with the Corrections Department. For example, one of us might have been appointed acting director for the period of time required to recruit a competent successor. We would have gained legitimacy and institutional power which together might have enabled us to develop a workable rehabilitative program. We might then have trained someone to assume the directorship.

By this example, we do not mean to imply that we had the answers and that all would have gone smoothly if one of us had been the director. Rather, we are suggesting that we could have supplied the staff with leadership and fostered the development of a "rehabilitative" ethos. Furthermore, we are suggesting that the role of the psychological consultant in a community setting may demand that the consultant not only be a skilled observer and interpreter but also an advocate of specific ideas, actions, and values. He must be willing to put himself on the firing line and accept responsibility. What actions need to be taken will vary from setting to setting and from situation to situation, but such action should be acknowledged as a valid alternative.

The emphasis on the study of the individual led us to assume that our client was the individual setting, i.e., the Mountville Camp, rather than the camp and its parent organization. The real importance of the fact that the camp was not an entity unto itself, but rather an appendage of the larger system and, as such, could not be treated in isolation, was not salient enough to us until it was too late. Institutions have varying degrees of autonomy from and involvement with the parent organization. Depending upon that degree of autonomy, whenever a setting is part of a larger entity that larger entity must become involved in the consultation effort if that effort is to succeed. The Mountville Camp is an example of an institution with very little autonomy. All major policies and decisions were made in the central office. As such, part of the initial agreement with the Corrections Department should have been that certain members of the central office staff would have to become involved in the consultation effort. Such an agreement would have insured the sustained interest of the central office as well as providing an opportunity to educate these individuals regarding their self-defeating behaviors toward the camp.

Our experience provides us with a vivid example of our deficiencies with regard to subject matters such as organizational structure and politics. We imagine that students of sociology and administrative sciences would have been tuned into the former, and students of political science, to the latter. However, each of these groups probably would not have been particularly aware of the influence of the individual personalities on these systems. Once the focus of a consultant's change efforts shifts from an individual to a community setting, it becomes imperative that the change agent be acknowledgeable of various phenomena to which no single discipline can lay claim. It becomes essential that a multidisciplinary approach be adopted in training programs in order to adequately equip students to deal with the situations and problems they will encounter in the field. There is a move in this direction in a number of community psychology programs which have been instituted in the past few years. Nevertheless, this shift, for the most part, is minimal. Yet, it is absolutely crucial if we hope to train first-rate social change agents and researchers.

Another crucial shift, which must occur in conjunction with the adoption of a multidisciplinary approach, is the enlargement of traditional value orientations within these training programs. The underlying value in all social science is that of *seeking* knowledge for the sake of *understanding*. This orientation must be maintained, but should be coupled with the value of *utilizing* knowledge for the sake of *action*. Without this pairing, we will continue to pit inappropriately inquiry against action, theory and research against practice. The end result can only be less understanding and less effective action. It is imperative that as new training programs develop that are focused on important social problems, they give equal weight to both understanding and alleviation.

We may have bombed in Mountville, but the lessons we learned there have had a major impact on our thinking and actions. As such, our experience has been invaluable to ourselves. We hope our account of these experiences and some of the issues they raised for us will be of interest to others and will help them to avoid similar pitfalls.

References

Berline, I.N. "Psychiatric Consultation on the Antidelinquency Project." *California Journal of Secondary Education* 35 (1960); 198-202.

Fairweather, G.W. *Methods for Experimental Social Intervention.* New York: John Wiley & Sons, Inc., 1967.

Goldenberg, I.I. *Build Me a Mountain: Youth, Poverty and the Creation of New Settings.* Cambridge: MIT Press, 1971.

Leavitt, H.J. "Applied Organizational Change in Industry: Structural, Technological and Humanistic Approaches." In *Handbook of Organizations,* edited by J.G. March. Chicago: Rand McNally, 1965.

Levine, M. "Problems of Entry in Light of Some Postulates of Practice in Community Psychology." In *The Helping Professions in the World of Action,* edited by I. Goldenberg. Lexington: D.C. Heath & Co., 1973.

Loomis, S.D. "Psychiatric Consultation in a Delinquent Population." *American Journal of Psychiatry* 123, 1 (1966): 66-70.

McCorkle, A.D and Bixby, F.L. *The Highfields Story – An Experimental Treatment Project for Youthful Offenders.* New York: Henry Holt & Co., 1958.

Sanford, N. "Will Psychologists Study Human Problems?" *American Psychologist* 20 (1965): 192-202.

Sarason, S.B. and Levine, M. "Graduate Education and the Yale Psycho-Educational Clinic." In *Community Psychology: Perspectives in Training and Research,* edited by I. Iscoe and C. Spielberger. New York: Appleton-Century-Crofts, 1970.

Sarason, S.B.; Levine, M.; Goldenberg, I.; Cherlin, D.; and Bennett, E. *Psychology in Community Settings.* New York: John Wiley, 1966.

Saunders, J.T. and Reppucci, N.D. "Reward and Punishment: Some Guidelines for Their Effective Application in Correctional Programs for Youthful Offenders." *Crime and Delinquency* 18 (1972): 284-290.

Shapiro, L.N. "Psychiatric Care and the Public Offender." In *Mental Health and Urban Social Policy.* San Francisco: Jossey-Bass, 1968.

10

Psychological Consultation at Attica State Prison: Post-Hoc Reflections on Some Precursors to a Disaster

Edward S. Katkin and
Ralph F. Sibley
State University of New York at Buffalo

[Editor's Note] : *When Attica State Prison "blew," the enduring and accumulated agonies of our adult correctional institutions finally became a greater part of our society's collective conscience and consciousness. In this chapter, Edward S. Katkin and Ralph F. Sibley, through an analysis of their attempts to design and implement a rehabilitative program at the prison, describe the "institutional soil" out of which the rebellion erupted. However, the timeliness and importance of their work (and this article) extend far beyond the question of Attica Prison. The Criminal Justice System as a whole is currently in a state of flux, with movement occuring simultaneously in such diverse areas as de-institutionalization, the creation of community-based alternatives to incarceration, and the utilization of neuro-psychological techniques (even psycho-surgery) and learning theory to control and/or change "deviant behavior." In addition, mental health professionals are more and more becoming a part of this system, often in positions of high responsibility and increasing power. This being the case – and unless we want, unthinkingly, to become our society's new "agents of deviance control" – it is important that we begin to examine the nature of our involvement in the system and the relationship between the demands placed upon us and our own analysis of the system's underlying goals, processes, and ideology. Katkin and Sibley begin to do this, and in the process raise the question: "Whose agent are we?" The ultimate answer to that question will certainly do much to define the role of the helping professions in the years to come.*

This chapter will describe the development of a program of psychological service within the walls of Attica State Prison – a program that set out to provide clinical service, and which found quickly that the very definition of such

We are indebted to a variety of people for their guidance and encouragement in the preparation of this chapter, but especially to those students who contributed so much to the development of the program – Mike Domencio, Emory Hill, Mike Moses, Kevin Mulholland, David Ragland, Karl Slaikeu, and Bob Tomkiewicz.

service was beyond discovery. Specifically, this chapter will discuss the development and frequent miscarriage of various programs over a three-year period and the circumstances which led us into a deep involvement in the administration of the institution, and thence into the politics of the institution, and thence into the Realpolitik.

In the summer of 1968, the Department of Psychology of the State University was contacted by the Division of Vocational Rehabilitation of New York State, and requested to enter into a contract with the project whereby the State University would provide graduate student interns for a project at Attica and Supervision of these interns by the university staff. The prison environment appeared to have potential as a particularly interesting internship setting for students in that the DVR (Division of Vocational Rehabilitation) director was eager to have the consulting psychologists experiment with techniques such as behavior therapy, encounter groups, and T-groups.

Thus, with a sense of "doing good," and unbridled optimism, two graduate students and the senior author entered the prison in the fall of 1968. Our optimism faded rapidly. Operating within the structure of the prison institution at the same time that one tried to operate within the framework of the traditions of DVR and of clinical psychology proved to be an unusual and almost impossible experience for us, primarily because the apparent mission of the corrections institution seemed at complete loggerheads with the mission of the rehabilitative and clinical institutions. Whereas the ethic underlying the rehabilitative approach is the recognition of each man's individuality and worth and the systematic attempt to encourage individual growth, the correction tradition (notwithstanding official pronouncements from wardens) is founded upon principles of uniformity for administrative orderliness and safety. These principles of uniformity demand equal treatment for all inmates regardless of individual needs and/or differences, for the prison institution and its traditions are structured so that the overall security of the prison complex must precede any consideration of individual need, whether of inmates or of staff. While this approach maintains the highest level of security with a minimum of overt distress or disturbance, it often appears to force the prison institution into an abrupt abdication of its rehabilitative responsibilities.

In the pages to follow we will briefly describe our attempts to provide traditional service. We will then try to explain some of the reasons why the traditional service orientation failed, and we will describe the emergence of a changed role for the staff psychologists, a role of institutional consultant and evaluator. We will describe a broadening of our own horizons and the realization of the importance of coming to grips with the new culture and new traditions of the institution to which we were called; and we will present some opinions concerning the role of a clinical consultant in an institution whose values and traditions are diametrically opposed to those from which he operates. Finally, we will describe the problems which arose when the senior author and his team left the project at the end of the year, and the junior author assumed leadership of a new psychological team.

Services Provided

Personality tests administered under conditions of imprisonment in a maximum security setting do not yield the kind of results a clinical psychologist is used to seeing. The results of such personality assessments, therefore, were difficult to evaluate within our intuitive and/or actuarial framework. Unlike the mental health setting, the prison atmosphere is one of severe suspicion and interpersonal instrumentality; test results indicating significant psychopathology might result with equal probability from deliberate falsification or fear of negatively affecting one's chances for parole. It became apparent to us also that the nature of prison life rendered many of the assessments we used inappropriate. The inmate possesses a permanent awareness of being observed and scrutinized. How then does a clinical psychologist interpret the Rorschach test of a newly arrived inmate in which there is apparent paranoid content such as eyes staring at him? How does the clinical psychologist interpret the TAT response of an inmate who describes the hero as feeling that he has no private life, that he is always being watched, that people are out to get him? It is too simple to conclude, as we might in a mental health setting, that these are pathological signs. Conversely, it is also too simple, and probably misleading, to conclude that these are signs *only* of the situational content in which the inmate lives. Finally the psychologist begins asking himself what is normal and what is abnormal for a man living in a cage? And how do these criteria relate to the criteria and norms which we have come to understand in the outside world?

In addition to these conceptual and interpretive restrictions, we found ourselves faced with severe restrictions on our actual administrative responsibilities. In hospital and clinic settings the mental health specialist is accustomed to being the central figure in a patient's schedule. Hospital routines are presumed to be secondary to the doctor's scheduling of diagnostic and therapeutic sessions, and the doctor becomes accustomed to the notion that the institution is organized around his services. Not so in the prison! The inmate is scheduled according to the mandates of "security." If the hospital is "doctor centered" then the prison is "officer centered," or more appropriately, "security centered," and the mental health specialist had better accommodate himself. For instance, inmates are only available for testing and interviewing during certian prescribed and limited daytime hours. The prison routine is relatively inflexible and no exemptions are made for the psychologist who is in the midst of an important interview. Not only do meal schedules interfere with the work at hand, but inmates are locked in their cells several times a day for security counts.

These factors forced us to choose, where possible psychological tests which did not require extensive time for administration. Early in the life of the project, we tried to circumvent these difficulties by asking inmates to take certain objective tests, such as the MMPI, back to their cells for completion. This plan failed. First, the fear of self-incrimination which is so prevalent among inmates tended to invalidate almost all such tests. Second, inmates asked other inamtes and even prison personnel for the "correct" answers to these tests and more often than not received well-intentioned replies. It is likely that most of the MMPI profiles obtained from inmates under such conditions were in fact group profiles jointly contributed by fellow inmates and officers. Finally, there was a perceived stigma associated with being selected for testing. No inmate wanted to risk being labeled "psycho."

Psychotherapy

Individual. At the outset of the project, a variety of inmates were seen in individual therapy both in formal sessions and informal consultations. These psychotherapy sessions were useful for two purposes. First, for some inmates they provided essential support which facilitated adjustment to the prison environment and helped them to develop greater self-understanding. Second, and importantly for the therapist, the sessions provided an excellent opportunity to acquire an understanding of the prison environment from a different perspective than might otherwise have been obtained. This new perspective, it was felt, enabled the clinician to work in the system with far greater understanding of his impact on the population.

Group. At the beginning of the project, the staff psychologists entertained the notion of group therapy as a viable alternative to individual therapy. Their thinking was quite traditional: group therapy could accommodate a larger number of inmates in the same time as individual therapy, thus maximizing the effectiveness of the small psychological staff. However, it proved impossible to carry out group therapy with any degree of effectiveness. First of all, the logistics of getting eight to ten inmates in a room with a therapist without correctional supervision were difficult because of prison security regulations. The presence of this security force made it very difficult for the inmates to talk openly about their problems because of the realistic fear that their comments might be taken directly to the warden. In addition, effective group therapy would require the inmates to trust the psychologists leading the groups. This, we soon discovered, was far from likely. Despite the high opinion we had of ourselves and of our integrity, we were little more than plainclothesmen to the inmates.

Attempts at group therapy were complicated further by yet another unexpected development. Not only were the inmates inhibited by the presence of correctional officers and unwilling to trust the plainclothesmen-psychologists, but they were equally afraid (for equally valid reasons) to deal openly with their fellow inmates. The prison culture is riddled with informers, extortionists, blackmailers, and a variety of other unsavory characters, against whom the average inmate is constantly on guard. The possibility of lessening one's defenses in a group therapy situation, and opening oneself up to possible attack is quite intimidating, and rightly so. In a prison group therapy session there is no way for the men to hide from each other between sessions, no large community for them to slip back into anonymously. What we did not know until we started is that it was unreasonable of us to expect these men to play by our rules!

Summary Comments. Before six months had passed the psychologists became aware that their traditional approach to diagnosis and therapy was considerably less than optimal in this setting. Standard procedures did not seem to fit the requirements of the institution and attempts to develop nonstandard procedures were thwarted either by inmate resistance or the institution's inflexibility. We had jumped into the fire too hastily and it was time now to climb back into the frying pan and try to gain a greater understanding of our immediate surroundings. Consequently, the consultants spent a great part of the next six months evaluating the institutional factors which affected inmate behavior as well as staff behavior.[a] The purpose of this evaluation was to enable us to plan new programs which, hopefully, would be effective *within the limits of institutional restrictions.* However, the notion was not ruled out that the evaluation might lead to the conclusion that these institutional restrictions and some institutional structures might have to be renovated.

Institutional Evaluation

The Perceived Role of the DVR Project in the Prison

The contract under which the DVR project was established indicated that a variety of rehabilitative strategies including environmental manipulation would be carried out; yet, there was little institutional cooperation in the accomplishment of these stated goals. For example, an inmate suffering from gross obesity related to physical and emotional isolation had been granted informally the priv-

---

[a] It should be noted that at this time we became acutely aware of the severe inadequacy of our preparation for the task at hand and the hubris manifested in jumping into a new professional context without consulting what turned out to be a voluminous literature on the problems emerging before our eyes. Of particular importance to us and to any member of the reading audience who may find themselves in our footsteps in the future are books by the American Correctional Association (1959), Cleaver (1967), Conrad (1965), Cressey (1961), Fenton, Reimer and Wilmer (1967), Kesey (1962), Menninger (1968), and Solzhenitsyn (1963). In addition, much was gained from studying papers by Kelly (1966), Graziano (1969), and especially Levine (1967, 1969).

vilege of an open cell door at times when other inmates were going to certain specified jobs or spending free time in the yard. The obese inmate, who could not work and could not exercise in the yard because of his physical condition, nevertheless requested that he be granted his hour of freedom simply by having his cell door left open. The staff psychologists decided to use this potential freedom as a reinforcement for a weight-loss program that the inmate needed desperately for his future medical safety; the extension of this privilege was discussed with a correction officer on the block and the privilege was granted. However, within a week the privilege already granted was repealed due to "orders" and the need for "security," and the inmate, feeling betrayed, rejected further approaches from the psychologist. An attempt to find out where the orders came from and what the security question was resulted in complete failure. The fact that the inmate in question was a virtual invalid, incapable of moving, and therefore a nonexistent security risk never entered into the final decision. There is simple a prison rule that an inmate must be either locked in his cell or locked out of his cell; the possibility of his remaining in the cell with the door unlocked during "free" time was never considered. This example reflects, through one instance, the notion that the institution perceives its responsibility primarily in terms of stated security rules and that these security rules are not readily modified in the interests of the rehabilitation of an individual inmate.

After a series of instances in which a psychologist requested minimal environmental change in order to facilitate treatment of an inmate and met with no success, the prison authorities were confronted directly concerning the stipulation in the DVR contract which called for "environmental manipulation." The institution, through the warden, indicated that environmental manipulation could be allowed only within the limits of defined security. We countered that the limits of defined security eliminated any and all environmental manipulation and that this must have been clear at the time the project was approved.

Later, it was discovered that the DVR project had been foisted upon the prison largely at the pleasure of the administrative hierarchy in the state capital, who felt that such a project would lend "class" to the prison and to the New York state system. The warden, for his part, had not been eager to welcome us to his house. The decision-making process which resulted in the placement of the project, then, was related to considerations of administrative prestige-seeking and institutional competition between the State Educational Department and the State Corrections Department at the highest level. The project itself and its success or failure, apparently, were never taken very seriously by the upper administration; the placement of the project within the prison was seen in Albany as a means of providing opportunity for high-level administrators to give talks to professional and nonprofessional groups about the state's interest in the vocational rehabilitation of inmates. In short, everybody in the state capital was happy as long as nobody in the prison rocked the boat. The staff psychologists could easily have fit into this pattern by acting as ballast in that boat, seeing inmates for superficial therapy and continuing to give projective tests irrespective of their value. What we did, in fact, was compromise; we agreed among ourselves to continue to provide the services requested while actively and discreetly lobbying and using whatever powers of argument and persuasion we had to change some of the prison regulations.

Initial Attempts to Modify the System

The first such attempt to modify the structure was a proposal to the warden that weekly training groups (T-groups) be established for purposes of enabling interested members of the DVR staff (including correctional officers) to improve their relations with each other. Essentially what was being proposed was a modified form of sensitivity training for all members of the staff. We hoped that by asking for a weekly staff meeting in which both uniformed and non-uniformed personnel could participate, channels of communication might open up and some of the walls of hostility between the correctional and rehabilitative staff might break down. This plan was rapidly undercut. First, the warden decreed that corrections officers would not be allowed released time in which to participate in such groups. Second, the warden ordered that the groups could only be attempted if attendance were mandatory for all members of the project, incredibly even for those officers for whom no time would be provided! Either of these restrictions alone would have impeded the effectiveness of the group; together they rendered the operation useless. Furthermore, these restrictions, coming as they did from the correctional authority rather than from the DVR authority, emphasized the open fact that the DVR project was being denied responsibility for developing its own programs. This was just one example of how the imposition of superior correctional authority on a specific psychological program proposed by the DVR project sabotaged an operation.

Upon reflection, we discovered that there were numerous other incidents which could serve to illustrate the destructive imposition of correctional authority upon the rehabilitative function. Our awareness of these new incidents was mind-expanding at first because of our gradual understanding that *the areas in which the imposition of such authority affects the inmate's psychological life are more often than not those areas which psychologists do not normally recognize as their province.*

For instance, constant censorship of inmate reading material is carried out, often by men who have no awareness of the abilities, interests, or needs of the inmate, nor any understanding of the literature being censored. Thus, black inmates from urban ghettos are denied access to relevant black literature, because white rural censors find the material in some sense "foreign." Books containing common obscenities are censored although the majority of correctional employees themselves can be heared using the same profanities in their common speech.

The critical point here is not the merit of the literature in question; rather it is the damaging assumption by the authorities that the inmate is to be protected from himself at all times and denied the simple human dignity of choosing for himself what he will read. This, we began to realize, is *inimical to positive mental health.*

What are the implications of functioning in such a system? The primary result is the development of extraordinary skepticism among inmates and to a large extent among officers. Thus, when a project such as ours presented its credentials to the inmate populations, they did not expect it to be serious; they just suspected that they were being "conned" again. To a large extent their expectations came true, because many of the promises made could not be carried out in the context of the prison rules. For instance, many inmates discovered upon entering the project that their idle time increased rather than decreased. They discovered further that actual training programs often waited until after parole while they waited on the project with little or no personal gain. They discovered also that the project was held suspect by the correctional authorities.

Inmates discovered further that they were being discriminated against by some members of the prison staff because of their affiliation with the DVR project. As tension between the rehabilitative personnel and the correctional personnel mounted the inmates became the victims of displaced aggression. Simple requests for privileges were kicked back and forth between the DVR office and the Corrections office in petty jurisdictional disputes while the inmate waited for an answer. Medical services offered by the prison hospital (administered entirely independently of the DVR project) seemed suddenly to deteriorate. Apparently the knowledge that the DVR project had a budget line for outside medical consultants influenced the prison physicians to resist offering medical services to DVR inmates. The rate of inmate complaints about poor medical service increased consistently as the project continued, and most of these complaints were seen by the rehabilitation counselor, whose responsibility it was to investigate them, as entirely valid. The medical staff and corrections staff interpreted formal complaints from the DVR staff as a combination of paranoia and trouble-making.

At about this time, the consulting psychologists tried to withdraw somewhat from the immediate stresses and strains of the situation and attempted to analyze the role demands placed upon the various staff members and inmates involved in the life of the project, hoping this analysis would indicate appropriate directions for future input to the system.

A Role Analysis of Participants in the Project

The warden's role is defined primarily by the State Department of Corrections to whom he is responsible. The role he plays for them is that of efficient chief administrator. To fulfill this role expectation, the warden concerns himself with a variety of administrative responsibilities such as the average daily cost of feeding a man, the average yearly expense for heat, and the costs for maintenance of the concrete. In addition, the warden is expected to preserve order. A prison with no disturbances or internal violence is a good prison. There is little evidence that the role definition of the warden includes reducing the recidivism (that is for the parole department to do), teaching skills that are in demand outside the prison, or creating an environment conducive to human development.

The correction officer, who is the interface between the inmate and the prison system, fills a role which is also defined primarily by those above him. The officer's role, as defined by his superiors, includes the task of dispensing rewards for behavioral expressions of conventional values on the part of inmates. These rewards include block jobs and their associated privileges; but "rewarding" is not extended definitionally to include encouraging or anticipating good behavior. An officer's role is not in any way defined as "assistant to the rehabilitative venture"; the correctional officer is told simply that he guards. The implications of such a job definition are extensive and distressing: a guard is alert, not relaxed; he is responsible for blaming or punishing but he is not receptive; he relates to inmates only on the basis of administrative rules; therefore his authority depends on his position, not on his competence; he makes no decisions on the basis of consistency with an overall goal.

An inmate's behavior must be directed towards satisfying the expectations both of his peers and the staff. An interesting facet of his role in the institution is that a variety of community members holding different values concur with each other in their anticipation of inmate behavior, although for different reasons. For example, the correctional officer may expect inmates to gamble because he knows they "intentionally try to get away with everything." The DVR staff member similarly expects gambling from the inmate since "he can't help but want to gamble" in such an oppressive situation. The inmate subsequently encounters expectations which are shared by officers and DVR staff, then generalizes that all prison employees are alike.

The inmate must also behave in accord with the expectations of other inmates. While peer pressure also is exerted by staff members upon each other, the existence of such pressure is clearest among the inmates. Just as it is considered bad form for a staff member to befriend an inmate (for fear that his authority will be weakened), it is considered equally bad form among inmates for one of them to befriend a staff member (for fear that he may be seduced into acting as an informer). Consequently, an inmate achieves esteem among his peers in proportion to the degree to which he is viewed as unfriendly or hostile to the staff.

Members of the DVR project defined their roles as essentially different from those of the officers. Yet the inmate, from his perspective, did not perceive the difference and the warden, from his perspective, did not want to perceive the difference. This conflict between the DVR worker's self-definition and the definitions imposed on him from below and from above often led to friction between him and the institution. For instance, the project director respected his staff's ability to use discretion in drawing a distinction between their rehabilitative function and their custodial function; consequently correctional authorities, who did not display such respect, felt compelled to warn DVR workers about the dangers of being "conned" into breaking rules. As might be expected the rules most likely to cause polarization between correctional officers and rehabilitation workers are usually those which the rehabilitation workers deemed least dangerous if violated and potentially harmful to inmates if enforced. For example, the reading of sexual literature and magazines is seen as dangerous by officers *because* it is outlawed; but the DVR staff may see it as a source of constructive tension reduction. Any resolution of such conflicts which arise as a result of the rehabilitation worker's lapses of rule enforcement and the correctional officer's prohibitions must come through the warden, who in turn *must be convinced that no negative consequences will follow his actions.* Naturally, under a situation where the warden perceives his role as stabilizer of the orderly status quo, decisions hostile to change predominate.

Given this basic structure in which pressure always flows towards preservation of the status quo, what is the proper role for the clinical consultant? The consultant entered the project as the agent of the institution, requested to fill a prescribed role, that of diagnostician and therapist. Yet, the consultant also was the possessor of a professional role as an agent of the inmates. Within the prison the conflict between these roles seemed unusually exaggerated. Whereas the mental health ethic prevailing in our culture labels the hospitalized as "sick," the prevailing societal code labels the imprisoned as "evil." This is especially so in those states (including New York) which provide specialized institutions for the "criminally insane"; for by definition, the inmates who are *not* "criminally insane" are just plain bad. In attempting to define his own role in this setting, therefore, the psychologist found himself in conflict between his role as agent of the inmates whose needs and rights he must serve, and as agent of an institution which perceived the inmate as unworthy of help and for which the needs of the inmate were at best a nuisance.

And yet the needs of the institution (to preserve order and increase efficiency) and the needs of the inmate (to develop along socially and vocationally acceptable lines) are not incompatible. Our plan was to present our views emphasizing the compatibility of the two models to the correctional administration with the hope of influencing them at the local level to allow the DVR project sufficient freedom to attempt to demonstrate that modification of the existing structure would be advantageous to the prison and to the inmates. We kept in mind, however, our observation that the local administration functioned in accordance with the role expectation perceived to emanate from higher state authority, and that is was possible that no changes would be allowed unless pressure for them was possible that no changes would be allowed unless pressure for them was perceived to come from the state. In that case, we had already begun to plan possible techniques for approaching the administration in Albany to plead our case.

Recommendations to the Institution

Proposals

Our first suggestion was that the demonstration block provide for the inmates a model of what an effective society can be. We suggested that a milieu based upon mutual trust (which must be constantly demonstrated, not just talked about) be established. This milieu should offer graduated degrees of freedom and responsibility as rewards for constructive behavior. In short, we proposed an attempt to carry out what was called for in the original description of the project — milieu therapy. The block, it was suggested, should guarantee each inmate complete freedom from informers, freedom from duplicity, and freedom from being prejudged because of past behavior. It should provide the inmate with free access to other people in the block without fear of being trapped or "conned." The block should demonstrate the rudimentary principles of democracy and encourage the men toward self-government, training them in principles of responsibility, rational bargaining with the authorities. It should entrust to the officers the responsibility for making daily decisions concerning responses to prisoner requests, thereby increasing the responsibility of the officer and placing the prisoner face to face with his keeper in mature confrontation. Naturally the block should enable all factions within it to develop methods by which their grievances may be heard by disinterested third parties. It should encourage education in civic affairs and politics as well as in vocational development and it should recognize the essential humanity of its inmates by allowing unrestricted private correspondence and regular conjugal visits.

What we suggested is that the risks involved in such an undertaking were worth taking. It was likely, we believed, that the number of inmates who would create serious problems in such an environment would be far outweighted by the number who would demonstrate growth and change toward more constructive living. Eventually such a milieu should provide *internal* correction for the troublemaker (i.e., inmate judiciary), relieving the institution from some of its current policing responsibility.

The first obvious problem facing us if such recommendations were accepted was the establishment of conditions within the prison environment conducive to the giving up of antisocial behavior on the part of the inmates and substitution of new behavior patterns consistent with the demands of society both inside and outside the prison. To these ends we proposed that the DVR block itself become an experimental unit in which prisoner behavior could elicit either rewards or punishment from the staff, both civilian and uniformed. The essence of the program was to give immediate reinforcement to inmates for their total behavior,

not just for isolated aspects of training and development; as inmates are processed through the project their success or failure should not only be evaluated but
rewarded. Inmates demonstrating clear-cut effort, motivation, and achievement
in educational training situations should be reinforced with some increased financial stipend. The prison environment currently makes this impossible because of the uniform regulations governing renumeration for all inmates. Although the institution approves of financial rewards for certain specific jobs, it
does not recognize financial rewards as reinforcement for sucessful rehabilitative
efforts. In general what we recommended was a type of "token economy" program for the demonstration block in which specific tasks would be described for
the inmates and limited goals established for them with reinforcements built in
as they achieved those goals.

The Politics of Implementation

The proposals were greeted with something less than enthusiasm and it became readily apparent that the institution was dissatisfied with the input it was
receiving. The general response to our proposals for change was total silence and
apparent inattention. It became clear that the warden was not responsive to suggestions from below, and that even minor changes in the system would be impossible to achieve unless the "system" directed him to start selling new and different products; that is, rehabilitation instead of detention. After discussion in-
voling the project director and various members of the DVR staff, a tentative
and optimistic conclusion was reached that the higher authorities in the state
would be willing to accept our viewpoint as long as we talked about trying it exclusively with the small number of inmates assigned to our project. Our job now
was to convince the state authorities of the virtue of allowing us to try, and to
convince them to communicate to the warden that no negative consequences
would result from allowing us more freedom within the prison.

Consequently, the project director, through the State Office of Education,
attempted to schedule a meeting with the Commissioner of Corrections, the
State Director of Rehabilitation, the warden, and concerned members of the
project staff to hammer out the dispute concerning the proper role of the DVR
project within the prison. But repeated attempts to schedule such a meeting
were met with delaying tactics. After months passed without a meeting, it became increasingly clear that the rehabilitation project had one of three choices
concerning its future role in the prison. One choice was simply to fold up our
tent and steal away, admitting that there was no conceivable way within this
context to carry out the mandate of the project. A second alternative was simply
to capitulate to the system, go through the motions, take home our salaries, and
provide the semblance of service requested by the institution. This alternative,
admittedly, was appealing because it would minimize conflict and maximize ease,

but it would result inevitably in failure for the project, and any further projects of this sort. The third position, which was tentatively agreed upon by the majority of staff members, was to force some sort of confrontation through the exercise of what little political power we had.

This plan was carried out in the following manner. The project director made clear his sense of dissatisfaction and impotence to the funding agency in Washington which had underwritten the project from the beginning, emphasizing to the funding agency that little progress was being made and little support was being offered. It was also made clear that it was unlikely that the demonstration project could succeed under the current conditions. The funding agency then notified the State Office of Education that it was placing the demonstration project on probation and that if there were not significant change in the nature of the project within a six month probationary period the contract would be terminated. The Department of Corrections, as mentioned earlier, was eager to maintain the project for the prestige it offered and the financial benefits to be derived from "over-head." The prospect of an abrupt termination of funds and severing of the project was sufficient stimulus to cause the Corrections Department to schedule a meeting at the commissioner's office within a relatively short period of time. The application of pressure had opened the door.

The meeting, which included the commissioner and deputy commissioner of corrections, the warden, the project director, and the chief psychologist was often acrimonious but nevertheless constructive. Sometimes functioning as a purely cathartic session, seomtimes as a constructive problem-sovling session, and sometimes as a sensitivity training group, the meeting wound down finally to a mutual agreement that the rehabilitation project would be given considerably more autonomy in the future and allowed to experiment with a variety of programs. A crucial factor in the meeting was the insistence by the deputy commissioner that the warden need have no fear of negative feedback if some of the attempted innovations failed. The deputy commissioner agreed to assume administrative responsibility for the changes that might take place in the DVR project, and continually reminded the warden that he was "safe." As a gesture of his interest in shifting the emphasis from security to rehabilitation the deputy commissioner proposed that the warden, the DVR program director, and the chief psychologist take a trip, at state expense, to a highly respected state Diagnostic and Treatment Center (DTC) specializing in the rehabilitation of the "criminally insane." The deputy commissioner suggested that a few days of observation of its innovative program, which emphasizes inmate independence and self-government, would be profitable for all of us who had been involved in the present conflict. The trip was later made, and all indications were that the warden, if not convinced of the wisdom of the different methods, at least understood the message from his chief that he was expected to allow some changes to be made.

Those programs which the warden agreed to implement immediately included the establishment of a block newspaper to be printed on a weekly basis and handled mutually by inmates and all staff members. In addition, the warden agreed that a token economy program could be established on the block as a demonstration project, and agreed to allow the project the necessary flexibility for changing rules and regulations to meet the needs of the token economy situation. Group counseling sessions without a security force were set up for all the inmates on the block. The DVR project director was also allowed to initiate a weekly gripe session in which the inmates could come together in a town meeting and air any and all grievances freely.

Some of the proposals which had been made were summarily rejected for reasons often unique and entirely unpredictable to us. For instance, the suggestion that officers wear civilian clothes instead of uniforms was vetoed on the grounds that it would cause a crisis with the union. Once again we had come up against a nuance which defied normal expectation. It seems that officers receive a special clothing allowance for the purchase of uniforms and that the union argued strongly during collective bargaining for relatively liberal allowances. The idea, of course, is for union members to receive an allowance considerably larger than they actually need. To establish a prison block in which uniforms were not required would be a threat to the union's ability to gain some extra funds for its members.

Nevertheless, the result of the applied pressure was generally positive. The second year of the project began with a renewed spirit. The inmates' morale was increased somewhat upon observing that the project staff had in fact accomplished something on their behalf and was able to make the institution bend at least some of its rules towards rehabilitation needs. The morale of the staff members themselves improved tremendously at the recognition that their efforts had been rewarded.

Eleven months had now elapsed since the senior author and his two graduate student intern-savants had entered the project. Just at the point when they might begin to gather momentum, all three of them were to leave the project. The senior psychologist was leaving for a sabbatical year in California, one of the interns was finishing school and leaving, and the second graduate student, feeling that he had learned as much as he wanted to and had contributed as much as he was capable of to the project, chose to leave. The junior author was recruited to replace the senior author as chief psychologist, and two new interns were assigned to the institution to replace the one leaving.

The problem of transferring clinical and political responsibility within the project, which constituted an important aspect of the total consultative experience, will now be explored. Whereas the description presented to this point has been primarily the responsibility of the senior author, the description to follow, which outlines the developments of the second year of the project, the problems of stepping into someone else's role, and some observations on the interpersonal dynamics within the project, is primarily the responsibility of the junior author.

First person references, henceforth, are offered by and refer to him.

The Second Year

As the senior author has indicated, the second year of the project was begun with high expectations for success. The warden had been both chastened for his past resistance to the program and relieved of responsibility for potential problems which might arise from a more imaginative and flexible approach. He now seemed to be offering us almost complete autonomy in operating the unit and told us we "could do anything we wanted except put a ladder against the wall."

Thus I began the year in an optimistic frame of mind, with the intention of focusing on the delivery of clinical services to our inmate clients, while providing the necessary supervision and training to the new team of interns, who, in contrast to their predecessors, had practically no clinical experience. Drawing on our observation of the program at the Diagnostic and Treatment Center (DTC), described below, the project director and I also determined to move our own program closer to the "therapeutic community" model.

Unfortunately, as we moved along into the year, it became clear that success was continuing to elude us. We were foundering on a series of unforeseen obstacles. With the clearer vision of hindsight, I am now able to identify and describe many of these impediments to progress. They include the failure to learn enough from the experiences of the first-year term, the fact that the organizational structure of the setting guaranteed the failure of any truly rehabilitative staff of the unique and favored role of the psychologist.

A Different Institutional Style

A brief description of the DTC will make clear some of the crucial differences between this program and our own. While administratively connected with a state prison, the Center is physically housed in a neighboring State Hospital for the Criminally Insane. This is significant, since the warden of the prison must actually go outside the wall of his own institution to see at first hand what is going on at the Center. Our project, by contrast, was inside the wall of Attica, and thus directly under the eye of our warden. A second major difference is that custodial officers at the DTC answer administratively to the director, a psychiatrist, who is a Department of Corrections employee. The officers on our project were responsible, through the usual prison chain of command, directly to the warden. Our director, who did not have an appointment in the Department of Corrections, could thus exercise no administrative control over the officers. This was a continuing source of frustration.

The program at the DTC includes individual and group psychotherapy for every inmate on a regular basis, daily community meetings, and a mandatory workshop experience. Obviously, doing individual therapy with 100 men puts a considerable drain on staff time. We learned that in many cases the relationship was "therapy" only in the broadest sense, consisting of infrequent meetings to assess progress. At the time of our visit the staff was considering dropping the rigid requirement of individual treatment for every inmate and offering this type of help only to those inmates who seemed likely to profit from it. They also felt that in most cases it was group, rather than individual therapy which proved most effective in developing insight. We noted, in this regard, much evidence in the community meetings of strong group pressures toward reality testing and psychological self-examination. Such pressures must have been even stronger in the smaller, more private, therapy groups.

Residents of the Center are divided into two companies of about fifty men each. Community meetings are held daily in each company, and there is a weekly joint session which brings together all Center residents. The meetings are chaired on a rotating basis by civilian staff members and officers. In the sessions we observed the inmates demonstrated considerable psychological sophistication in exerting strong group pressures on deviants. Inmates who were "not with the program," who were "conning" themselves or others, or who acted out their hostilities were subjected to exposure and recrimination. Staff members told us that peers are much tougher on an inmate than any Center officer would be, and that aggressive acts are particularly strongly sanctioned. An inmate who strikes another will probably still be hearing about it from his fellows months later.

A possible explanation for these self-imposed norms may be found in the relative absence of restrictive rules imposed by the administration. The atmosphere at the Center is quite friendly and relaxed. Inmates are allowed to wear "civilian" clothes, cell doors are left open and lights on until 11:00 P.M., and there is relative freedom of movement with the possibllity of casual socializing with both civilian staff and officers as well as other inmates. The most striking example of the difference between this and other prison settings, however, is the presence of an attractive young female psychologist moving about the unit unescorted, chatting with inmates, even closing herself in a room with a man for a therapy session. In our prison, by contrast, most inmates never get to see, much less talk to, the few female employees, and if they should glimpse one, it would be through a barred door.

As one might expect from the nature of the program, psychologists and psychiatrists make up the bulk of the professional staff at the Center. In our project, by contrast, a majority of the professionals came from a rehabilitation orientation. No psychiatric staff was assigned to our project, and direct psychological services were provided by graduate students with varying degrees of clinical experience.

I have described the program at the DTC because it illustrates what can be accomplished when one is not forced to operate under the constraints of physical setting and administrative organization to which our project was subject. The DTC well deserves its reputation as a showcase. At the time of our visit relations among inmates, civilian staff, and custodial staff were open and warm. There was an atmosphere of genuine interpersonal concern among the inmates and a willingness to accept responsibility for deviant group members.

The main lesson I take from the contrast between this program and ours is that *it is absolutely essential to the success of a rehabilitative project within a correctional setting that the project director have direct administrative control over all "uniformed" as well as "civilian" personnel working in the project.* Given this base, it may be possible to operate successfully inside the wall of a larger institution, but it would certainly be preferable to have a physically seperate building outside the wall. But this was a lesson taught through the often frustrating and sometimes bitter experience of trying to function in a setting where the rehabilitative staff had very little control over anything.

Continuity and Discontinuity

The senior author and his graduate student interns were associated with the project throughout its first full year of operation, and they played a major role in the political maneuvering which was necessary to keep the project operating in the face of obstructionist tactics; suddenly, on August 1, 1969, they were gone. I had been to the prison for one visit prior to the senior author's departure, but I was actually an unknown entity, except to the director, on my first workday. I had, of course, talked with the senior author and was somewhat familiar with his view of the situation, but I found myself totally unprepared for many of the crucial issues which arose in the very first week.

Furthermore, I did not know the students who would be working with me until the week before we started. The two interns were also totally new to the clients and staff members of the project. One of the civilian staff members in discussing this turnover among psychologists emphasized the importance of continuity to me in this way: "It takes a guy about six months before he finds out what's going on around here. Then he can settle down and do his job." It was this fellow's contention that you couldn't be told what it was like, that you had to gradually build up the correct view through direct personal experience. Perhaps I am still naive, but I would disagree, at least in part. I feel that a few broad-ranging preliminary sessions with the "old hands" before a new student's first trip to the prison, plus a thorough but loosely structured orientation program once he is on the job, could materially help to smooth the transition from one year's staff to the next.

The Role of the Clinical Supervisor-
Consultant

My role was somewhat unclear from the start. The original proposal had
called for the university faculty member to supervise the clinical students. However, the extraordinary administrative problems which the senior author had encountered during the first year had forced him to spend the majority of his time
as administrative consultant to the project director and as therapist to the system; little time was left for intern supervision. Fortunately for all concerned, the
graduate students serving during the first year were advanced clinical students,
highly experienced, and quite sophisticated. Close supervision was not required,
and its absence was not missed. In addition, these students were eager to participate in the developing political problems and the resultant institutional analysis.
But now we were starting a new year — a year in which we had been given our
freedom by the state administration, which now expected us to produce. I soon
discovered that my fledgling clinicians needed more supervision than I was able
to provide in one day a week, although they were not always willing to admit it.
Because of this, I spent a greater portion of my time on the unit with the students and inmates than "up front," in another building, talking with the project
director. Consequently, I never achieved as close a relationship with him as the
senior author had, and it may have taken me longer to come to a clear understanding of his conception of the project and of psychology's role within it.

My meager stock of time was further eaten into by my involvement in direct
delivery of services. The project director and I had decided after our visit to the
DTC that all of our clients should be involved in group counseling. Since there
weren't enough other professionals to handle all the groups, I had to become involved in order for the program to function. This was a very valuable experience.
First, it acquainted me directly with the problems the students were having with
their groups. Second, I got to know the men in my group reasonably well, and
they got to know me. We psychologists were thus able to participate more intel-
ligently in planning and decision-making concerning those men we knew from
our groups, and the inmates learned that they could count on a fair hearing, and
frequently, support for their grievances from us.

Sources of Conflict Within the
Psychology Staff

The psychologists from the previous year had taken an extreme position on
confidentiality. They not only refused to divulge to any other staff member
what sort of progress they were making with their therapy clients, they even refused to say who they were seeing. This decision for extreme confidentiality was
not arrived at lightly. Rather, it was felt by the interns who worked on the proj-

ect during the first year that they had to move to such extremes in order to achieve any degree of trust in their relationship with the inmates. Consequently, they felt that they must demonstrate by their actions that their conversations (therapy) with the inmates would be treated as sacred material, not even to be discussed with their own professional colleagues. To ease administrative problems concerning diagnostic evaluations, when psychological evaluations were requested, the student on the team who had no prior contact with the client did the testing. If the client was in therapy, his therapist would read the report based on this testing and either approve it or veto it without offering any additional comment. In informal meetings with the second-year interns their predecessors convinced them that such absolute confidentiality was the sine qua non for therapeutic functioning in the prison setting. My own point of view was that the need for confidentiality had to be tempered by our responsibility to function as members of the team, and that taking a hard line on confidentiality could only be interpreted as arrogance by other staff members. I also felt that it was sensible for a client's therapist to be involved in writing his parole report, since he was the one staff member who was in the best position to comment on the man's psychological status as this related to the likelihood of his repeating his crime. Since our report writing was, for teaching purposes, usually a collaborative effort, I was often able to get the therapist to contribute in an informal way, though he would never take responsibility for authoring the report. I was also able to convince the students to share with the project director information as to whom they had been seeing, for how long, and how the treatment was progressing in general terms.

A second area of conflict was what I will call "overzealous nurturance." Every student who worked with me during the year came into the prison with the attitude (which I shared to some degree) that our clients were relatively blameless products of a society characterized by unequal opportunity, and that this was particularly so for the blacks, who represent about 60 percent of the present prison population in New York State. In short, they viewed the inmates more as victims than victimizers and felt that they deserved whatever acts of humanitarian concern and kindness one was able to provide.

Unfortunately, such laudable humanitarian instincts fly directly in the face of traditional prison attitudes and specific prison regulations, which prohibit doing the slightest favor or giving the smallest gift (even a stick of gum) to an inmate. Bringing anything whatever into or out of the prison for an inmate is sanctioned as a criminal act. Because of the possibility of our being expelled from the prison for violating this rule, I argued against doing prohibited "favors" for inmates. I felt it was wiser to work within the limits of this restriction to try to effect change in the system as a whole. I later learned that all the students did not share this view.

We suffered our first casualty to the clash between "idealism" and "authority" after about five months. Our intern had written to a court in another state on behalf of a client he had been seeing, asking them to dismiss an outstanding charge against the inmate. The court agreed to do so if the man would make good on a $40.00 bad check. Unfortunately, the money order was made out to the wrong party, and was therefore returned — to the warden! The intern was dismissed summarily, and this occurred within a week of the firing of our project teacher, who reputedly had smuggled out a valentine card to an inmate's wife.

Poor communication was the common thread connecting the issues of confidentiality and nurturance. It wasn't until our last day at the prison that one of the interns told me about having been influenced by the previous year's students regarding the confidentiality issue. He felt at the time that having been in this unique situation for a year they were in a better position than I to determine the requirements for clinical effectivness. Furthermore, the intern who was dismissed had told me nothing about his letter writing and money lending until after the fact. The nature of the situation, plus the fact that I was at first unknown and unproved to them, seemed to produce a "do your own thing" ethic on the part of the students. This ethic not only created problems for me in my supervisory relationship with the interns, it also created serious problems of communication with other staff members, both civilian and uniformed.

Relations with Civilian Staff

The major figures with whom we interacted on the civilian staff were the project director, a rehabilitation counselor with extensive experience in prison work; a project coordinator; a full-time rehabilitation counselor, who screened and selected clients, coordinated rehabilitation services for them, and helped them with plans for release or transfer after completing our program; a parole officer who arranged for appearances of our clients before the Parole Board and wrote reports for the board; a prison service unit counselor who updated the client's prison file and processed matters concerning the inmates' correspondence lists and requests for special privileges. There were, in addition, a workshop evaluator and an institutional teacher assigned to the project, but our relations with them were infrequent.

There appeared to be general agreement among these staff members that the proper role of the psychologist involved: (1) writing parole reports based, at least in part, on projective testing; (2) interviewing "problem" clients, i.e., those disruptive of the ordinary routine of the project, reporting back on the nature of their problems, and if possible, changing the clients so that they would no longer be perceived as problems; and (3) developing informal social relationships with other staff members, i.e., being cohesive with other civilian staff vis-à-vis inmates, officers, and the prison administration. In the eyes of our colleagues, we were miserable failures in regard to all these expectations except, perhaps, the second.

Considerable consternation was generated by our lack of enthusiasm for routine administration of the Rorschach test. The parole officer wanted it given because one of the Parole Board members was very interested in the outcome of "projectives." Furthermore, the project coordinator had very definite ideas on the importance of testing in psychological evaluation. There was also a problem in getting from the parole officer the names of inmates requiring reports prior to their Parole Board appearance. This probably can be explained by the fact that the parole officer felt that reports should be made on all clients, while we held out for investing our limited time in cases in which psychological factors were clearly involved in the crime or there were questions about the man's current psychological status.

Additionally, our view of "problem" inmates differed from that of most other staff members. As the senior author has already described, we tended to construe problem situations in interpersonal and situational rather than intrapsychic terms. For example, in one particular chronic conflict situation between an inmate and an officer we felt that both were contributing to the problem and that it would be artificial to deal only with the inmate, in an attempt to "straighten him out." In this case we were able to involve both parties to the conflict in discussions which led to at least a temporary defusing of the situation. Frequently, however, we went along with staff expectations and interviewed the inmate alone, and the student invariably reacted to such sessions with a sense of uneasiness and inappropriateness.

Finally, we fell far short of developing good informal social relationships with other staff members. My belief is that we were viewed by the others as clannish, uncooperative, and benefiting from special privilege. We differed from the rest of the civilian staff in two major ways. We were part-time employees, and we lived more than twice as far from the prison as most of the others. Each of the two graduate students worked two days per week, and I was present one day a week. Unfortunately, as I now see it, our schedules were arranged to overlap maximally. Thus all three of us were present on Mondays, and both students worked a second day together. The requirements of the situation dictated that the students be available on my workday in order to allow for supervisory time. Also, this was the day of the weekly staff meetings, which I was interested in attending.

The unfortunate result of this arrangement was that a psychologist was never on duty alone. There was always another psychologist available to talk to during free time, and since the students shared similar problems and a similar outlook, they tended to seek out one another rather than staff members from other disciplines. We must, therefore, have been perceived as clannish, and with good reason. As another offshoot of our schedule, the weekly staff meeting was usually overloaded with three or four psychologists, including an additional research consultant. We must have seemed a powerful bloc indeed.

Our overlapping schedules had one other deleterious effect. For three days every week there was no psychologist on the unit. This fact, I'm sure, trained people not to need a psychologist in a hurry, since they might have to wait as long as five days to get to talk to one. Also, this meant that we were not present when certain crucial decisions were being made. We were particularly missed at the "interim staff meetings" at which the progress of clients who had been with the project for a moderate length of time was discussed informally.

We did succeed in rearranging the schedules so that we could participate in those meetings at which it was decided whether to transfer a client who had complete the mandatory aspects of our program to another institution, to the general population at our prison, or to retain him on the project. Some inmates however, left the project on very short notice through the mechanism of a drum-head court consisting of the project coordinator and the rehabilitation counselor. The latter, I finally learned, had the ultimate power to decide whether a man stayed or left, even despite an opposite recommendation by the final staffing group. I was disturbed to discover, in about my third week, that the inmate who had emerged as the natural leader of my counseling group had been cut from the project without my having been consulted. This was a particularly strong blow to my effectiveness with the group, since I had been trying to convince them that they were wrong in their contention that anyone who opened his mouth to complain about the system would be removed from the program.

Despite definite assurances from the project director after this incident that no one else would be removed before his group counselor had been consulted, there were at least two recurrences of this during the year. Both cases involved alleged violations of prison rules, in one case fighting, in the other, homosexual activity, and the project coordinator maintained that an immediate decision had been necessary in both cases. Since the psychologist concerned was unfortunately not on hand on the day of the incident, it had been impossible to include him in the decision making. Again our schedule was working against us and perpetuating a chronic source of conflict.

A final factor which interfered with the development of good reciprocal relationships with other disciplines was the psychology staff's apparent pro-inmate bias. The inmates try to force every new staff member into one of two exclusive categories: "for us," and "against us." Those in the first group are exploited; those in the second, rejected. This is not to say that inmates are incapable as individuals of responding to a combination of firm limit-setting and humanitarian concern, but in general they tend to distrust such an approach and operate more comfortably in a black and white world. Full-time staff members, for their part, have been so long exposed to the lies, intrigue, and manufactured complaints which are associated with inmate behavior that they sometimes act as if it were impossible for an inmate to have a legitimate grievance. Also, some of these staff members had invested a good deal of energy in attempting unsuccessfully to correct obvious deficiencies in the prison, such as inadequate medical care, and they had reached a point where they could no longer identify strongly with legitimate grievances and remain in the setting.

Being naively thrust into this situation and communicating primarily with inmates and each other, it is not surprising that we tended to take the inmates' side in their complaints of unfair treatment. Over-enthusiastic support of questionable client grievances by psychologists was generally viewed with tolerant amusement by the full-time staff. Yet, even after our "education" we did not achieve their cynicism and tolerance for the status quo, and our continual harping on certain basic injustices of the system must have changed from amusing to downright bothersome before the year was out.

Relations with Uniformed Staff

Since they responded to a different chain of command and performed custodial rather than rehabilitative functions, the officers assigned to the project tended to see all civilians as outsiders who were interfering with the smooth operation of the prison. If the attitude of the guards towards civilians in general was lukewarm, their attitude toward the psychologists was positively cool. The groups could not be much more different. Prisons in New York State are usually located in small rural communities, in which they are the dominant economic and social influence. Because of their inaccessibility, the prisons draw most of their custodial personnel from the local residents, who appear to be the descendants of the subsistence farmers who originally populated these small towns. In any case, their speech and manners are definitely "rural," and their attitudes clearly conservative. The psychology students, on the other hand, were attending the largest branch of a burgeoning state university, boasting a cosmopolitan student body with generally liberal values.

There was a good deal of activism on the campus during the spring of our second year at the prison. After a clash between students and the campus security force, the city police were called on campus. This resulted finally in a violent confrontation between the police and several hundred students. There were fire-bombings of the library and other buildings, and forty-five faculty members were arrested for staging a sit-in outside the president's office. These events served to underline certain basic differences in values and outlook between the psychologists and officers at the prison. We were frequently greeted with such witticisms as "Haven't you been arrested yet?" and neither guards, inmates, nor most civilian staff could understand our sympathy for certain of the student's demands.

Our physical appearance alone was enough to make many officers uncomfortable. In complying with the norms of our own peer group, we wore longish hair and "modish" clothes. This simplified our categorization as "students," "hippies," and, very likely, "radicals," with all the surplus meaning these terms carry for a rural, conservative-minded group.

Toward the end of the second year, there was an incident which disturbed the fairly comfortable informal arrangement for work-sharing which had grown up between uniformed and civilian staff. Much of an officer's time is spent in turning his keys in locks and "supervising" inmates, i.e., keeping an eye on them to prevent any unacceptable interaction, such as fights, gambling, or homosexual activity. Since we were understaffed with officers on the unit, the warden had agreed that a civilian could "supervise" the men he was dealing with, e.g., in school, workshop, or therapy group, without an officer being present. In some cases, civilians, including psychologists, had even unlocked a man from his cell to interview him and then locked him in again. This arrangement was working well until we acquired, late in the year, a new hallkeeper (the top custodial position on the unit) who, while rigid in his interpretation of most rules, also insisted on testing the limits as to how much of his staff's work he could get the civilians to do for them.

Matters came to a head when this man called upon a psychology student who had been with the program for a very short time to conduct a group of inmates to the commissary some distance from our unit. The student didn't want to do it, but there were no other psychologists at hand to support him. Not wishing to create an incident, he complied with the hallkeeper's request.

This incident led to an overt examination of the role definition of psychologists vis-à-vis prison officers. The project director was, of course, eager to return to the status quo ante, since "helping out" served to reduce the impact of the officer shortage on his program. Furthermore, the policy of helping out was a direct outgrowth of the analysis of our role problems which had been carried out by the senior author and his interns the year before. It was felt strongly that some sharing of responsibilities with uniformed personnel would alleviate somewhat the friction between civilian and uniformed staff. It had not been anticipated that such sharing would lead to limit-testing and exploitation, nor had it been anticipated that role-sharing would cause friction between us and the inmates.

The interns, however, began to look more closely at the effect of role-sharing on inmate attitudes and the implications of this for clinical effectiveness. As a result, they took a hard line, refusing to perform any custodial functions beyond supervision of inmates in their therapy groups. The officers naturally resented this, since it was clearly a denigration of their function. It may well be impossible to find a solution to this conflict until the role of the prison officer can be broadened to include rehabilitative as well as custodial functions.

*Program Innovations During the Second
Year*

The mandatory group counseling program. In response to questioning as to which aspect of their program had been most significant in developing adjustment-oriented inmate attitudes, the psychologists at the DTC which we had visited at the beginning of the year agreed that it was the mandatory group therapy experience. The director and I therefore decided that it would be worth trying a similar experiment with our population. On our return to the prison we divided our population into seven groups of approximately ten inmates each, assigned a counselor and an officer to each group, and set a weekly meeting time. The experiment went on for about eight months, at which point we realized that it had failed in its major aim of making group members consciously aware of certain self-defeating interpersonal behaviors which were preventing them from adequately satisfying their needs. Unexpectedly, however, the experiment succeeded in a completely unintended way by stimulating the formation of informal inmate-led groups.

In our post-mortem on the counseling groups we discovered a number of probable reasons for their failure to achieve the expected goals. We had made the mistake of believing that we had resolved three major issues after what was actually only superficial discussion: mandatory attendance; arbitrary assignment of men to groups; and finally, the presence of officers in the groups.

Distrust and dislike of officers proved too deeply ingrained in the inmates to be erased through infrequent contacts in the groups. The officer participants responded reflexively to the posting of group assignments and meeting times by rounding up the men assigned to their group and seeing that they were at the meeting on time. This emphasized the mandatory nature of the groups and heightened inmate resentment.

Another factor which prevented the groups from even really getting started was their changing composition. The turnover rate on the project forced us, we felt, to make the group open to new members as the original members left. Unfortunately, the turnover was so rapid that it prevented the initial establishment of a group culture which could be passed on to newcomers. We found ourselves being forced back to a discussion of ground rules and basic issues, such as confidentiality, in nearly every session, and it seemed that leaders no sooner emerged in the group than they were paroled, released, or transferred.

Resistance to the mandatory groups at first took the form of nonattendance. This put us in a bind because we were unwilling to impose the usual sanction for rule infractions — keeplocking the man in his cell. And we could not get an open airing of the man's reasons for wanting to stay away if he was never there.

As the mandatory groups continued to flounder, interest in inmate-led groups was increasing. A "self-help" group with a fluctuating attendance ranging from five to ten had actually existed since the previous year. After the mandatory group program had been operating for a few months, regular attendance at the self-help meetings increased to the extent that the group had to split to accommodate all interested inmates. In addition, a new group focusing on the drug problem was formed on the initiative of a few ex-addicts. They asked the project director to attend their meetings, but in an advisory rather than a leadership role. The participants were quite enthusiastic about these groups and obviously felt they were getting something out of them.

References to what was going on in the voluntary groups became more frequent in the mandatory sessions as time went on. There were also indications that professional involvement might be welcome in the voluntary groups, but on the inmates' own terms. This was stated quite openly in my own group. Some of the men who were also active in an inmate-led group said they would like to have me attend one of their session, but they would only offer the invitation when attendance at the staff-led groups was no longer compulsory.

We realized finally that the group counseling experiment was, in itself, a failure and must be either drastically reorganized or dropped entirely. After much discussion we decided to scrap the existing groups and start a new voluntary group with one of the original interns and a new student as co-therapists. There was little difficulty in attracting an initial membership of about eight men, some of whom were already involved in one or more of the inmate-led groups. The new intern also offered assistance to the inmate group leaders. His offer was eventually accepted, and he started training sessions for the four clients who took some leadership role in the voluntary groups, with a focus on understanding and dealing with group process.

Thus, while the compulsory groups failed to become effective therapeutic settings in themselves, there is strong evidence that they spurred the inmates' interest in helping each other through group discussion. Also, I think that the helping attitudes of staff members were seen as sincere, despite the shortcomings of the group, so that staff participation was later welcomed in the client-initiated groups. Finally, I feel that involving officers in the groups, while it created problems, also started some cracks in the stereotypes which inmates and officers had been maintaining about one another.

The community meeting.   The daily community meetings at the DTC had impressed us as a central part of that program. We felt that if we were ever to establish a therapeutic community atmosphere in our project, we must have some such mechanism to establish a feeling of group identity and shared responsibility among the clients. A weekly "gripe session" of all project members had, in fact, been initiated a few months earlier. We decided to continue these meetings, but modify them somewhat to achieve our desired aim.

The plan to establish a therapeutic community was hampered from the start by certain structural aspects of the social setting. First, our decision to meet weekly rather than daily guaranteed that the level of group sentiment and involvement would be less than optimal. More frequent meetings seemed impossible, however, because of conflicts with other aspects of the program, such as group counseling and education, and the ever present restrictions of the custodial routine.

The director called the meetings to order and served as chairman. Much of the meeting time seemed to be taken up with individual complaints and questions directed to him, and after the meeting adjourned there were always a few men eager for a private talk with him. I soon realized that this was the one time during the week when the men could be sure of seeing the director, who spent most of his time in his office "up front." Obviously the men were not going to work out their own solutions to shared problems in a meeting which was so dominated by a powerful central figure. I urged the director to adopt a rotating chairmanship and, as soon as the time seemed right, to turn the chair over to an inmate. I also asked if he could make himself available to the men at another time for personal matters, so that the community meeting could address itself to issues of concern to the clients generally.

The director went along with my suggestion to the extent of occasionally allowing me or one or the interns to chair the meeting. Even when we were conducting the meetings, however, we would frequently find ourselves turning to the director, or the project coordinator, for answers to questions raised by the inmates. This pointed up the largest single obstacle to the establishment of a therapeutic community — the fact that the inmates were so totally powerless in this situation that they could not take the smallest step toward independent action without official approval. They turned to the director for this approval, but he, in turn, had to clear everything with the warden, who very seldom endorsed his proposals. The men couldn't even get replacement of worn out ping pong balls without the warden's sanction.

Incredibly, however, a sense of group identity emerged from this sterile soil. The earliest sign was the occurrence for the first time in the client's vocabulary of the words "we" and "the community." This was prompted initially by the presence within the group of certain members with an uncertain status: a deaf-mute, a blind man, and a very young black militant who couldn't do anything right and was in danger of being dropped from the project. In each of these cases a spokesman came forward to urge the group to accept responsibility for dealing with the special problems presented by these inmates so that they could be retained in the project. And, in each case, there was a generally favorable response from the group as a whole.

Another development which pleased some of us was the open airing of conflicts between inmates in the meetings. This happened only twice during the second year. There was one discussion around the issue of a particularly noisy and hostile inmate, and, at another session, there was the beginning of a dialogue on racism within the unit. The raised voices and open expressions of hostility disturbed some staff members and inmates, but, as far as I know, there was no consequent physical violence, and a potential confrontation may even have been averted.

Finally, the community meeting did continue to be a forum for personal gripes, which I think is fortunate. The men gradually came to realize that they could criticize the program without being summarily eliminated from it. Further-

more, it was rare for a man with a complaint to fail to find support from other
inmates. All in all, then, the community meeting came to serve several valuable
functions for the men in the project. The robustness of the spirit of group identity was surprising and gratifying. I only wish that we could have provided more
favorable conditions for its further growth.

Some Comments Upon the Problems of
Entry into the Maximum Security Prison
Setting

As we look back on the events of the first two years of operation it appears
that most of our difficulty derived from two sources, our inadequate preparation
for the task of dealing with those institutional problems unique to the prison
setting and our inability to come to grips with the problem of whom to serve.

Inadequate Preparation as a Source of
Trouble

It seems almost absurd to have to say that a professional who is inadequate-
ly prepared for his job is likely to fail at the task; yet, it may be helpful to state
this fact explicitly at a time when the demands and pressures for the extension
of services to the community are increasing rapidly. The crucial problem here is
the wide gap between the job for which most professional psychologists were
trained ten years or more ago and the reality of the responsibilities they will be
asked to assume in extending their services to new settings in the community.
Graziano (1969) has described the difficulties encountered in attempting to provide innovational service even in a rather standard setting for mental health workers; the problems seem even worse when one moved to a setting such as Attica,
where mental health workers are truly foreign agents.

Our failure was not just a failure to anticipate the problem. It was also a personal failure of attitude — a belief that existing knowledge and existing skills
were sufficient to cope with whatever difficulties might arise. It was a homely example of professional "arrogance," and unfortunately may have resulted in a
temporary worsening of the entire situation. By the time we became aware of
the need to *treat* the institution and its administrators rather than to fight it, it
was almost too late to save the situation. By the time we learned to diagnose the
organizational ills and to negotiate successfully within the system itself, we were
almost out of the professional ball game. But we gained a reprieve at the last min-
ute, and we now have to work at double time to alleviate difficulties created by
past mistakes.

Who Is the Client?

Clinical psychologists usually are clear about whom they serve — they are hired by patients in distress and charged with the responsibility of relieving that distress; or they are hired by an institution and requested to relieve the distress of the inmates of that institution (although, obviously, conflicts emerge in mental hospitals also). The situation in a maximum security prison was entirely diffemt. The institution saw us as its agents, whose responsibility was to serve it; dealing with inmates was merely incidental to the task.

The psychologist's job was complicated further by the institution's implicit belief in "intrapsychic supremacy" as the primary determinant of deviant behavior. "Intrapsychic supremacy," as Levine (1967) discusses it, is the notion that deviant behavior can be attributed almost exclusively to intrapsychic disturbance or psychodynamic disequilibrium within the individual. In a prison setting this doctrine leads to the conclusion that the social deviance which resulted in imprisonment and any subsequent social deviance within the prison may be attributed in large part to an inmate's intrapsychic disturbance. This enables the entire correctional institution (police and penal) to conveniently kick the ball to the psychologist, neatly absolving itself from major responsibility for understanding the deviance as an outgrowth of social forces, and, more importantly, relieving the institution from any guilt for outrageously high recidivism rates. The high incidence of recidivism, incidentally, serves to reinforce strongly the doctine of "intrapsychic supremacy," being interpreted as evidence that some guys are just plain bad.

When we arrived at the prison for the first time we were not sure what to expect. Basically, we adhered to an oversimplified view of Goffman's (1961) notion that an institution is an institution is an institution; consequently, we mistakenly thought that previous experience in VA hospitals, state hospitals, community clinics, and private practice would serve us well in dealing with the problems of a maximum security prison. It did not take long to realize that we were unprepared for the challenge; and we soon understood Goffman's essential point — that if we were to function effectively we would have to deal with the institution itself as a client. In order to do this we had to learn (often the hard way) to understand *its* needs, *its* values, and *its* potentialities for change.

References

American Correctional Association. *A Manual of Correctional Standards.* New York: American Correctional Association, 1959.

Cleaver, E. *Soul on Ice.* New York: McGraw-Hill, 1967.

Conrad, J.P. *Crime and Its Correction.* Berkeley: University of California Press, 1967.

Cressey, D.R. *The Prison: Studies in Institutional Organization and Change.* New York: Holt, Rinehart & Winston, 1961.

Fenton, N.; Reimer, E.G.; and Wilmer, H.A. *The Correction Community: An Introduction and Guide.* Berkeley: University of California Press, 1967.

Goffman, E. *Asylums: Essays on the Social Situation of Mental Patients and Other Inmates.* New York: Anchor Books, 1961.

Graziano, A.M. "Clinical Innovation and the Mental Health Power Structure: A Social Case History." *American Psychologist* 24 (1969): 10-18.

Kelly, J.G. "Ecological Constraints on Mental Health Services." *American Psychologist* 21 (1966): 535-36.

Kesey, K. *One Flew Over the Cuckoo's Nest: A Novel.* New York: Viking, 1962.

Kohl, H.R. *36 Children.* New York: New American Library, 1967.

_____. *The Open Classroom: A Practical Guide to a New Way of Teaching.* New York: New York Review, 1959.

Kozol, J. *Death at an Early Age: The Destruction of the Hearts and Minds of Negro Children in the Boston Public Schools.* Boston: Houghton-Mifflin, 1967.

Levine, M. *Some Postulates of Practice in Community Psychology and Their Implications for Training.* Paper presented at the University of Texas Symposium on Training in Community Psychology, Austin, Texas, 1967.

_____. "Problems of Entry in Light of Some Postulates of Practice in Community Psychology." In *The Helping Professions in the World of Action,* edited by I. Goldenberg, Lexington: D.C. Heath & Co., 1973.

Menninger, I. *The Crime of Punishment.* New York: Viking Press, 1968.

Solzhenitsyn, A.I. *One Day in the Life of Ivan Denisovich.* New York: Praeger, 1963.

11

Clinical Innovation and the Mental Health Power Structure: A Social Case History

Anthony M. Graziano
State University of New York at Buffalo

[Editor's Note:] *Lest the reader persist in the belief that the major obstacles to change are invariably located in the systems or settings often termed "responsible" for the creation or exacerbation of problems (e.g., the school system, the welfare system, etc.), this chapter should provide needed perspective. The author focuses attention directly on the machinations of the "helpers" themselves, detailing with clear and documented precision the ways in which programs, however innovative or potentially helpful, are subverted by the professional helping "establishment" when such programs are perceived as ideologically threatening to that establishment itself. In the present instance, the struggle revolved around attempts to implement a behavior modification-oriented program for autistic children in a community dominated by a psychoanalytically-oriented mental health power structure. This chapter, the only one in this volume to have previously appeared in a professional journal, was one of the first (and best) attempts to analyze the resistance of the helping professions to the winds of change that characterized the 1960s.*

The 1960s have been a decade of increased involvement by social scientists and educators in the problems and welfare of society. Turning their professional acumen to the very old problems of employment, housing, education, poverty, mental health, and others, many have heard the repeated call to innovate creative and bold new approaches to our vexing social problems. The ensuing increase in new programs, all actively seeking humanitarian goals, has led many of us to suspect that humanitarian aims and scientific methodology have finally come together and melded into a broad new mobilization of the previously unfocused humane and scientific strengths of our culture. In the field of mental health we have seen new developments in the use of subprofessional manpower, the development of behavior modification approaches to therapy, and plans to develop new comprehensive community mental health centers, designed to increase the scope of services.

The common sound in those approaches is "innovation"; it is in the air, and in these conceptually fertile sixties, many innovative ideas have been conceived

This chapter is a reprint of an article originally published in *American Psychologist,* vol. 24, no. 1, pp. 10-18. Copyright 1969 by the American Psychological Association, and reproduced by permission.

and put forth. However, it should be clearly noted that the *conception* of innovative ideas in mental health depends upon creative humanitarian and scientific forces, while their *implementation* depends, not on science or humanitarianism, but on a broad spectrum of professional and social politics!

The main points of this chapter are (1) that these two aspects, conceiving innovation through science and humanitarianism on the one hand, and implementing innovation through politics on the other, are directly incompatible and mutually inhibiting factors, and (2) our pursuit of political power has almost totally replaced humanitarian and scientific ideals in the mental health field. Innovations, by definition, introduce change; political power structures resist change. Thus while the cry for innovation has been heard throughout the 1960s, we must clearly recognize that it has been innovative "talking" which has been encouraged, while innovative *action* has been resisted. It has been the "nature of the sixties" as it were, to simultaneously encourage and dampen innovation in mental health. A major question for the next decade is, following this "reciprocal inhibition" of both innovative and "status quo" responses, which of the two will emerge strongest, and what are we, as psychologists, doing about it?

The following discussion is an attempt to trace the progress of innovative ideas to the level of action, by examining a single case history in which a group of people with new ideas about the treatment of severely disturbed children encountered the resistance of the local mental health power structure. The developments, which cover some eleven years, are briefly described and, recognizing the danger of generalizing from the single case, we nevertheless do so and attempt to suggest conclusions about our contemporary mental health professions.

The Case History

About eleven years ago a small group of parents sought treatment for autistic children, and found available only expensive psychiatrists or the depressing custodialism of back-ward children's units at the state hospital. Local clinics were of little help since they operated on the familiar assumption that their services were best limited to those who could "profit most" from therapy, and, given a choice between a rampaging psychotic child and one with less severe behavior, the clinics tended to treat the latter and send the others off to the state hospitals. Unwilling to accept either deadly placement (private therapists or state hospitals), parents cast around and were eventually referred to the "experts," i.e., the same clinics and private-practice psychiatrists who had previously failed to help those children. They were nevertheless still considered to be the proper agents to carry out a new program, now that a few determined *lay* people had thought of it. This is an important and recurrent point, suggesting that any new mental health service or idea, regardless of its origin, is automatically referred back into the control of the same people who had achieved so little in the past, perhaps insuring that little will be done in the future. The territorial claims of professionals, it seems, are seldom challenged, despite what might be a history of failure, irrelevance, or ignorance.

Following some two years of work, the lay group arranged with a local child clinic to create special services for autistic children. The result, a psychoanalytically-oriented group program, operated uneasily for four years, amidst laymen – professional controversy over roles, responsibility, finances and, finally, of the program's therapeutic effectiveness. The lay people, rightly seeing themselves as the "originators" of the program felt that they were being "displaced" by the professionals. The professionals, on the other hand, saw the laymen as naive, not recognizing their own limitations and trying to pre-empt clearly professional territory. Threatened and angered, both sides retreated to positions which were more acrimonious than communicative. "Don't trust the professional!" and Beware the layman!" were often heard in varied ways.

Hostilities grew, the groups split and, after four years of their cooperative program, these two groups, the "insider" professional clinic with its continuing program, and the "outsider" lay group now determined to have its own program, were directly competing for the same pool of local and state funds.

The clinic, imbedded within the professional community, had operated for some twenty-five years and espoused no new, radical, or untried approaches. It argued that it was an experienced, traditional, cooperating part of the local mental health community; that it was properly medically directed; that its approaches were based on ". . . the tried and true methods of psychoanalysis." The clinic based its arguments on experience, professionalism, stability as a successful community agency, and offered to continue the accepted psychoanalytic methodology.

The "outsiders" having acquired the services of a young and still idealistic psychologist who was just two years out of graduate school, contended that because psychoanalytic approaches had not resulted in significant improvement for autistic children, the community should support many reasonable alternative approaches rather than insisting upon the pseudo-efficiency of a single program to avoid "duplication of services." One alternative was proposed, the modification of behavior through the application of psychological learning theory; that is, *teaching* adaptive behavior rather than *treating* internal sickness. Further, because this approach was psychological, it therefore would properly be psychologically and not medically directed.

Thus the "outsiders" criticized the establishment and proposed change; attempting new approaches based on a psychological rather than medical model, and insisting on including poverty children in the program. Naively stepping on many toes, they said all the wrong things; one does not successfully seek support from a professionally conservative community by criticizing it and promising to provide new and different services which are grossly at odds with accepted certainties, essentially untried, and, in many respects, ambiguous. Early in 1963, to offer psychological learning concepts as alternatives to psychoanalytic treatment of children and to insist that traditional clinics had failed to help low-income children, was not well received. From the beginning, then, this group (henceforth referred to as ASMIC — Association for Mentally Ill Children), were cast as "radicals" and "troublemakers."

Hoping to avoid competing within the clinical structure, ASMIC proposed to the local university in 1963, a small-scale research and training project to develop child therapy approaches from learning theory, and to select and train non-degree, undergraduate, and master's level students as child group workers and behavior therapists. It was hoped that after a year or two of preliminary investigation, federal support would be available through the university. Approved by the chairman and the dean, the proposal was rejected at the higher administrative levels because: (1) the project was too radical and would only create continuing controversy; (2) the local mental health professionals had already clearly indicated their opposition to it; (3) the university, always cognizant of Town-Gown problems, could not risk becoming involved.

The message was clear; the project was opposed by the local mental health professionals, it had already caused controversy, would create more, and the university was no place for controversy!

Thus denied the more cloistered university environment, ASMIC moved to compete within the closed-rank mental health agency structure, where they soon encountered what we shall refer to as the United Agency. That agency's annual fund-raising campaign is carried out with intense publicity, and donating through one's place of employment seems to have become somewhat less than voluntary. Operated primarily by business and industrial men the United Agency had some million and a half dollars to distribute to agencies *of their choice,* thus giving a small group of traditionally conservative businessmen considerable power over the city's social action programs.

Having been advised that ASMIC's proposed program could not long survive, the United Agency's apparent tact was to delay for a few months, until ASMIC demised quietly. That delaying tactic was implemented as follows:

1. The United Agency listened to ASMIC's preliminary ideas but could not act until they had a written proposal.
2. A month later the United Agency rejected the written proposal because it was only a "paper program"!
3. ASMIC's program was started and expanded, but after six months of operation was again denied support because it had been too brief a time on which to base a decision. The group was advised to apply again after a longer period of operation.
4. After a year of operation ASMIC's next request was denied on the basis

that the program had to be "professionally evaluated" before the United Agency could act. And who would carry out the evaluation? The local mental health professionals, of course. ASMIC objected to being evaluated by their competitors, but agreed to an evaluation by the State Department of Mental Health, although they, too, had previously refused to support the program. This was to be the "final" hurdle and, if the evaluation was positive, the United Agency would grant funds for the program.

5. Completing its professional evaluation the State Department returned a highly positive report, and strongly recommended that ASMIC be supported. Apparently caught off guard the United Agency was strangely unresponsive, and several months elapsed before the next request for funds was again deferred, on the basis that the question of "duplication of services" had never been resolved.

6. After additional state endorsement and high praise for the program as a *nonduplicated* service, the United Agency rejected ASMIC's next request, replying that if the state thought so highly of the program, then why didn't *they* support it? "Come back" they said, "when you get state support."

7. Six months later and nearly three years after starting the program, ASMIC had a state grant. The United Agency then allocated $3,000, which, they said, would be forwarded as soon as ASMIC provided the United Agency with: (a) an official tax-exemption statement, (b) the names and addresses of all children who had received ASMIC's services, and (c) the names of the fathers and their employers.

For three years ASMIC had met all of the United Agency's conditions; they had provided a detailed proposal, launched the program, had successfully operated for three years, had expanded, had received high professional evaluations, had resolved the duplication-of-service issue, had provided the tax-exemption voucher but could not, they explained, provide confidential information such as names, addresses, and fathers' places of employment.

The United Agency, however, blandly refused support because ASMIC was, after all, "uncooperative" in refusing to supply the requested information.

ASMIC's final attempts to gain local mental health support was with an agency we will call "Urban Action" whose function, at least partly, was to help ameliorate poverty conditions through federally supported programs.

Arguing that the city had no mental health services of any scope for poverty level children, ASMIC proposed to apply and evaluate techniques of behavior modification, environmental manipulation, and selection and training of "indigenous" subprofessionals, mothers and siblings, to help emotionally disturbed, poverty level children.

The written proposal was met with enthusiasm, but, the agency explained, in keeping with the concept of "total community" focus, more than one agency had to be involved. They therefore suggested inviting the local mental health association to join the project, even if only on a consultant basis. The mental health association, of course, was comprised of the same professionals who had opposed ASMIC's program from the beginning. Skeptical, but nevertheless in good faith, ASMIC distributed copies of their proposal to the mental health association, again referring something new back to the old power structure. Five months later a prediction was borne out; the mental health association returned the proposal as unworkable and, in its place, submitted their own highly traditional, psychiatric version, which was ultimately rejected in Washington. Those poverty level children who received no mental health services in 1963, still receive no services, and there are no indications that the situation will be any different in the next few years.

The "outside" group, its new ideas clashing with the professional establishment, repeatedly encountered barriers composed of the same people and never did receive support from the local mental health agencies, the United Agency, the university, or the Urban Action Agency. For the first two years it subsisted on small tuition fees and a spate of cake sales organized by a few determined ladies, and eventually did receive significant state support from the Departments of Education and Mental Health. Thus it carried out its programs, in spite of the opposition and lack of support of the local mental health professionals.

This case history of an innovation ends on two quite ironic points. Moving into its fifth year, ASMIC had successfully overcome all major external obstacles and, having been evaluated by both the State Department of Education and Mental Health, was receiving significant support. The first irony is that having successfully overcome the external opposition, the agency began to disintegrate internally. Having achieved some status, success, and continuing support, it no longer had the cohesive force generated by battling an external foe. Its own internal bickering, previously overshadowed by the "larger battle," now became dominant, and the agency splintered, again along laymen-professional lines. The precipitating factor this time was the professionals' insistence on including poverty level children, who were nearly all black and Puerto Rican. A few lay perons, actively supported in their anger by the professional director of an actively competing agency, objected to the "unfairness" of allowing blacks into the program "free," i.e., supported through a grant, while their "own" children had to pay a small fee. Poverty funds could not be used to support the more affluent white children, as the lay people demanded, and the professional staff was then faced with two main alternatives: (1) abandon the poverty program and work with only middle-class, white children; (2) resign from the agency and continue the program under other auspices. The staff decided on the latter alternative.

The second irony is that while the staff successfully continues its behavior-modification group program, netiher the originally sponsoring agency, ASMIC, nor the opposed, traditional and still well-supported child clinic has been able to maintain its group program for autistic children!

Thus turning innovation *concepts,* i.e., group behavior therapy and the inclusion of low socioeconomic-level children, into actual programs required a good deal more than humanitarian beliefs and scientific objectivity. The eventual reality of the program depended upon its ability to maintain its integrity throughout all of the political buffeting. The program continues today, well supported by the state, but no support was ever obtained from the local mental health area.

The Local Agencies as a Field of Parallel Bureaucracies

In spite of the expressed support of the state and of many "outside" professionals the local, traditional agencies such as the hospital, the clinic, the mental health association, United Agency, city clinics and Urban Action, all maintained a closed-rank rejection of the program. It seemed apparent that a workable set of relationships among the various mental health agencies had developed over a period of years. In fact "interagency cooperation," ostensibly in the service of clients, seemed to also provide important reciprocal support for the agencies.

Despite overlap, the agencies were differentiated according to major functions: some were referral sources (schools and churches); some provided services (the hospital, the clinic, the center for retarded children); some were financial supporters (United Agency, Community Chest); some acted as community planners (the Mental Health Association); some had dual functions, such as the State Department of Mental Health and the antipoverty agency, both involved in community planning and in funneling federal money to agencies of their choice.

Each agency had its own administrative structure with its own bureaucracy, decisionmakers and line personnel. Thus there existed several autonomous, parallel bureaucratic structures, some larger than others, but all trying to deal with some aspect of human health. Their work was clinical, practical, dealing with issues of immediate reality. On the assertion of too much pressing immediate work, these agencies had no use for research of any kind, and therefore no adequate evaluation of the few available services was ever made. The agencies tended to give support to each other through their mutual referrals, and maintained an uncritical acceptance of the various territorial claims, never openly questioning the value of their own or other agencies' work.

Gradually, another level of interagency cooperation became apparent; for example, the director of the leading mental health agency which received funds was also a ranking member of the major mental health planning group, which made recommendations about what agencies would receive funds; some persons were not only important members of agencies which allocated money, but also of agencies which received the money; some sat on boards of several agencies; some positions were held concurrently, while some people "rotated" through the various agencies. In a period of four years, the same relatively few people were repeatedly encountered in various roles associated with one or another of the agencies and making the major decisions regarding local mental health services. In other words, while the parallel bureaucracies which made up the "mental health community" were ostensibly autonomous, each with its own demarcated area of functioning, interagency sharing of upper level decision-makers occurred, and the situation approached that of the "interlocking directorates" of big business.

There was yet another way in which the parallel bureaucracies cooperated; based on some immediate issue or problem, temporary agency "coalitions" were formed. The composition varied according to the nature of the issue, and the coalition relaxed when the issue was resolved. One such coalition was the original cooperation of ASMIC and the clinic, while the United Agency stood opposed. Later, when conditions had changed, a new set of coalitions formed, this time finding the United Agency and the clinic together.

Thus the active mental health field in this city was made up of parallel bureaucracies, i.e., various social agencies which, by virtue of their "expertise," had been granted legitimate social power by the community in the area of mental health. Despite the essential autonomy of the bureaucratic structures, they closely cooperated in several major ways which tended toward mutual support and perpetuation of the existing bureaucratic structures. This cooperation occurred through (1) normal and clearly legitimate professional channels, such as reciprocal referrals of clients; (2) tacit, uncritical acceptance of agency "territories" and functions; (3) interagency "sharing" of upper-level decision-making personnel; and (4) temporary, variable-composition coalitions which briefly intensified agency power in order to deal with specific issues.

The Mental Health Power Structure

We have thus far described the practice of the mental health professions as a legitimized special-interest segment of a community. That segment, or field, was composed of parallel bureaucratic agencies which, by virtue of their control over professional and financial resources, cooperated in their own mutual support and tended to maintain decision-making power within that field. There thus existed a definable and relatively stable social structure through which agencies shared leadership, made cooperative decisions and wielded legitimized social power which tended to support, strengthen, and perpetuate the viability of the structure itself. Schermerhorn (1964) notes, "The power process frequently crystallizes into more or less stable configurations designated as centers or structures of power (p. 18)." Clearly what has been described is a *power structure*, a ". . . temporarily stable organization of power resources permitting an effectual directive control over selective aspects of the social process (p. 24)."

Polsby (1963), who takes issue with the prevalent "stratification" theory of authority power structures, nevertheless notes that:

> By describing and specifying leadership roles in concrete situations, (we) are in a position to determine the extent to which a power structure exists. High degrees of overlap in decision-making person-nel among issue-areas, or high degrees of insitutionalization in the bases of power in specified issue areas, or high degrees of regularity in the procedures of decision-making — any one of these situations, if found to exist, could conceivably justify an empirical conclusion that some kind of power structure exists (p. 119).

We have tried to show that such conditions did obtain and therefore con-clude that there existed a viable *mental health power structure* which made all major decisions in the "mental health field" of this community. Never static, the mental health power structure continues to react to new pressures, and to maneuver, in a changing world, in order to maintain and further strengthen it-self. In so doing, it becomes a defender of its own status quo. It is our conten-tion that local mental health power structures across the country have become so thoroughly concerned with maintaining themselves, that the *major portion* of their committment has been diverted from the original ideals of science and hu-manitarianism, and invested instead in the everyday politics of survival.

Selznick (1943), writing about bureaucracies noted:

> Running an organization as a specialized and essential activity gen-erates problems which have no necessary (and often opposed) relation ships to the professed or 'original' goals of the organization . . . [these activities] come to consume an increasing proportion of the time and thoughts of the participants, they are . . . substituted for the professed goals . . . In that context the professed goals will tend to go down in defeat, usually through the process of being extensively ignored (p. 49).

Thus we maintain that contemporary mental health practice is carried out within power structures which are primarily concerned with justifying and main-taining themselves, while they pay scant attention to the scope of mental health services and even less to the objective evaluation of quality or effectiveness. They maintain their own self-interest which conflicts with humanitarian ideals, science, and social progress. Such conflict is clearly evident in the power structures' rela-tionships to (a) their clientele and (b) to any intruding innovator.

Relationship to Clients

Because of the proliferation of agencies with their territorial claims on one community, there must be some means of parceling out the available client pool.

Some agencies deal with children, others with adults; some deal with poor children, some with retarded children; some with Catholics and some with Jews; some with immigrants and others with unemployed. None deal with just people, but all deal with "certain kinds" of people who are categorized and parceled out. To whatever category he might be assigned, it is implicit that the client is, in some way, a failure; that he has folded up and dropped out; that he is marginal; that he is not as bright as "we," or as well-adjusted as "we," or as well employed as "we," or as nicely colored as "we." There is always an implicit, and very real distance, which separates the clinician from the client. And at the upper end of this breech is the righteous and very certain knowledge of the professional that he is behaving nobly, in a humanitarian cause. While the clinician focuses on each "client-failure," society is busy producing several more. We too often fail to recognize that our individual, internally-focused ministrations have little if anything to do with the amelioration of those social conditions which have shaped the individual's disorder in the first place. To say that the mental health professionals have failed to recognize the crucial importance of external *social conditions* in shaping disturbed behavior, is another way of saying that *professionals refuse to recognize that we labor to rebuild those lives which we, in our other social roles, have helped to shatter.* Nowhere is this more obvious than in the area of civil rights, where a clinician might occasionally help some poverty-level minority group member, and later go home to his restrictive suburb, attend his restrictive club and play golf on a restrictive course and share a restrictive drink in a restrictive bar with businessmen who hire blacks last, in good times, and fire them first in bad times. By fully accepting the "official" power-structure view of the "sick" individual in an otherwise fine society, we clinicians never admit the validity of such nonscientific analysis as Kozol's (1967) shattering *Death at an Early Age;* and we therefore need not admit that the restrictiveness of our own lives has anything to do with the frustrations of someone else, in another place.

The power-structure clinics tend to limit their services to white, middle-class children with mild to moderate disturbances. That is, to those children with the best chances of improving even when left alone; those children whose parents would be most cooperative in keeping appointments, being on time, accepting the structure, and, of course, paying the fees; those children who do not present the vexing and, to the middle-class clinician, *alien* problems of lower-class, minority groups. Certainly a clinic is much "safer," much "quieter," more neatly run, when it limits itself to the most cooperative clientele, and, we might suggest, when it *selectively creates a pool of cooperative clients.* The waiting list is one of the selective devices used to weed out the impatient and retain the most docile clients. By insisting on the incredibly lengthy and largely irrelevant traditional psychodynamic study, the clinics refuse to deal immediately with a client's problems. Instead they artifically create a waiting list which then serves as an objective validation of the continuing "need" for clinic services over the next year or so. The length of the waiting list is, in fact, often seen as a positive indication of the value of the clinic. Thus, in some perverse manner, the slower and less efficient the clinic and the longer its waiting list, the greater is that clinic's claim to importance and to increased money and power! It would not be surprising to find that a clinic which efficiently handled all new referrals within an hour, would be considered of dubious quality because it had no customers waiting at the door.

Thus the structure, responding primarily to its own needs for self-perpetuation, has created a mythical client beset by dramatic internal conflicts, hidden even from himself, but who is apparently little affected by the realities of external social conditions. The professional, with his role clearly delimited by the power structure, continues his myopic psychodynamic dissection of individuals, and never perceives the larger social, moral or, if you will, *human* realities of that client's existence. The power structure, further insuring its own perpetuation, carefully selects clients who best meet the structure's needs, and rejects the great majority who do not. The "most hopeful" but still doubtful psychiatric services are offered mainly to bright, verbal, adult, neurotic, upper-class whites. In the context of contemporary social reality, the mental health professions now exist as expensive and busy political power structures which have little relevance for anything except their own self-preservation. In this process, we suspect, the client might too often be exploited rather than helped.

Response to Intruding Innovations

The mental health power structure, committed primarily to its own preservation, is alertly opposed to any events which might change it. Thus when innovation intrudes, the structure responds with various strategies to deal with the threat; it might incorporate the new event and alter it to fit the preexisting structure so that, in effect, nothing is really changed. The power structure might deal with it also by active rejection, calling upon all of its resources to "starve out" the innovator by insuring a lack of support.

The most subtle defense, however, is to ostensibly accept and encourage the innovator, to publicly proclaim support of innovative goals, and while doing that, to build in various controlling safeguards, such as special committees, thereby insuring that the work is always accomplished through power structure channels and thus effecting no real change. This tactic achieves the nullification of the innovator while at the same time giving the power structure the public semblance of progressiveness. The power structure can become so involved in this pose that the lower-line personnel come to honestly believe that they are working for the stated ideals such as humanitarianism, science, and progress, while in reality they labor to maintain the political power of the status quo.

This has occurred in civil rights and antipoverty programs where federal money has been poured into the old local power structures which have loudly proclaimed innovation, improvement, progressiveness, while all the time protecting themselves by actually nullifying those efforts. After several years of public speeches and much money, it becomes clear to the citizens of the deprived area that nothing has changed. Then, frustrated and angry, many submerge themselves into nonprotesting apathy and others, perhaps the more hopeful ones, erupt into violence, smashing their world, trying, perhaps, to destroy in order to rebuild.

Hence while the power structure continues to proclaim innovation, it expends great energy to insure, through its defensive maneuvers, the maintenance of its status quo. Innovation is thus allowed, and even encouraged, as long as it remains on the level of conceptual abstractions, and provided that it does not, in reality, change anything! The hallmark of this interesting but deadly phenomenon, of spending vast sums of money and effort to bring about no change, all in the name of innovation, might be summed up in what I recently suggested as a motto for one of those agencies, *Innovation Without Change!* This motto reflects a central tendency of mental health services in the 1960s: maintaining our primary allegiance to the power structures, rather than to science and humanitarianism, and continuing our busy employment, creating innovations without changing reality.

Every community has its built-in safeguards which, in the mental health field, guarantee rejection, neutralization or at least deceleration of any new approches which do not fit the prevailing power structure. Significant progress in mental health, then, will not be achieved through systematic research or the guidance of humanitarian ideals, since they are neutralized by being filtered through the existing structure. In order for those scientific and humanitarian conceptual innovations to remain intact and reach the level of clinical application, they must avoid that destructive "filtering" process.

Likewise progress will not be initiated by or through the power structure, but will depend upon successfully changing or ignoring that structure. It does not seem possible at this point to join the structure and still maintain the integrity of both areas, i.e., the essentially political power structure, and the humanitarian and scientific ideals. The two areas are incompatible; science and humanitarianism cannot be achieved through the present self-perpetuating focus of the power structure.

A case in point is the present interest in the development of comprehensive mental health centers. When a community commits itself to the vastly expensive reality of a mental health center, and then *refers control of that center back to the existing power structure,* it has created "innovation without change." The major result might be to enrich and reinforce the old power structure, thus making it vastly more capable of further entrenching itself, and successfully resisting change for many more years.

Our personal experience in contributing to the planning of comprehensive mental health services led us to the conclusion that the comprehensive centers would provide only "more of the same." Instead of trying to determine the needs of the people in the urban area, and then create the appropriate approaches, the planners asked questions such as: "How can we extend psychiatric services to treat more alcoholics? How many beds do we need for acute cases? How can we increase our services to schizophrenic children? How can we pool our resources for more efficient diagnostic workup of cases?", etc. The questions themselves assumed the validity of the existing power structure and were aimed at *extending old services* rather than determining needs and *creating new services.* Only the scope and not the relevance or effectiveness of existing approaches was questioned.

Thus, surrounded by the modish aura of "innovation," the existing structure not only remains intact, but becomes enriched, and continues its existence irrespective of the real and changing needs of its clients. By allocating a great deal of money to the existing power structures, whether through mental health centers, antipoverty programs, special education, or other action, we are playing the game of the "sixties," innovation without change," and, win or lose, we run the risk of insuring our own stagnation.

In summary we have maintained that contemporary U.S. mental health professions have developed viable, community-based professional and lay power structures which are composed of mutually-benefiting bureaucracies. Scientific and humanitarian ideals are incompatable with and have been supplanted by the professionals' primary loyalty to the political power structure itself. By virtue of their focus on self-preservation, these power structures (1) maintain a dogmatically restrictive view of human behavior and the roles of the professionals within that structure and (2) prevent the development of true innovations. The basic, self-defeating weakness in the variety of current attempts at innovative social action is their unintended strengthening of the existing power structure which is incompatible with innovation. Thus future advances in the practice of mental health will most readily occur outside of the current mental health power structures.

Contemporary American mental health professions base their major decisions neither on science nor humanitarianism, and certainly not on honest self-appraisal, but on the everyday politics of bureaucratic survival in local communities. As Murray and Adeline Levine (1968) have pointed out, while the professions operate to maintain themselves, society changes, and the two grow farther apart. Eventually the mental health professions become grossly alienated from the human realities of the very clients they purport to help, and the professions soon achieve the status of being irrelevant. Admitting no need for critical evaluation, the professional continues to provide services which are, in fact, of limited scope, questionable value, and extremely high price. As long as we continue to uncritically refer all new developments back into the control of the old power structure, we will continue to insure "innovation without change." Then, as professionals, we can all continue going about our business, keeping our private lives out of phase with our professional pose, and keeping both of them alienated from larger social realities. In this way, we need never allow the restrictiveness of our lives to mar the nobility of our profession.

References

Kozol, J. *Death at an Early Age.* New York: Houghton Mifflin, 1967.

Levine, M. and Levine, A. *"The Time for Action: A History of Social Change and Helping Forms."* Unpublished manuscript, Yale University, 1968.

Polsby, N.W. *Community Power and Political Theory.* New Haven: Yale University Press, 1963.

Schmerhorn, R.A. *Society and Power.* New York, 1964.

Selznick, P. "An Approach to a Theory of Bureaucracy." *American Sociological Review* 8; (1943): 47-54.

Part III

The Future: Implications for Professional
Training, Research, and Service

12

The Search for Boulder: Three Perspectives on Graduate Education and Research Training

Murray Levine, Steve Tulkin,
and Michael Domenico
State University of New York at Buffalo

[Editor's Note] : *In almost every chapter of Part II of this book, the authors raised questions concerning the efficacy of their own professional training for the kinds of problems they eventually found themselves addressing in the "real world." Clearly, changes are needed in the preparation of future professionals. The question remains, however, as to what kinds of changes, from what perspectives, and toward what ends. One hopes, naturally, that whatever changes eventually occur will be based on the assessments of people who are at very different points of development both as individuals and as members of the helping professions. In this chapter, a dialogue is established between such people, each with a somewhat different perspective on, and set of experiences in, the field of clinical-community psychology. The authors for all their apparent differences (e.g., age, past professional accomplishments, status in the field) are nevertheless united in their commitment to improving and up-dating the field. Their chapter represents an important step toward the development of the kind of dialogue through which this process of up-dating can occur both reflectively and rationally.*

In keeping with the phenomenological orientation of this volume, each of us will offer personal statements about aspects of graduate education and our separate relationships to it. One of us is a senior faculty member and director of training programs whose experience goes back more than twenty years. Another of us is a new Ph.D., and a first-year faculty member, just now experiencing the various dimensions of the role, and the relationship of his own education and experience to new responsibilities. The third writer is currently a graduate student in a clinical program in transition.

The reader is invited to put himself in our respective shoes and to try to see the world through our eyes.

Our method for approaching the problem is based on the epistemological premises that there is no truth independent of the means of observing that truth; and that profound differences and even contradictions deriving from different modes of observing need not be synthesized but can co-exist as truths

211

of considerable consequence. Objectivity consists of the acceptance that a phenomenon indeed looks different when it is viewed from different perspectives. Common understanding, to the degree that we are capable of achieving it, consists of our ability to explain or to describe phenomena viewed from different perspectives, in common language.

Translated into social psychological terms, we note that graduate education and education for research necessarily take place in an organized social system, that each of us has a role in that social system, and that each of us relates to the same set of issues by virtue of role and personal history. We selected three roles. Obviously these do not exhaust the perspectives which need to be understood and which might have been included. We might well have included the perspective of an undergraduate, a dean, or a university president, the chief psychologist of a service setting, or a state legislator, to name an incomplete list of role groups with an interest in graduate education.

For purposes of achieving understanding of different viewpoints, competent description is helpful. We may call such descriptions truths, but while truth might set us free, truth does not necessarily set us free of conflict. To acknowledge that different perspectives each provide their own truth does not automatically resolve a conflict. For purposes of knowledge, perspectives are independent of each other, much as different modes of observing can be independent and often mutually exclusive. However, in this instance the people-in-roles exist in dynamic and mutually influencing relationship to each other and are not independent observers. The presence of the other is an element in the field of action and observation for each of the parties and as such each exerts an influence on the other. Our intent is not necessarily to minimize or to reduce conflict by presenting different perspectives. Rather we wish to emphasize that a certain order of difference may be inevitable, and not at all undesirable. At the same time, our view from different perspectives may help us to understand how we develop unnecessary conflict, or how we sometimes structure relationships to be self-defeating.

In keeping with our epistemological premise, we have not attempted any integration, but we feel that the pages which follow are a form of data from which the reader may develop his own understanding about the problems of graduate education.

Why a Ph.D.?

We are all involved in a Ph.D. program. If we ask *why* a Ph.D. in clinical or community psychology, we can get a whole range of answers which will include educational objectives and professional objectives. If we ask individuals why they wish to work for a Ph.D., we get answers of a different order. Those differing answers can be a beginning point to understand the problems of contemporary graduate education.

Q. Why did you want a Ph.D.?

A. Graduate Student:

My reasons for getting a Ph.D. have undergone many transformations, related to the positions that I have held at any given point in time. When I first
thought about getting a Ph.D. I was an undergraduate student, searching for
that one field which would catch my fancy, to which I could devote my life,
and with which I could gain fame, riches, and immortality. When I decided I
was interested in psychology as a profession, I was soon informed that if
you wanted to make it in psychology, and especially in clinical psychology (which
I had been considering) you would need a Ph.D.; a master's or B.A. were simply
not enough to set you on your way. This sounded reasonable to me and
besides my family wanted a doctor in the family no matter how you spelled
it (M.D. or Ph.D.). So I applied and was accepted to a training program which
offered an APA approved (nothing but the best) Ph.D. program in clinical
psychology.

A. New Faculty

I can remember that during my last year in high school and first year at
college I thought about becoming a social worker. My parents tactfully and
gently led me to feel that social workers didn't earn too much money and didn't
have many options open to them. I took some vocational guidance tests, and
was told that clinical psychology appeared to be a very suitable career choice
for me. It allowed me to help people and to work on social problems; it also
allowed me to teach and do research. Thus, as I look back to my vocational
choice point, ten years ago, I see that I wanted to be a Boulder psychologist.
I never questioned why I was getting my Ph.D. It just seemed natural: After
high school, of course, you go to college; and then if you want to be a psychologist, you go to graduate school and get a Ph.D. There is no other way to be a
psychologist.

A. Senior Faculty:

It is hard for me to remember now why I wanted a Ph.D. I don't really
remember thinking about it. I remember that to be a psychologist one had to
go to graduate school. That state of mind is more than twenty years behind
me now. In the course of those years I have viewed my degree in very different
ways. After I finished, it got me a job in a psychiatric clinic. It got me into
professional organizations, and it enabled me to offer myself to various pub-
lics. I could take some private cases, address PTAs, do psychologist testing for
a management consulting firm or for a juvenile court. It let me apply for
research grants, and before I went into the university, I could supervise students.
At that point in time, it was a thing that opened doors to me.

It was also something that affirmed my sense of community with other
psychologists. In the struggle against our inferior position vis-a-vis psychiatrists,
we could feel we were better than those without degrees. It gave me a certain

status in the clinics and hospitals in which I worked. I was called doctor, and treated accordingly. When I decided to move toward an academic career, my degree, and my research background, again got me a job.

As a faculty member, the Ph.D. degree became less important to me personally. My title as professor superseded the significance of the degree. After all, everyone had one. It then became my task to decide whether others should get the degree, and later when issues of training became prominent in the field, I had to think about the question of why one should get the degree and for what. The integrity of the degree became something one had to protect. The quality of work for which it was granted became an issue, and the reputation of the program became an issue. How would our program be viewed by the audience of our colleagues in general, and by the APA or NIMH accrediting bodies? As I get older and know more people, to some extent the program's reputation becomes identified with my own. Students come to our program in part because of its reputation, and we send them on to other jobs in part on the strength of our reputation.

Over time, then, my concern changed from wanting to get a degree, to using the degree, to participating in the granting of the degree. At each level, its meaning to me was something else. I am not sure that I recall the different meanings the degree had to me when I relate to my students in my present role.

The Graduate School Experience

While professors are concerned about the meaning of the Ph.D. in a broad social sense, in a narrower sense those entering the field have few detailed notions about what a Ph.D. is or ought to be. For most, the degree is the ticket of admission to a professional world, whose meaning is very vague. However all arrive in graduate school with expectations and unstated fantasies and anxieties about being there, and encounter the realities of the graduate program.

Q. How did you look upon what you were learning in graduate school?
A. Graduate Student:

As a new graduate student my ideas about the Ph.D. began to be more realistic. I began to see exactly what was involved — four to five years of my life, for one thing. I began to ask myself things like do I really want a Ph.D. and is it worth the effort? Once I had decided that it was indeed worth it and that I could live on $1,800 (the USPH stipend when I started) a year, I began to try in earnest to do my best in school. For me now the Ph.D. was a goal in the distant future which was: (a) desired, (b) quite involving mentally and psysically, and (c) *might* bring me fame, riches, and immortality.

The next phase in my thinking came as I began to feel more independent as a student — as I began to want to shape my world and my program to fit me rather than vice versa. As this happened I found that I still wanted the Ph.D.;

that it still involved a lot of time and energy; and that it probably *wouldn't* bring me fame, riches, and immortality. However, I was less willing to take what was handed to me as sufficient for my purposes. I began to question the value of some of the things I did (psychological testing, for example) and wondered if they were essential skills that a Ph.D. should provide. Thus I was looking at my future as I could best project it and wondering if my Ph.D. would prepare me to meet the future better equipped than any other four or five year experience. I began to gauge my courses and their usefulness against the yardstick of my future needs. I actively sought information about what my world as a professional would be like; I was especially interested in asking professors if their training was helpful to them. Much to my chagrin, the overwhelming answer to this question was that their training was for the most part irrelevant to their present work. And I said to myself, "Why do I want a Ph.D.?" The answer to that question is my present dilemma. I have decided that I want to work in an academic setting and for that I need a Ph.D. As for the relevance of my training to my future needs, I have come to want my graduate training to teach me ways of working and approaching problems in addition to specific skills. I know now that these four or five years will never give me all the skills or ways of working that I will need, and that I will constantly be exposed to situations in which I will have to learn new techniques. I think that a helpful attitude is one that says, "I don't know everything but I can learn what I need to know." I want the Ph.D. to provide me with ways of thinking which will not graduate into obscurity before I graduate from school. Finally I want to use the experience of my own training to serve as a guide for the time when I will have the job of training graduate students. I think I will probably try to reproduce the good experiences and attempt to avoid the experiences which I did not find helpful. For this reason I have found it helpful to be aware of the training I am receiving and its effect on me.

A. New Faculty Member:

While I was in graduate school I doubted that a lot of what I was learning would be much help to me professionally, as an applied psychologist. Many of my fellow students voiced the same concern, and we set out to develop courses which we felt would meet our needs. Faculty members were very cooperative. The chief psychologist at a local mental hospital agreed to teach (without pay) a seminar in advanced psychopathology, which at that time was not formally offered. A senior faculty member agreed to teach a course (above load) in theories of personality. These additions to our coursework were welcome, but we were still angered by the fact that the philanthropy of faculty members was needed to provide a curriculum which we felt should have been there in the first place. We were also frustrated because we knew that these changes would not be permanent, and that succeeding classes would again have to wage battles to develop coursework in applied areas.

Graduate school was also frustrating because of the program's implicit and explicit bias toward producing researchers. I myself enjoyed research, and planned to do research after getting my degree; but I wanted to do *clinical* research, and felt that I had to be familiar with clinical theories and clinical skills as a prerequisite for doing clinical research. The program's emphasis seemed to be on research that did not have a great deal of clinical relevance, and therefore it was very difficult for me to get excited about various aspects of the curriculum.

Thus, there is little doubt that much of the content of the graduate curriculum left something to be desired in terms of career preparation. When I think about my graduate school years now, however, I do not feel that it was a waste of time (partially, I'm sure, because of the effects of cognitive dissonance). Although the content of many of my courses may not be applicable to my present interests, some of the personal characteristics I developed, and my approach to the study of psychological problems, is of value to me – and, in fact, is what I feel differentiates me from a non-Ph.D. I developed these skills through close contact with role models who helped me to develop the ability to conduct intellectual inquiries and to become an innovative problem-solver.

In my present role as a teacher of graduate students, I am trying to communicate the importance of developing various methods of problem-solving, and developing the ability to see issues from multiple perspectives. I do not feel that we should ignore the content of our training program; on the contrary, an exciting curriculum which is relevant to the tasks faced by community psychologists in the real world makes graduate school both more palatable and more profitable. However, many authors (e.g., Kelly 1970) have predicted that the work of community psychologists can be expected to change continually over the next decade, so that what is relevant content today may be less relevant for the 1980s. Thus, if we train a psychologist to depend on particular theories or specific skills, he may be less likely to function effectively in a profession which demands maximum flexibility, and which demands that in order to succeed, we must train people to replace us.

I don't want my students to approach a problem with a standard bag of tricks – we know that we can train paraprofessionals to do many of our "tricks." I don't want my students to respond to a problem in an S-R fashion, e.g., kids who cause trouble in school are acting out and showing pathological lack of impulse control; or people claiming the government is spying on them are paranoid. Maybe the students in this hypothetical school causing trouble are doing so because they were not allowed to discuss the Kennedy assassination when it was uppermost in their minds (see S. B. Sarason, Personal Communication) – and the school needs to be changed rather than the students referred for therapy. Maybe the government *is* spying on its citizens – and its practices need to be changed rather than its citizens hospitalized.

At this point, I find that I am questioning myself: Was it really my Ph.D. training that taught me to approach problems of people's needs with an open mind? Not really, although people I met while I was in graduate school helped me to formulate many of the ideas that I now have. Again, then, the formal curriculum was less important than extracurricular experience and contacts.

Even if my Ph.D. did not formally train me to look toward social systems to understand problems of individuals, the Ph.D. does give me power to act on these ideas, and I have come to feel that increased power is, in fact, one of the main benefits of the Ph.D. degree. Regardless of how good one's ideas are, a power base is necessary in order to effect change. A Ph.D. is a power base; and I will be disappointed if my students do not recognize their power and use their power properly. Community psychologists will be intimately involved in power issues, as can be noted in recent case studies by Graziano (1969) and Katkin and Sibley (Chapter 10 in this volume); and even with Ph.D. degrees, our colleagues are often powerless to effect the changes which they see as necessary. Without a Ph.D., there would be less chance that they could exert pressures. The power of the Ph.D. is manifested by the influence we can have on the training of future psychologists, by our easy entrance into society's systems of control, by the increased likelihood of our ideas being considered as "expert testimony," and by our better-developed interpersonal skills. Psychology has typically either not used its power, or else abused it; but it is possible to reverse the trend.

In summary, then, I too felt that the content of my graduate training was largely unrelated to my work as a clinical-community psychologist; but upon reflection, I found that there was more to graduate school than the *content.* I developed an orientation toward being a conceptualizer and a problem-solver, and I developed an appreciation of the increased power which my degree was giving me.

A. Senior Faculty:

When I was in graduate school there was very little discussion of why one learned anything, or whether it was better to learn one thing or another. Occasionally someone would say, with anguish, "Why do we have to learn that?" but it was more a cry of pain or outrage than a serious question about curriculum. Everyone knew you learned psychology. We accepted that we were complete psychologists, and that we could talk with equal facility about psychophysics, learning theory, psychophysiology, personality, and psycho-therapy. It was several years out of graduate school that I began to realize that not only wasn't I interested in most of what was in the *Psychological Review,* but that I could no longer even read it and make sense of most of it. It took me several more years to sever my connections with my past and cancel my subscription to it. The field had grown and specialized in such a way that it really became necessary to think about what one should learn and why.

When I was in graduate school there was no question about what we should study. We studied what we were told to study because that was psychology. There were good courses and poor courses, good teachers and bad ones. But the idea of relevant or irrelevant, or the idea that we should shape our own studies, beyond choosing some specialty, was never in anyone's awareness. We just did it. I think we reacted so because there were no serious questions in anyone's mind at that time, at least none that we were exposed to. Psychology was far more unitary, and there was no substantial experience with the clinical world as yet. Since few had had any length of career, there was no real way of saying what was irrelevant.

There are many actions that I take now in my professional work which are very different than anything I did during graduate school, internship, or during the first several years of professional life. There are other things I simply don't do any more. The content and form of our graduate training program hardly reflects those differences.

I would like to see the curriculum and, to a large extent, modes of teaching change. I don't think it is entirely because of a personal desire to have an impress on my world. For example, I cannot justify spending significant chunks of time in clinical training in projectives. Neither the literature, contemporary professional practice, nor economics supports the use of projectives as an effective clinical tool (Zubin, Eron, and Schumer 1965). I note that my colleagues in personality or social research can learn to use projective instruments for their purposes very rapidly, because there is a usable technology (Atkinson 1958). I see that we are teaching such techniques in ways not terribly different from the way I was taught twenty years ago. I look at the literature on therapeutic interventions, and find that most of what we do can be done by people with considerably less training with little apparent loss in effectiveness, and perhaps even with some gains (Meltzoff and Kornreich 1970; Magoon, Galann, and Freeman 1969).

I note that we take but very few students, perhaps in a ratio of one in thirty applicants, and I know we select these according to criteria which guarantee they are at the upper levels of intellectual ability for the nation. Our students constitute a portion of the intellectual resources of the nation, and will contribute to the pool of leaders in the profession. There is little point in having graduate programs if leadership is not the goal. It is simply absurd to train people to do the work of the world when a large program accepts ten students a year. Our university is located near the periphery of an ellipse of territory covering several thousand square miles, and covering several million people. We turn out six or eight Ph.D.'s in clinical psychology in a good year. That's barely enough to replace deaths, retirements, and pregnancy leaves among those in the field.

All of that tells me that our curriculum and approach to teaching ought to be different. I attribute my motivation toward change to a rational assessment of the state of the field. I do not feel comfortable going along with the way things have been. I am less convinced by the various arguments for continuing training more or less as is even though I value my own broad training. When I make these particular arguments, I sometimes antagonize my colleagues. Perhaps it is my way of doing it. However, if the arguments are not made 'forcefully, I feel that not much will happen because my position requires considerable modification in graduate education. If the arguments are not made forcefully, they will be met with pleasant nods, and inaction.

I think I can understand part of the reluctance to change because I can find the same inertia in myself often enough. I am sure I have not sought out opportunities to enlarge my own skills and experiences nearly as much as I might have. I frequently feel very much tied to my own background, and often find that I have to hold myself in check, when my professional mind automatically draws itself into channels which I know from the past lead into dead ends. I am not sure I have a clear idea of what ought to be done, and that uncertainty on my part must convey itself, but I believe deeply that something different needs to be done.

As we try to move, I find that the complexities of change are enormous, even within a relatively small section of a department within a large university. University organization provides little power to people in departmental administrative positions, and all that goes on requires persuasion. University organization supports the tendency to do your own thing, and it supports the selection of people into senior positions who have their own careers, or their own immortality in mind. Loose coalitions of interest are possible, but the impulse to get your own grant, to have your own following of students, to do your own book, to be a well paid and respected consultant on your own, are powerful and undercut efforts at cooperation. Even though I understand the social dynamics, I get very impatient when I can't even get the group together to plan change. Our efforts to move something within our own structure give us perspective on the expectations we have for change in other large and complex institutions in the society.

The Work World

We have been concerned with the graduate school experience for its own sake, and because of the latent and covert attitudes which are shaped in it. Graduate school, however, is ultimately designed to prepare for the world of work.

For a student the world of work is only a part of his life space. As a student he is still in a temporary, transitional role. He can still draw a distinction between academic life and the "real world." Once out of the student role, one's definition of the work world changes. Where the student sees his academic career as temporary and removed from the real world, the fully fledged professional *is* in a real work world, be it academia, or the clinic.

Q.   What does that work world look like, and how does the experience in
graduate school relate to the "real world?"

A.   *Graduate Student:*

I find that the phrase "real world," the world "out there," is an accurate
description of the way I view the work world. That is because for me the work
world has always been "out there" as compared with "in here," the academic
world in which I have spent a great part of my life. In many ways I have
always felt that I have been constantly preparing to go "out there." When I
was in grade school I was told it was important to go to high school or else
"you'll have to go 'out there' and get a job." When I was in high school I was
told that "you can't get a good job 'out there' unless you go to college." And
when in college I was told that "nowadays college isn't enough for you to
get a good job 'out there'." Now I am in graduate school and I face the prospect
of possibly choosing an academic career and never really going into the world
"out there." The point is that the academic life that I have led has in many
respects insulated me from aspects of the world in which I hope to work. I
think that it is for this reason that as a graduate student I am so eager to get
experience outside the walls of academia.

My view of the world out there has always been heavily influenced by my
position at any given time. I have seen it through the eyes of a child, an adolescent, a college student, a teacher: in short, I have seen it in as many ways as
there have been positions I have occupied. Perhaps the most drastic shift in
my view came with my decision to pursue a career as a clinical psychologist.
Until then I had seen the world from the perspective of a participant in it, *seek-*
ing counsel and advice from those who I felt could best give it to me. But
the decision to enter a "helping profession" placed me in another perspective.
I began to see the world as a place with a lot of hurt, and I entered the perspective of one who would alleviate that hurt, who would *give* advice and
counsel. I was not sure where my decision would lead but it was an important
personal decision that I had made, and I had committed myself to live with
that decision, at least until I got my Ph.D.

Since my first day at graduate school almost four years ago, I have had
many contacts with the world from within this new perspective. Each has provided me with data and each has influenced me in many ways, some of which
I may never know. I stayed in graduate school only six weeks after I arrived.
Having made my choice to be a clinical psychologist my next act was to question
that choice. I decided to take a leave of absence and consider my choice from
a different perspective. I knew that only then could I be sure about my decision. I eventually spent two years away from school, with one of those years
being spent as a public school teacher. When I finally returned, my greatest
desire, besides staying in school, was to keep some contact with the "real"

world. I had come to relish the feeling of dealing with problems which needed immediate solution, and which could not wait for suspended judgment.

My real world contact in graduate school came with several assignments in which I was working with people outside of the university setting. I spent part of my first year working with new teachers in the inner city. These teachers worked at schools in the area where I had spent my year teaching. Consequently I had the unique experience of being a teacher one year, and then working with and helping teachers the next year. I think the most interesting part of this work was the fact that I could anticipate the teachers feelings toward me as an outsider trying to help them with their problems. When I was a teacher I was quite intolerant towards anyone who was not a teacher trying to give me advice about teaching. And since I was no longer a teacher I feared that I would be of little utility to these teachers, especially if they felt the way I did about outsiders. However, I soon found that my distance from the everyday affairs of teaching was my biggest asset. By viewing the situation as an observer I was able to help teachers place their problems in perspective. I was able to help them sort out their feelings in an atmosphere which was removed from the everyday strains of the teaching situation. The work had many frustrating aspects but its importance to me was a sense of *doing* as well as *thinking*; and it meant that I would not have to delay my desire to help people for three or more years until I could go on an internship. In many ways it helped me keep the affairs of school in perspective through the first year.

My next experience was to spend the summer after my first year working in a maximum security prison. It was there that the full measure of my desire to help people was fulfilled as never before. There were more people there who wanted my help than I could ever spend a lifetime helping. I felt that many of the skills needed for such work were secondary to the fact that I was simply a person willing to listen and care. That feeling stayed with me. I began to question the value of my education, and wondered whether it gave me more skills to help people like those men in prison, or whether it might be dulling the thing that seemed to be most effective: my desire and willingness to help another person.

A more recent experience has been working with student teachers entering the inner city for the first time. In addition, I have had extensive contact with a family which can be best described as having multiple problems. These experiences are very close to me now and it is hard for me to evaluate their effect or their meaning to me. I do know, however, that one feeling remains: I savor my contacts with people and the immediacy of present problems crying for solution.

As I begin to think about these contacts with the world out there, several thoughts emerge. I have consistently found that each experience calls directly on my skills in many ways. I am constantly forced to *act* and to *move*. People ask me for service: therapy, testing, to run a group. I am constantly stretched to the limits of my skills. I am struck by the range of skills that I may need, especially if each new situation makes as many different demands on me as these have.

In a real world setting you have no time to review your theoretical assumptions about a situation. Many times I must act and accept the consequences without the luxury of suspending judgment. This is a new experience for me. In school I have been taught to weigh and look at the merits of all positions. I find I do not have that luxury when someone is staring me in the face and saying: "What do we do now — Right Now!" I find that I must not only be aware of the body of knowledge at my disposal, but I must be willing to act on it, to believe it or disbelieve it, at an instant's notice. People's hurts cannot wait for analytical decisions and suspended judgments.

After being in a situation I begin to question the things I have done and wonder if there were not others I might have done, had my scope not been limited by my training. My view of where the hurt comes from is constantly changing. I find that helping those who seek help is not just a matter of applying the bandaid in the right place. Most people do not know where the hurt is and many times the hurt is not in any individual. Many times, especially working with teachers, I hear people, all with good intentions, hurting others and hurting themselves. I find that I cannot stop the hurt. I wonder if my training is not aiming me at only a small portion of the places where hurt really comes from.

Finally, I think the most frustrating thing about working in the world out there is coming back "in here" to my academic base. Out there I am the expert, the person with counsel and advice who can solve problems; in here I am the student, the person who receives counsel and advice and who needs help solving problems. The reason that this is so frustrating is that many of the things that I learn in school are directly counter-productive to the demands of the world out there. I must often learn things that my own experiences have proven to be useless. I do not claim knowledge of all that is good for me. But I cannot forget the teachings of my experiences and I cannot resist the urge to believe the teaching of my experiences rather than the teachings of my teachers when the two conflict. However, since I need a Ph.D. to do the work which I want to do, I've returned and remain in the program. I've accepted the fact that I will have to do some things I do not like or understand.

A. New Faculty:

It is interesting to me that when I started thinking of what the work world was like, my thoughts turned to my clinical and community work. I was not yet fully socialized into seeing academia as my job. When I come into my office at the university I talk about it as "going to school" — the same expression I used when I was a student. This is an example of a more general conflict between student role and faculty role that I've experienced throughout this past year, and is therefore worth elaborating.

Throughout the year, I found myself identifying with the graduate students who were often complaining about various aspects of the program because their complaints were very similar to the ones I had as a graduate student. Things were different now, though. Instead of being a member of a peer group who complained about exams, poor supervision, and irrelevant coursework, I was now in a new peer group — being complained to! I found myself attempting to be an ombudsman — an interpreter — telling the students that faculty members were not all that bad, and suggesting to faculty members that some of the students' concerns might be legitimate. I became close friends with several graduate students this year, and I hope that this does not change. As the year progressed, however, I could feel myself being pulled (or pushed) more and more into the faculty role. This happened mostly as a result of responsibilities I felt toward the program. It happened as graduate students procrastinated in the completion of work for my courses, and I had to say, "Yes, there is a firm deadline." It happened when a student wanted academic credit for doing volunteer work and couldn't understand why I would want any written product. It happened when undergraduates balked at being graded and instead wanted everybody to get an "A." I found that there was a definite limit to my identification with students and it seems to me that I am somewhat less identified with students now than I was at the beginning of the academic year. My present identity is as an understanding faculty member, and I am pretty content with it.

The more I think about my first year as a faculty member, however, the more I feel that it was (and still is) valuable to be identified with students; and in fact, all first-year faculty members can make a unique contribution to their programs by utilizing the full potential of their dual identity. For example, I traveled in both faculty and student circles and thus developed a multifaceted perspective of our program. Having been dissatisfied with various aspects of my own clinical training, I was enthusiastic about becoming a change agent here. I will probably never have as much time or enthusiasm for changing our program as I had during my first semester on the faculty. Various factors contributed to my seeing myself as a potential change agent, and spelling these out might be helpful to other programs which might want to use a new faculty member in this capacity:

1. My initial teaching load was light, and I was told that I should "get to know the system." Informal contact with both faculty and students was facilitated.

2. I had immediate and extensive contact with both new and advanced graduate students, and didn't teach undergraduate courses until the second semester. Had my major initial responsibilities been limited to undergraduate teaching, my role as a faculty member would have been

reinforced and my identification with the graduate students would have been reduced – thus making it more difficult to see things from the eyes of people in both major subsystems of the training program.

3. Program innovation seemed to be something that was positively valued. Neither students nor faculty talked as though they feared change; in fact, they seemed to look to new people for innovative suggestions and continually sought an exchange of ideas.

4. I was discouraged from fitting into a mold, and encouraged to do my own thing with the courses I taught, the students I supervised, and the positions I took on departmental issues.

5. Perhaps most important was the curriculum's emphasis on community psychology theory, which I felt could be applied to our own training program. Levine (1969) stated that:
    "A problem arises in a setting or in a situation . . . because there is some element in the social setting that blocks effective problem-solving behavior." Thus I had ammunition for arguing that problems were not the *fault* of particular individuals, that various problems in the program might be interrelated, and that proposed solutions needed to consider how the system (the entire training program) may be causing, triggering, exacerbating, or maintaining various problems (Levine 1969).

I began to see that psychological theory was applicable to our own training program. Let me give one example. Crisis theory (Caplan 1964) suggests that changes in life situations are likely to produce periods of stress, and that interventions can be introduced at strategic points to ease tension and to help people cope with the heightened stress. Entrance into graduate school would definitely qualify as such a change in life situation. Moving to a new location is itself a cause of disequilibrium (Levine 1966). Many settings provide orientations for newcomers, but graduate students are often forgotten. Undergraduates attend Freshman Orientations; and as a new faculty member I attended orientation meetings, orientation cocktail parties, orientation luncheons, and so on. The lack of such programs for graduate students is an important system fault. I started talking with present graduate students about things they could do to ease the crisis of entry into graduate school which they had experienced themselves (this may be considered primary prevention). The graduate students were enthusiastic about developing this project. They sent incoming students information about the city and the program, and invited them to visit and stay with them. Various orientation meetings and parties are planned for the fall. We expect that with this type of crisis intervention we can reduce some of the typical anxieties of first-year graduate students.

Recommendations made to the faculty also were received enthusiastically. Faculty action on those suggestions has been much slower in coming, however. I found that program change is an incredibly slow and tedious process, and that the only way to change things rapidly is to institute changes in the courses that I teach myself — which I have done. I see that I am beginning to sound like an old faculty member in my statement that system change has to be slow and tedious. I think that in reality I have lost some of the spark for my change agent role that I had when I first came. That's why I think it's so important to really exploit the first-year faculty member in this capacity, for rarely will someone have so unique a perspective on the program and as much enthusiasm for change.

I found the real world of the clinical settings difficult to change also. During my internship year, staff members proposed and initiated various changes, but it felt to us like we were battling decades of apathy. We were allowed (and even encouraged) to do our thing, but we felt that many people might have been happier had we not attempted to be creative problem-solvers. Thus, the real world of clinical psychology is not really what we think it is. We talk as though it will be a challenge to the new Ph.D. and that we need to train innovators. This may be true of some programs, but it is probably not an accurate reflection of the field in general. Let's not kid ourselves: the real world is not demanding that we produce innovators. I find that the real world is just as happy to accept traditionally trained clinicians; provided, of course, that they are community oriented — which means that the clinic is in their own neighborhood rather than downtown. It is acceptable for me to consult with front-line people like teachers, police, welfare departments, etc., and to offer some training to these people. But, when I start talking about making these institutions more effective by changing their power structure, or changing the front-liners' perceptions of their roles and their interactions with their clients, or paying nonprofessional therapists at the same rate as professional therapists, or giving community members more administrative control of mental health services, people think I'm crazy. I'm trying very hard to resist losing my enthusiasm for what I see as meaningful change in the real world, but it's not easy. There have already been moments when it seemed appealing to me to go back to doing research — where it matters less whether you are producing "meaningful change" — and to resign myself to the fact that I have to separate my professional interests from my social and political interests.

In summary, my work world — both in academia and in clinical settings — is one of frustration in trying to change systems. This world requires political savvy and frustration tolerance. It is a world where I constantly have to be aware of subtle changes taking place in myself as a result of my "socialization," and where I continually have to evaluate whether my activities are really leading to the outcomes I value.

A. Senior Faculty:

I remember the day I took my Ph.D. oral examination very clearly. I don't know how others felt about it. I really felt on top of everything that day, but that was one of the last days that year I felt good about things. The year after I completed my degree was one of the toughest for me, in a personal, psychological sense. It was the first time in my life that I didn't know where I was going to be a few years later, or what my goal was to be. I searched anxiously, even frantically, over the next few years for a place. I toyed with private practice, management consulting, and research consultation outside of my full-time job, which was as a clinician in a VA outpatient clinic. I went seeking other jobs, and never really connected anywhere. I finally settled down in the position I had. After a few years I decided to leave it when another opportunity came along. Partly I felt there was declining institutional support for research activities, and partly I felt myself going around in circles.

I don't ever remember thinking about the field, or about the nature of practice in the field, or about training. I think I felt that we knew how to do things, in research anyway. The major problem was to do what we knew how to do well. At any rate, at that point in my career, the problem of what to do professionally was a personal and not a social issue. I had to find my own salvation. The field could very well take care of itself.

In my next position, I had much more opportunity to blend clinical work with research. At Devereux Schools in Pennsylvania, George Spivack and I had a free hand, and considerable administrative support to develop a research department. These were productive years, in the sense that we developed a research program, obtained external support for some of it, developed research training for interns, and we developed concepts and instruments which obtained gratifying professional recognition. In another sense though, we were victims of our own training. We developed ideas in that context which came out of a clinical bag. We probably lost far greater opportunities for contributing in areas which were later to be strongly developed by others, because we were blinded to them by our clinical perspective, and our previous training.

There were other things happening as well. I became involved with local professional societies, and was active in committee work, and in community education. While I had left clinical practice in a setting dominated by medical people, discussions of professional life were largely devoted to competition with or cooperation with psychiatry. At that time (the fifties) advanced training in psychoanalytic institutes was considered the ideal, but such training was largely controlled by medical people; most psychologists were excluded unless they were willing to pledge themselves to second-class citizenship. An APA survey at that time revealed that most psychologists said they would not do it again. I fully understood the feeling that was expressed although I don't believe a similar survey now would produce the same results. The many and varied opportunities now available to psychologists were not clearly available at that time. I made a personal decision to move toward a university setting. That decision, for me, was based on the rational estimate that opportunities would be opening up rapidly in the universities, and my observation that university-based psychologists seemed to be in the most independent and highest prestige positions.

During the years that I did a lot of clinical work, I was always nagged by the sense that the scientific base of whatever I did was not solid. I sometimes had to fight off a feeling of guilt, or a sense that I was a fraud whenever I sold professional skills. When we sought consultation in research, it was usually from the university-based people we admired, and while we often got sound methodological advice, we never received real stimulation or encouragement to seek out the new and the different. Working with the typical university psychology department as a basic reference group was helpful in one sense, but it promoted a deep ethical conflict on one side and a deep snobbery on the other that led us to feel that our research tools and not our experience would find the answers.

In retrospect, I think that my own training and my tendency to look back to the university for forms of social support for my activities led me into much narrower pathways than would have been true had the university culture not been so bound up with teaching and valuing confirmatory research above search and discovery. It was not until long after graduate school that I could feel comfortable with the idea that we still had to do the best we could, even though the knowledge base was far from firm.

Yet as I think about the work world, we cannot wait for the development of a knowledge base to act. The day's problems require immediate decisions, and strong action, in conditions of great uncertainty. That's the way the world is now, and that's the way it is going to look for a long time to come. I can't feel comfortable with those who claim panaceas, or with those who base their doing upon unexamined platitudes and myths, without reflection. I feel sympathetic with the need to act and to accept responsibility, even when the basis for action is uncertain. I wish I knew ways of conveying to students the schizophrenia which says that you act in clinical roles with full confidence as if you know what you are doing because you can't work any other way; and that when you step out of a clinical role you mercilessly expose every defect and deficiency in the modes of practice and in the conceptual base for practice so you can work to make it better the next time. University training tends to stress the critical, and to denigrate the action. I am sure now that's a mistake, as I am sure it is a mistake to train people at the Ph.D. level only to do the clinical work.

For me personally and professionally the most important growth period came during my years with Seymour Sarason and other colleagues at the Yale Psycho-Educational Clinic. There a number of things came together for me. First, the university base, my basic social reference group, supported the new efforts we were making. Secondly, Sarason provided the skilled and experienced leadership to get a diverse group to pull together. Third, the group of colleagues was able to share ideas and problems over a period of several years, regularly. Fourth, because we were somewhat interdisciplinary, and because my wife was in graduate school in sociology, I was exposed to wholly different modes of thinking. That period was one of professional retraining, in mid-career, as much as it was anything else. We were enabled to try and to learn in an atmosphere which supported the doing and the learning.

If I were to generalize about the conditions of the work world in which students will function, I would have to say that it is a world characterized by ambiguity and uncertainty, especially if we want our students functioning at the forefront of knowledge and practice. Secondly, there is a need to act with assurance when the basis in knowledge for such action is weak; there is the need to maintain a highly self-critical approach toward our work, without crippling ourselves with an overaggressive criticality. Thirdly, my own career and my own efforts have been marked with frustrations, failures, and disappointments. I don't know how to teach frustration tolerance, but I know that it is a necessary and inevitable requirement for professional life. I think that graduate training programs ought to teach tolerance of ambiguity, responsibility for action, a critical attitude toward practice, and frustration tolerance. Moreover, I think that educational institutions need to become more hospitable to the retraining needs of the field, if we are to see progress in practices.

When I think about the design of graduate education, it is against a background of such issues. When we attempt to translate these ideas into practice we encounter the weight of tradition, institutional inertia, and realistic criticism and opposition stemming from different life experiences.

Research and Training for Research

Most of us involved in training Ph.D.'s feel pleased when we believe our students plan to incorporate research as a part of their careers. Our aim, both for ourselves and our students, is to work toward making some truly important contribution to the discipline of psychology. But do we act that way? Do the conditions of academic life and graduate education support lively research into significant problems?

> *Q. How do you feel about your own research training, and about the place of research in your professional life?*
>
> *A. Graduate Student:*

My first awareness of research in psychology came when I was an undergraduate student hoping to attend graduate school in clinical psychology. At that time my main desire was to get a Ph.D. so that I could spend my time doing individual therapy. However, at that same time I began to have more contact with the clinical faculty and saw that they enjoyed their work in an academic setting. Consequently, I began to think that I too might like to pursue an academic career. This is when I first realized that to work in an academic setting required a commitment to research and to publication. As I inquired about the nature of the research that faculty and graduate students were doing I heard a lot of sentiment to the effect that research was boring and tedious and took away from time for other more pleasant tasks. Furthermore, the folklore among undergraduates and many graduate students who worked for professors was that most people disliked research and wouldn't do it if they didn't have to. Again I found myself leaning toward clinical work outside an academic setting. I could see the research requirement in an academic setting only as a hindrance to my plans for doing clinical work.

In my senior year, as a part of my honors program, I was assigned to work with Vic Raimy, a clinician whom I respected highly. In working with him I found an exciting marriage of research and clinical work. He was not only doing research in areas related to his own clinical practice, but was doing research which was creative and exciting. It was at this time that I decided that there was a possibility of doing both research and clinical work and surviving in an academic setting, and that clinical practice and research were not mutually exclusive activities.

After I entered graduate school it was not long before I began to talk to students and faculty about research and clinical training. I found that the same issues I had encountered at my undergraduate school were quite alive in my graduate school. In fact, there were many times when I felt that I was duplicating conversations which I had had as an undergraduate student. It was as if I had run into some universal unconscious which was in the minds of clinical students everywhere. I found clinical students doing research which had no relationship to their interests and hating the whole process. Others did work which was clinically related but trivial. Among the faculty there were those who had simply disengaged themselves from clinical concerns and whose main interest was research. Some enjoyed doing clinical work but had no faith in anything happening as a result of that work. And a few enjoyed clinical work and research and could find satisfaction doing both and still survive in an academic setting. At this point I was undecided about the way things would work out for me.

My decision was helped along by a curiously consistent phenomenon among graduate students in areas other than clinical psychology. Many of them had a different view about why clinicians did not do much research and did not like to do it. They felt that clinicians were basically "soft headed" and did not like research because they really didn't know how to do it. I recall this theme or variations on it several times throughout my first year, and although it was said jokingly many times I began to think that there was some truth in it. Thus my decision was made. I promised myself that I would not be vulnerable to this kind of criticism, and that if I chose not to do research it would not be because I didn't know how to do it. I took two courses in research methods the following two semesters and buried myself in books on research, tooling up for the time when someone would ask me about it and would try to show that I was "soft headed" in the area of research. My own reading, as well as the reading from the two methods courses, culminated in a lengthy paper which had an immense influence on me. I looked at the laboratory experiment as a research strategy and found that (for many people) research was synonymous with experimentation. Intrigued by this thought, I began to look for other research strategies. This search took me to books like Webb and Campbell's *Unobtrusive Measures* (1966), which widened my view of what can be called research.

A critical factor in my thinking about the range of research strategies was the support I received from the faculty I came into contact with. Those who taught research methods and statistics stressed the narrowness of the laboratory experiment as a research model. They felt that it was important to approach problems with a view to fitting a research design or statistic to the problem rather than having only one design which is applied to all problems. Further, I saw the faculty and students engaging in a wide range of research strategies including field studies, participant observation, historical analysis, etc., as well as doing laboratory studies. I was encouraged to be creative and flexible in approaching my research.

This atmosphere had a strong influence on my choice of an original research project. I chose to do a field study which required a longitudinal design and which utilized the methodology of participant observation. As I planned the study, I became quite involved in it and had a lot of my time and energy invested in it. However, when I put the idea in the form of a proposal I began to find constraints on the study which I had not anticipated. I found that the methology of participant observation was not a prestigious one among psychologists. Furthermore, I had just received a rejection from the program committee of the Eastern Psychological Association on a study utilizing this methodology.[a] Another problem was that my research was to be part of the requirement for prelims and this meant that there was a deadline for the completion of the research. I began to have fantasies about missing the deadline and having all that work go for nothing. My anxiety about being dropped from the program increased immensely. My first inclination was to forget my first idea for the research and do something which I was sure I could finish by the deadline — like measuring eyeblinks in turtles, or studying rats in mazes. Finally, with encouragement from several persons (faculty and students), I decided to return

---

[a] I have no way of knowing why the study was rejected, but it is interesting to note that there is no category which lists this type of research on the forms they send out; and in fact there is no provision for field studies of any kind. Our program and others that I know about are encouraging a wide range of research strategies, and yet the reward structure in academic settings remains oriented toward a narrow model of what constitutes research. At this point in time it might be difficult for Piaget to have a paper which reported a developmental study of his own child (N = 1) accepted by the EPA program committee.

to my original idea and request an extension of the deadline, which was subsequently granted. Now I face the prospect that any of the difficulties which can plague field studies will make it difficult or impossible to meet that new deadline. As I plan the finishing touches on the project I am equally aware of both the design of the experiment and the importance of meeting the deadline.

As I think about my current attitudes toward research, there are a couple of influences which my training for research has had on my thinking. One of these influences is the ability to criticize a piece of research. I find that my training has given me the ability to look critically at things like design and statistical assumptions; I have been taught to be skeptical of generalizations and to constantly look for alternate explanations. Yet I have found that these skills have been a handicap in other situations. Often I see myself taking the critical attitude into situations and finding that I should suspend judgment because of lack of data or because more research is needed. This leads to a tendency to avoid making decisions and to ignore areas I might be interested in even though they might not be well developed. I find the rigor of the research attitude a hindrance in situations where I must act regardless of the amount of evidence available.

A second influence on my thinking has come from my clinical contact with a young girl who was refusing to attend school. My supervisor directed me to a piece of research which claimed a high rate of success with school phobias using the authors' methods. I found that the decision to use the method re-required a quite different kind of decision than I have made in looking at literature in a vacuum. I found that my confidence in using the method was considerably different from the kind of confidence given by the .05 level of significance. By believing the research and utilizing the method I was placing my success in dealing with this girl in the hands of those who did the research. As a result of this experience I have come to an awareness of the possibilities of applying research evidence to my other work. I find that this is not something I do easily and that I do not see others do it regularly. And in fact this issue for me transcends the area of research and is reflected in all facets of my training. The more contact I have with work that I will be doing as a psychologist, the more I become aware of the need to translate theory into practice and to utilize abstract notions by relating them to everyday problems. I think this is one of the most important skills that should be cultivated by students in my position. As the research literature expands, as new areas of inquiry develop, and as we feel the effects of the information explosion in all areas, we must not only be able to interpret all of this data and information, but also to determine its applicability to the problems we will face as psychologists. The luxury of scholarly activities for their own sake is rapidly being challenged by the immediate problems of a rapidly changing and growing technological society. Therefore I do not see my task in graduate school as the accumulation of a body of knowledge or the acquisition of specific skills. Rather I hope my training will provide me with ways of working and thinking which will help me bridge the gap between the theoretical and the practical and which will make me able to constantly utilize new information. Therefore I do not look at the end of my training in graduate school as the end of my learning. In many respects it is only the beginning.

A.   *New Faculty Member:*

There are two separate aspects to my professional self-concept: the research psychologist and the clinical-community psychologist. I hope that within the next few years I will be able to synthesize my two lives, but I see forces working against this synthesis. I feel that in many ways my own struggle reflects the conflict within the profession of psychology; thus it seems relevant to examine how I got to where I am, and what my options are at present.

My first exposure to real-world psychology came during my sophomore year at the University of Maryland, when I took a part-time job working on a research project for J. R. Newbrough at the Mental Health Study Center of the National Institute of Mental Health. The job was exciting because it allowed me to work closely with a psychologist and thereby learn how he operated, and to begin to ask questions and investigate things independently. I was successful at this job. The compulsive-like orderliness of my approach to problems was a real asset, and I found that I was productive. My honors thesis developed from my work in this setting and this was also a rewarding experience.

I had very little experience with clinical work. I did unsupervised volunteer work at St. Elizabeth's Hospital, and at various orphanages and homes for retarded children, but there didn't seem to be much of a relation between this "social activity" and psychology as I knew it from the books. At the Mental Health Study Center, the clinical section was separate from the research section, and it was not until after I left the setting that a Clinical Research Section was established. I talked a great deal with Bob Newbrough about my dual interests in clinical work and research, and tried to understand how he chose which professional road to take. I remember his saying that Albert Schweitzer and Jonas Salk were both great men, but that in terms of total impact on the world, Salk probably had the greater influence. I guess that this triggered off various savior fantasies in me, and I found myself leaning toward the Salk route.

I went to graduate school oriented toward becoming a psychologist who was going to change social institutions and evaluate these changes. I wanted to learn about personality, psychopathology, clinical psychology, community psychology — I wanted to learn about people. My graduate courses were very frustrating; the work-load was immense and very little of it afforded any opportunity to wet my feet in the real world. Very little of it afforded me any opportunity for personal growth.

The first real exposure to clinical psychology came during a second-year course in interviewing and projective testing. I found that my compulsive-orderliness, which was a valuable asset to my research work, was a hindrance to my clinical work. I remember various times when the professor, Irving Alexander, along with my fellow students, hinted that I ought to loosen up a bit; I wish that they had worked harder on me. In any event, I recognized that my classmates were "better" at clinical work than I was and this reinforced my view of myself as a researcher.

I did not enjoy my course in psychotherapy either. The classroom aspects did not give me a feeling for the diverse approaches to therapy, and my practicum was oriented toward the psychoanalytic model, which just did not sit right with me. At the same time, my research world was becoming brighter and brighter. Journal articles were being published, reprint requests were coming in, my work was being cited by other writers, and I had begun to work steadily on my dissertation under Jerome Kagan, and even received a small grant. Since the goal of the Harvard program was to produce researchers, there was no reason for the faculty to be unhappy with my direction.

Two experiences from those years stick in my mind as further reinforcing my emerging professional self-concept. After working with Jerry Kagan for a year or so, and coming to see him as a human being as well as a renowned psychologist, a collegial relationship began to develop. I can remember my utter amazement when he first sought my opinions on issues he was pondering. At first I saw this behavior as kind of paternal, and didn't believe that he was seriously interested in my views; but when I realized that he really was seeking an exchange of ideas with me, my professional self-esteem took a quantum jump.

The second influential experience of the dissertation years involved teaching an undergraduate course and working with a first-year graduate student on the development of a research project. Here I found that I had something to offer; I had learned something in graduate school and I was able to get my ideas across to others. I guess it was around this time that I clearly began to see myself in an academic job. I still wanted to learn about community psychology, however, and I still wanted to work with people. I enjoyed the research that I was doing, but I didn't feel that it was the type of research that I wanted to devote my life to. I had not yet been able to break away from the mold that I entered in my sophomore year at Maryland.

My internship showed me how the "other half" lives; I was introduced to practicing clinicians. I loosened up, developed some clinical skills, and came to see myself as a person who could work effectively with clients. But I was not totally happy with the clinical work either. Many of the clinicians didn't seem to be in touch with psychological research and theory that was relevant to their work. Some, like my friend whom I spoke about previously, were genuinely upset about being isolated from "academic" psychology. My friend had fantasies of some day applying for a grant and doing a large-scale study of the institution where we worked. But there didn't seem to be much support for this. Just as most academic psychologists saw clinical training and clinical work as secondary, so also did most practicing clinicians see research as a luxury for which there was little time. I began to wonder if I would ever be able to find a setting in which I could do applied work and evaluate the effectiveness of the work I did.

My still incomplete professional self-concept made job-hunting difficult. I was still searching for a setting where I could learn about community psychology. Some departments quite frankly told me that their needs dictated that I had to be available to teach what I knew (developmental psychology, abnormal psychology, etc.) and that they could not provide me with additional "training." Murray Levine simply said, "If you want to learn about community psychology, come here and we'll teach the course together," — which is what I've done. So, I have finally made it — I'm learning about community psychology. Then why did I say that I still had doubts about whether I would be able to synthesize my two lives of researcher and clinician? First, I have become fairly knowledgeable in a specific area of psychological inquiry; it will be difficult to leave the area where I have begun to develop my reputation and move on to an area where I will be unknown. This, however, is a "personal" decision. In addition, however, I feel some pressure to remain in my area of expertise if I want to be productive enough to obtain tenure. I'm not sure if academia values "dabbling" — doing a study in one area and then moving on to something else. I've spent this year dabbling, and I like it. I want to feel that I still have choices to make regarding my career in psychology; I don't want to withdraw into an isolated work-world where I grind out articles in my area of expertise and do nothing else. I'm no longer sure I want to push myself to be a Salk. I want to try out various alternative models of psychology careers and then choose. Up until very recently, I was hampered from doing this — both by my own needs to remain a specialist, and by a history of training experiences that made it difficult for me to develop into the kind of psychologist I wanted to be.

Implications. What lessons does this personal history have for current training programs? For me, the lesson is that we seem to be stacking the deck against the production of Boulder-model psychologists. Many of my instructors talked about the need for scientist-practitioners, but few were role models. Many instructors were dedicated to one role and demeaning to the other. Few seemed to feel that "scientist" and "practitioner" roles may each lose something if isolated from the other.[b]

---

[b] This does not imply that I myself am opposed to professional schools of psychology. We need programs to train psychologists for leadership roles in applied areas, and many of our academic programs have failed in this regard. I do feel, however, that psychology's uniqueness as a profession is that it critically evaluates the services it provides, and thereby gives itself corrective feedback which leads to improved services — and greater understanding of psychological processes.

In my first year of teaching I have tried to communicate my enthusiasm for research *and* clinical work. In my undergraduate Abnormal Psychology course I have arranged field work opportunities and scheduled weekly supervision sessions with my graduate assistant and myself. I have tried to point out the relevance of various research studies to the understanding and treatment of emotional problems. I have tried to get students to think about how their ideas may be investigated empirically.

I see my major "mission", however, as being with our graduate students; because if they buy the Boulder-model, they will become role models for *their* students and gradually the face of clinical psychology will change. One implication is that we as a faculty should consider good, innovative applied work as a part of our tenure decisions — not just give it lip-service as many of us now do. We should have more half-time faculty appointments in our programs so that colleagues who want to be scientist-practitioners can have time for their applied work. We need to bring practitioners back into academia — so that students don't develop a schizophrenic professional life, so that they can study with people who do clinical work and research, and so that there can be an exchange of ideas between academics and clinicians.

I see my mission as helping my students see a relation between research and clinical work. Discussions of clinical work often suggest researchable questions — with answers which are relevant to practice. I also feel that we need to revise our conception of the internship. My academic training and field training (internship) were almost completely unrelated, leading me to think that I had to choose one or the other professional activity. We need to involve our students in field experiences from a very early point in their graduate career, and *integrate* the field experiences into the academic work; use the field experiences as both clinical settings and research settings. In sum, I want to help my students develop their professional self-concept as scientist and practitioner together.

A. Senior Faculty:

I was brought up in the Boulder model, and I have largely absorbed its ideals. An important condition predisposing my acceptance of the Boulder model was my involvement in clinical settings, very fully, from the beginning of my graduate experience. I was in the original Veterans Administration program where we spent a minimum of twenty hours a week in a clinic or hospital, from the day we began graduate school.

The period from the mid-forties to the mid-fifties was vintage, for we were coming into our own. We had high hopes of achievement, we were learning, and we were taking on responsibility. Interdisciplinary battles were there, but the social order was relatively unquestioned. We accepted our place in the clinic, did our job, and were grateful when we were permitted to do more psychothereapy. In the battle, the one place where we clearly had the edge was in our research training. An important element was my exposure to men (Jerome L. Singer, Julian Melzoff, Howard Mitchell, Sheldon Korchin, Julius

Wishner, and Mort Garrison), some still trainees themselves, who undertook clinically relevant research in clinical settings. I could accept and understand what they were doing, and when I wanted to engage in clinically relevant research myself, I received encouragement from those around me.

I didn't receive that encouragement from too many around the university. I still remember the shocked and stony silence coming from one of the senior professors when I told him of my discovery that his discussions of perception, learning, and memory had something to do with the Freudian ego. Perhaps I conveyed my discovery in a way which was insulting, or naive. Be that as it may, I found that the university setting was not the place for the free discussion of ideas. (Now, perhaps too often, I feel an impatience with the naiveté of students. I think my impatience has increased in recent years, as that naiveté is accompanied by an increase in student challenges to authority, but I hope it doesn't extend to a restriction on the ideas which are permitted examination.)

Through my experience in the VA as trainee and staff member, and because of other clinical work, I feel competent in doing a variety of clinical jobs, but I value my ability to think and to conceptualize most of all. In those moments when I assess myself, my sense of personal satisfaction derives from my sense of mastery of a broad range of psychological ideas and literature, and from my ability to understand psychological problems conceptually. Right or wrong, I feel I have an edge on others, particularly those without research training.

I am reflecting my professional socialization in my views, and I am reflecting the fact that the model has worked fairly well for me personally. I have achieved a reasonably secure place in the world and I have a job which offers me about as much freedom to use my time as any I could conceive. I have made many friends through my profession throughout the country, and enjoy those signs of recognition which indicate that I have attained a modest reputation.

My feelings are ambivalent. I often feel that the value attributed to work in psychology, my own and others, is greater than the work deserves, particularly when one is faced with the problem of implementing ideas in practice. While scholarly research ought to be conducted on the basis of timelessness, there are urgent social problems before us. When I compare the status of knowledge against reality problems, I frequently suffer a sense of futility. I have stopped reading a lot of the more academic research literature because I find it mostly unhelpful, and mostly going around in circles. Having played the publishing game, I am also well aware of how much is done wholly for that purpose. Yet I am also aware that the giants of our field were typically highly productive people. Perhaps one needs the ground of bad and mediocre research, and the social organization of a field, so that a contribution can stand out as figure.

Research in academic settings. But there are other problems as well. In many ways research training, particularly in academic settings, contributes to the difficulties in undertaking meaningful work, and in integrating the scientist and professional roles. Academic research training emphasizes the ability to be aggressively critical. We teach our students to find all of the flaws, the artifacts, the extraneous variables which could account for a given finding. Moreover, we use a variety of committee procedures in doctoral research, presumably to insure quality control. Too often the committee members impose a demand for perfection in design, as a consequence of competition among themselves, taking the life out of the problem. Later when the student comes up with some trivial finding, or when he comes up with nothing but good reliability coefficients, the committees conspire to approve the form, confirming for the student that it is all a game after all. The sense of intellectual excitement and discovery have long since been killed off in many. We send people out into the world who are convinced research is tedious, painful, and probably a lot of crap, or who are so sure they are incapable that they never undertake any more work on that score, and sure that it has nothing at all to do with their applied interests.

We have demanded certainty of ourselves and our students, and in the process we have killed off the value of risk taking, or the value of experimentation in its broadest meaning. The academic attitude we train says that we cannot offer anything unless we are certain — and we are never certain. I wouldn't want to give up the tendency to be deeply critical of the state of our field, but I think it is necessary that we learn how to say, "This is the state of the art, and this is my best guess." The danger of minimizing critical and scholarly values is best reflected in the outcomes of advice given on the basis of romanticized or incomplete understanding of the basic literature of a field (Herzog 1970; Moynihan 1969). Too many of us do not study problems carefully, yet do not hesitate to assert the conclusions forcefully, and in my view foolishly. I am appalled at how often I see large-scale treatment programs planned and implemented without reference to available literature which could predict the outcome of a given course of action. How to get a blend between action and scholarliness is our problem in research education, and in accepting a research role in the world.

I am part of the academic world now, and while I try in my own way to encourage a broad range of ideas, I have to fight battles within myself continuously. I want my students to take on important problems, and to do them in grand style, but I know field problems are immense. Because there are pressures to get people through, I find myself encouraging and supporting little problems. I find myself opting for practicality, and encouraging students to take on do-able problems rather than important and exciting ones. I find myself hesitating to encourage students to do descriptive work, or to do case histories. I get anxious lest I put a student in the middle of some ideological battle, and I am fearful lest an intemperate, impatient outburst of mine will alienate colleagues with whom I live and on whom I am dependent.

Little by little we are getting people to try some different things, but I hope some of my students will be able to carry matters further than I am able to do now.

I am freer myself to engage in whatever intellectual activity interests me. The constraints come more in trying to get support for offbeat work than in doing the work. The lack of financial support is more an annoyance than a real handicap, since I have long since learned to do with very little, and to bootleg support when necessary. Most of the things that I think I do well really require time rather than support. That's a set of issues which I have resolved for myself.

More important is the fact that I would be hard put to finding social support to get students to engage in the kind of work I find most congenial for myself. I am certain that I could not have gotten a Ph.D. in psychology for my work on either the Rorschach test (Levine and Spivack 1964), in community psychology (Sarason, Levine, Goldenberg, Cherlin, and Bennett 1966), or in social history (Levine and Levine 1970a,b). Applications to obtain support for each of those activities were turned down by one or more federal granting agencies, and I assume a dissertation prospectus would have met the same fate. Right or wrong, I think that too many of my colleagues would object to that kind of "loose" work in students. I may be underestimating my colleagues, and I may be reflecting some personal restriction or lack of courage, but I am reluctant to test the issues when a student may be in the middle.

The problem of authority. The authority of professors over students is another problem in educating for research. I am not advocating that professors relinquish authority by any means, but it is a problem that both professors and students have to solve. The latent consequences of the authority relationship for education need to be assessed. As a teacher, I must confess to a peculiar ambivalence when I see my students cite my work or use it in shaping their own. On the one hand I am pleased and flattered. On the other, I am concerned lest the student is simply giving me back what I wish to hear; that he has given up some of his independence of mind to give back what he has learned.

Intellectually, I encourage students to criticize my work. Emotionally, I am jealous of its status and feel wounded whenever that work, which is an extension of my ego, is attacked in any way at all. The social and economic organization of scholarly and professional activity promotes competitiveness, but other issues are at stake as well.[c]

---

[c] I think that anyone who has accepted the publish-or-perish view of the world, and researchers in non-academic settings, functions in a social system which supports grandiose and narcissistic fantasies. No matter how a person assesses his work realistically, inwardly he wishes himself a place among the greats. Inwardly each strives to achieve immortality. On my travels around the country, and in English-speaking foreign countries, it is one of my small pleasures to check library catalogues to see which of my books are included

I am sure it must be difficult for students to disagree with me. The various ways in which professors hold power over students has been exaggerated, to be sure, but professors can certainly make life easier or more difficult for students. The asymmetry of the relationship is handled in different ways by different people, but it needs to be solved, and it is an inherent issue in how both students and professors come to view themselves. The problem is no different in training for research and clinical work. Students who disagree with the clinical formulations of their supervisors sometimes find themselves subject to attacks on their competence or psychological health. Students parrot and chant the clinical formulations of their clinical teachers with the same, or worse, thoughtlessness that they cite the theoretical formulations of their academic instructors.

The problem of authority is in part the problem of the need for heroes, by both students and faculty. The student wants to believe that his faculty are powerful figures so he can identify with them. The faculty nurture the fantasy for their own reasons. I am not an advocate of the "reveal your most intimate thoughts and feelings" school of honesty in relationship, but I do think it is necessary to do something to reduce the reliance on heroes so the student can be freer to think for himself. I don't know that we would develop many more geniuses if we tried to reduce heroism, and we might lose something important, but I do think we would reduce the slavishness to concepts that makes men blind to the evidence of their senses. It may also be helpful to reveal more of the frustration and failure in order to encourage more students to persist when they do encounter difficulties. Professors, by concealing error and frustration, may inadvertently convey the view that the student is frustrated because he is incompetent.

Faculty do make mistakes and while it is not apparent to students, faculty are subject to critical review almost daily. It is not easy to walk out of a lecture room not knowing how your audience of blank faces has received you. Professional writing is subject to comment by anonymous journal editors, reviewers, and grant committees. The commentary fed back to the author is not noted for its tact, its kindliness, and frequently not for its helpfulness either. Articles that are published are subject to public attack, while books are reviewed publicly. Every book author is vulnerable to the criticisms of reviewers who, after an hour or two of reading and thought, may blithely tell him in journals read by his colleagues that the work into which he has sunk years of time, energy, emotions, and ambitions is worthless or worse. Reviews for tenure

---

in them. I feel a sense of smug satisfaction which I "hit" and a sense of being miffed and disappointed when the catalogue doesn't list my work. Thus far, I have successfully avoided the temptation to order my books in strange libraries, but the impulse is there and is accompanied by the thought that libraries exist forever. Having browsed through and used dusty books which haven't been handled in forty years, according to the date slip, the reality of the fantasy of immortality has been emphasized for me.

and promotion involve the public assessment of a man's worth. The wounds left to the professional ego take a long time to heal, and some never recover. Some refuse to run the gauntlet, and do not ever publish on that account alone.

Research is also frustrating. A great deal of time, money, and hope may go into a research project. After a year or two of devotion to a given problem, nothing of value may emerge. A research worker may be left with a batch of data which demand a report to a granting agency, but he may have little heart to do the necessary analyses and writing because eyeballing of the data already revealed that little of any importance or interest will emerge. While we know that we can expect few ideas to pan out well, we still need to justify our existence to ourselves, and failure is not infrequently accompanied by depression.

I do not wish to overstate the case of the suffering professor, because most of us adapt to the difficulties more or less successfully. I think that research success early in one's career can help one through later periods of despair, but failure in the early phases of a student's career may well turn him away from research problems forever. It may be helpful for teachers to share something of their difficulties with their students, if only to emphasize that a certain degree of failure is an expected part of life.

Implications. I still engage in some clinical work, although most of it tends to be community oriented rather than individually oriented. I still engage in research and scholarly activity of a variety of kinds: quantitative, library, and observational, and I still enjoy what I do. Although I have serious questions about a lot of what we do as research, I must confess that I feel a distinct thrill when the printout turns up with the hoped for significant chi square. One of the more freeing activities for me has been the writing of clinical and non-quantitative theory, history, and commentary. Accepting such activities as legitimate has literally been mind expanding for me, because I have allowed myself to think more broadly and to read more widely. I think the intellectual quality of the work I have produced has matured over the years, and that on the whole my nonquantitative work is better than the quantitative. I don't know if that's because it is easier, or because my own aptitude for the kind of thinking that experimental and quantitative work requires is limited. I am as sure that my scientific training has enabled me to reason more carefully as I am that for many years aspects of my scientific training limited what I was able to do. Both for myself and my students, the goal is to retain the benefits of rigorous thinking while losing the features of scientific thinking which have proven constricting.

Summary

We are in transition in many ways. The outside world has presented our profession with urgent challenge. That challenge, as expressed in the society at large, has exerted an influence on the academy through the infusion of new demands and a new spirit in graduate students and in young faculty. Those more senior people who have keenly felt a dissatisfaction with the nature of their own profession, that dissatisfaction rooted in career experiences, contribute by criticism of their own profession, by ideas, and most importantly by their own actions. Ideas, enthusiasm, and action all encounter the realities of social institutions; and efforts to find expression of ideas in new social forms for research, for training, and for clinical practice are marked by some advances, but almost always accompanied by conflict and frustration. The pull of tradition is strong, but new generations of students and faculty approach the problem with very different freight, and very different outlook. As the next professional generation absorbs new ideas, what seem to be risky advances will seem to be plodding, old hat, and something to be carried still further. Change takes time. We are in process.

References

Atkinson, J. W. (ed.). *Motives in Fantasy, Action, and Society*. Princeton, N.J.: D. Van Nostrand, 1958.

Caplan, G. *Principles of Preventive Psychiatry*. New York: Basic Books, 1964.

Graziano, A.M. "Clinical Innovation and the Mental Health Power Structure: A Social Case History." *American Psychologist* 24 10-18 (1969).

Herzog, E. "Social Stereotypes and Social Research." *The Journal of Social Issues* 26, 3 (1970): 109-125.

Kelly, J. G. "Antidotes for Arrogance: Training for Community Psychology." *American Psychologist* 25 (1970): 524-31.

Levine, M. "Some Postulates of Community Psychology Practice." In *The Psycho-Educational Clinic: Papers and Research Studies,* edited by F. Kaplan and S. B. Sarason. Boston: Massachusetts Department of Mental Health, 1969.

Levine, M. and G. Spivack. *A Rorschach Index of Repressive Style*. Springfield, Ill.: Charles C. Thomas, 1964.

Levine, A. and Levine M., (eds.). *The Gary Schools*. Cambridge: MIT Press, 1970a.

Levine, M. and Levine A. *A Social History of Helping Services*. New York: Appleton-Century-Crofts, 1970b.

Magoon, T. M.; Golann, S. E.; and Freeman, R. W. *Mental Health Counselors at Work*. New York: Pergamon Press, 1969.

Meltzoff, J. and Kornreich, M. *Research in Psychotherapy*. New York: Atherton, 1970.

Moynihan, D. P. *Maximum Feasible Misunderstanding: Community Action in The War on Poverty*. New York: The Free Press, 1969.

Sarason, S. B.; Levine, M.; Goldenberg, I.; Cherline, D.; and Bennett, E. *Psychology in Community Settings*. New York: Wiley, 1966.

Webb, E. J.; Campbell, D.; Schwartz, R.; and Sechrest, L. *Unobtrusive Measures: Nonreactive Research in the Social Sciences*. Chicago: Rand McNally & Company, 1966.

Zubin, J.; Eron, L.; and Schumer, F. *An Experimental Approach to Projective Techniques*. New York: Wiley, 1965.

13

Problems of Entry in Light of Some Postulates of Practice in Community Psychology

Murray Levine
State University of New York at Buffalo

[Editor's Note] : *Traditionally, members of the mental health professions have always devoted a small amount of their time to the problems of consultation, usually with or within mental health agencies. Recently however, especially with the development of Community Psychology, this situation has begun to change and mental health professionals have become increasingly involved as consultants in a variety of different settings including schools, welfare departments, community action agencies, and even City Halls. This being the case, the field of consultation has become a professional specialty in and of itself – and one in dire need of both theoretical explication and practical guidelines. In this chapter, Murray Levine addresses himself to these issues, and provides a unique, even radical approach to the meaning and implications of consultation. His definition of the consultant as a "problem-solving leader catalyst" goes far beyond current role definitions which are embedded in orientations stressing "intrapsychic supremacy" and "deviance control." As such, Levine's chapter is a particularly appropriate one, for it forces us to re-think – in very concrete terms – the conditions under which we can (or should) operate in community settings.*

Let me begin by defining my concept of the community psychologist and the consulting function, for what I have to say is relevant within a context which views consulting not as an extension of the clinical process, but as professional activity in and of itself embedded within a theory of practice. The word *consultant* is a poor one for my purposes, for that term implies a person who has specialized knowledge which can be applied to problems brought to his attention. The consultee asks for help of a kind he believes the consultant has to offer, and he can either accept or reject the consultant's advice. The consultant accepts a limited responsibility for what happens thereafter. If somehow "good" follows from his visit, he gets a reputation as a helpful person, and his practice grows. If "bad" follows, it is the consultee who acts on

This chapter has benefited from suggestions and criticisms offered by Adeline Levine, for which I am most grateful. It is based on work and ideas developed at the Yale Psycho-Educational Clinic, in collaboration with Seymour Sarason and my co-workers there.

the advice who is responsible. The consultant is an outsider who brings professional objectivity and specialized skills to a situation and he offers solutions which are meaningful within his professional understanding of the problem. He does not, usually, accept responsibility for implementing his solution. Such a consultant serves a very valid function, and many are quite effective in this role.

In the mental health field, in school consultation, and in other areas of community work, however, such a consulting role is very limited. Most of us, when we have functioned as consultants, have tended to adopt the classical consultant model. We have tended to work with caretakers, as the current phrase goes, around the problem of the people who are dependent in the setting — children, social agency clients, applicants for job-training, etc. Usually, the caretakers in the setting refer deviants to us, deviants being defined as people who either cause the caretakers trouble in some fashion, or for whom the particular institutional setting has no good solution.

In such settings we are usually brought in by some power in the setting, who negotiates with us on the basis of his judgment that he or his employees are having some difficulty which requires expert help. Frequently, the issue in school or similar settings is one of screening out "sick people" with whom they cannot work, of making referrals to treatment for these people. On a sophisticated level, the issue is one of helping the caretaker to do a better job by offering expert information, or expert suggestions about how to handle the person who is defined as the problem.

Note that the contract we accept is one of helping the agency or the institutional setting to deal with the *people it serves*, people whom the institutional setting defines as the problem. It is those people who don't fit in, in some fashion, who usually constitute the problem. In schools, the referral is likely to be the disturbing child — the active, aggressive child — and less likely to be the child who is not learning, but who is not bothering anyone. Frequently, when we do get another kind of referral, we discover the school is concerned about an aggressive parent, and needs the prestige or the strength of the consultant to deal with the parent. We almost never get a referral which says help us to think about what we are doing to contribute to the problems people have with the way we do business.

The contract, to help the setting deal with what it defines as its problems, presents the consultant with two important issues. First, those of us who come from the mental health professions, and who are used to thinking of ourselves as the agent of the individual in distress, find that we are the agent of deviancy control. Not that we do not frequently serve such a position in society anyway; it is usually more hidden, and less direct. In the consulting situation we find that we are placed in the position of validating the judgment of the caretaker in the setting that the person is disturbed, and that something ought to be done about that person.

The disagreements, the problems, the conflicts come about when the consultant finds himself, for example, identified with the child in the school situation, and in marked disagreement with the way in which the problem is being handled in the setting. The anger and distress that such a position elicits in the caretaker, teacher or principal, comes about only in part because of the implied or stated criticism of these people. It also comes about because the consultant may be viewed as having broken the contract. He is no longer supporting the caretakers in the institutional setting in their judgment of what constitutes a problem, but in fact he has aligned himself with the opposition to their judgment. What I am saying is that the terms of the contract are not always clear to both parties when they enter into the contract. Since it is clear that it was not the child or parent who asked for the consultant to intervene, he was hired by the caretaker, so to speak, it follows that the consultant under such circumstances is the agent of the caretaker.

The second issue follows from the first. The consultant who functions with a contract to help caretakers deal better with "sick people," (a term we use to set up our own areas of competence, and a term which causes more trouble than it helps), aligns himself with the major goals and values of the social setting, and accepts these as unchangeable givens, or at least as none of his business. By accepting the consulting function, as it is usually defined, the consultant himself defines the problem in a certain way, and cuts himself off from a large and important class of data, data about the social structure of the setting in which a problem is manifested.

An extreme of this blind position may be found in Scheff's (1966) description of the functioning of court appointed psychiatrists in relation to petitions for commitment to mental institutions. Scheff found that the probability of commitment once brought before such a person is almost 1.00. The psychiatrists operated with an implicit, if not an explicitly stated presumption that anyone who came before them must be "sick," that interview and case history were remarkably biased toward finding pathology, and that the interview to determine competence consequently lasted an average of only 9.2 minutes and rarely exceeded 17 minutes.

Scheff describes how such a situation can come about. The judge is under public pressure not to make a mistake by releasing a man who might cause trouble in the community. If a psychiatric consultant releases too many individuals, the judge's anxiety level is increased, with the result that he will question the professional's judgment, and stop referring or using those men who do not support his own position in the social scheme. Within a relatively brief period of time it is possible to get docile professionals, who accept the role given them and who, out of their own needs, act in ways to support the system. For example, if the professional is relatively poorly paid, he can increase his rate of payment by reducing the amount of time he spends with each person. If there are four people for him to see, and if he is given fifty dollars for the morning, he can increase his rate of pay to a respectable level by seeing the people in an hour or an hour and a half. At the same time he reduces the possibility that he will find data to refute the presumption of mental incompetence in the brief interview, and he makes the diagnosis with a clear conscience, rationalizing that had he had a longer interview more florid pathology obviously would have shown up.

To get back to our main point, the psychiatrist is hired by the court to serve the purposes of the court. There are a variety of economic and social pressures on the psychiatrist to fit in with the system, and he even comes to view himself as functioning as a helping agent in the situation because he can say that he is helping to get sick people to treatment. What happens when the psychiatrist views the system itself can be seen in the reception Szasz (1963) has had. Scheff's book (1966) contains a restrained, but exceedingly powerful attack on the whole system of legal commitment, as well as a thoughtful statement of an alternative to the model of mental illness as contained within the skin of the patient.

In part, it is our theory of human behavior which defines the kind of role we see for ourselves and how we relate to social settings. Contemporary concepts of psychological illness, and psychological therapies can be summed up in the descriptive, deliberatively provocative term, "intrapsychic supremacy." The concept of intrapsychic supremacy assumes that the important events in determining problems in living are invariably intrapsychic ones. It is not so much the circumstances of life, but the meaning and perception, conscious and unconscious, of the circumstances of life which are of importance. Any deviant in a social setting is deviant because of what he brings to the setting. We do not have to consider the setting. Meaning and perception of incidents are determined by a set of intrapsychic events whose basic characteristics were fixed in earlier experience. Therefore, we say, it does not make any difference if there are changes in a person's outer circumstances. He will remain the same, because the intrapsychic events will be unchanged. Moreover the assumption of intrapsychic supremacy also holds that changes intrapsychic events can take place only within a certain set of very narrow conditions, conditions not usually found in the normal course of social relationships, but conditions which are produced only in a psychotherapeutic relationship with a skilled, professionally trained psychotherapist.

This viewpoint, whatever validity it has, tends to overlook situational determinants of problems in living, tends to underestimate the strength of environmental events to foster change, and tends to ignore the problem of transferring gains from the psychotherapy situation to the life situation. Most importantly in our minds, it tends to isolate the person from the social setting. Our theory forces us to look at the person and not at the *person-in-a-setting*.

What I would like to do is offer another kind of viewpoint of the behavior of people, a viewpoint which derives from our work in community psychology, and one which permits the development of a rather radically different conception of the consultant. As I tell you about this different conception, you will see why it brings one to consider the relationships between the consultant and people who have power in settings in a different light. The viewpoint is expressed in a set of postulates which I would like to state briefly here. The postulates and their implication for training are discussed more fully elsewhere (Levine 1967 a,b).

1. *A problem arises in a setting or in a situation; some factor in the situation in which the problem manifests itself causes, triggers, exacerbates, or maintains the problem.*

This postulate states that the setting is always involved in some way in a problem person. (Paul Weiss, the eminent philosopher, was puzzled by my use of the term "problem" in this context. As I attempted to explain my meaning to him, he suddenly caught on. "Oh," he said, "you don't mean problem. You mean tsores!") We can offer any number of examples of this postulate. Perhaps the best one may refer to our observations of a child in a playground. The same child who was clearly the leader, the center of activity, ordering others to their positions and being obeyed, organizing his team, shouting encouragement, making good plays, was sullen, depressed, and negativistic in his classroom, unable to do the work of the classroom, and refusing to try. Or in a project I have with student teachers who act as tutors for first grade children, I can show you several examples of children who can read for their tutors, but who freeze, stumble, and act stupid and incapable in front of a group and in front of the classroom teacher.

In our book (Sarason et al., 1966) we cite examples of children who were clearly aggressive, and hyperactive, whose behavior changed radically, almost at once, when placed in a different classroom with a different teacher. The behavior disappears in one situation, is replaced by other behaviors, and reappears when the environmental contingencies change. Moreover, under some circumstances, for example, after two days of a thoroughly inadequate substitute teacher, a class which was not too well disciplined in the first place, made a total shambles of the classroom, with almost all of the children participating in the destruction of the classroom, even children who were normally well controlled.

It is not only the person who is the problem, but the person is a problem in a setting and the setting is part of the problem, in some way.

2. *A problem arises in a situation because of some element in the social setting which blocks effective problem-solving behavior on the part of those charged with carrying out the functions and achieving the goals of the setting.*

This postulate says that human behavior becomes of concern to others only when the system of deviance control or of conflict resolution is ineffective for some reason. For example, a young man who had been released from a state institution for the mentally deficient was accepted in a neighborhood youth corps program. His behavior, consisting of loud outbursts, complaints, mumbling to himself, cursing, was viewed as a sign of mental disturbance by those in the setting. Interviews with the personnel charged with supervising him suggested that they were reluctant to interfere with him for fear that he was mentally ill, and their interference would make him worse. Moreover, there was a fear that he would make a scene on the job site, causing the host on the job site to complain and perhaps losing the job site for the future, a serious concern in this organization. The boy also had a skill in argumentation concerning the rules, a form of adaptation that people in institutions sometimes develop to a high order of competence, and which in this situation led to considerable distress for some of the personnel because this supposedly mentally deficient lad could out argue a number of them. A part of the problem was resolved when a consultant was able to assure the nonprofessionals that discipline would not cause him to go insane, that the general supervisor would stand behind the boy's supervisor in the event of a scene on the job site, and others were not to argue with the young man, but only to insist that he complete his work as given to him. There was a fairly rapid improvement in the situation, following the imposition of controls. At least it became more livable for all concerned.

In another instance, a referral to the consultant came at the point when the supervisor on a work site had her duties changed so that she could no longer pay attention in the same way to the young lady who was her charge. The girl became a problem when the supervisor could no longer provide for her.

The two postulates together suggest a view of human behavior in which deviance, or abnormality, is defined as a problem in a social setting. The setting is viewed as part of the problem, and one defines a situation of a setting to include the capability of the setting to make provision for or to resolve the problems presented by the individual served within it. Given this view of behavior, it follows that a consultant must be in a position to diagnose the setting as well as the individual who is defined as a problem.

3. *Help to be effective has to be located strategically to the manifestation of the problem, preferably in the very situation in which the problem manifests itself.*

This postulate follows from the first two, and emphasizes the consultant's need to know the setting. It also argues that one should not bring the person to help, but the reverse should be true.

4. *The goals and values of the helping agent or the helping service must be consistent with the goals and values of the setting in which the problem is manifested.*

This postulate is also of critical importance for the consultant. Much misery which now occurs in consulting relationships comes about because the consultant, particularly in the mental health field, assumes that he and others share common values and goals. It frequently is not the case that mental health consultants and others share common goals and values, and in fact the reverse is often true. Recommendations for action come in a value context, and one needs to be acutely aware of value contexts. When the helping agent comes to the conclusion that the basic goals of the setting need to be changed, he is preaching revolution, and he can be expected to be greeted with the same enthusiasm that all revolutionaries elicit from those in power. The tactics necessary to achieve changes in goals and values may be very different from those in which one introduces help as a form of deviance control.

5. *The form of help should have potential for being established on a systematic basis, using the natural resources of the setting, or through introducing resources which can be come institutionalized as part of the setting.*

This postulate recognizes the principle that problems which arise are not to be considered individual examples of difficulty, but they are to be considered as members of a class of problems which can be solved by some systematic solution. Otherwise one is in the position of the man who swats at mosquitoes.

Given this principle, the role of the consultant becomes one of identifying the problems, and diagnosing them as reflections of the dynamics of situations, developing solutions which can be institutionalized, given the nature of the situation and available resources, helping to introduce the new form into the ongoing situation, helping to train new workers if such are necessary, and providing a form of leadership, or leadership support to help develop and carry through necessary institutional changes. Given the other postulates one can safely deduce that introducing changes will run into the same kind of system blocks that let the individual problem arise in the first place.

Let us look at the issue of power, and let me point out there is an important difference between power and influence. Power refers to the ability to give orders and to enforce these orders by suitable rewards and punishments. Influence refers to the ability to have others heed one's counsel without actually having the wherewithal to enforce the orders-read as counsel. I would like to illustrate the issue by describing a situation in which an individual without power achieved an important position of influence in a school. The story has much to tell us about our position as consultants, and about how to achieve a position of influence in a new setting.

In one situation, a weak, white, female principal, who has a number of fairly timid frightened teachers, mostly white, in her school, had an aggressive, male black community relation worker introduced into the school. In many schools, community relations workers are relegated errand boy duties, but in this situation, due to a combination of the principal's uncertainty, the teacher's anxiety, a fear of offending a black, a superstition that a black would know how to handle problems with black children, and the angry aggressiveness of the male worker, the worker practically took over the principal's job. He was ordering teachers, children, parents, and the principal around with impunity, and getting compliance with his orders. Actually holding the lowest powered and a low status job, the worker achieved a high degree of influence in the situation. There was no way he could enforce his orders, except by brute physical strength, a tactic he did use with some children, but he gained a great deal of compliance with his orders. Of course he also performed some valuable functions in the situation. He could frighten some children into brief periods of quiet, and he could forcefully stop a fight in the school yard, a situation which brought out great fears, understandably, in many of the teachers. He was able to make home visits, to check up on absentees, an activity which also frightened many of the white workers in that ghetto neighborhood, and which was a very important service from the point of view of the principal, who is charged with enforcing compulsory school attendance laws.

Let us look at the situation in terms of understanding the roles and positions. The community relations worker gained a position of influence, if not power, because of the uncertainty and anxiety among those with whom he worked. He had no power in his own right. He gained his position of influence by virtue of magical thinking and superstitution which attributed certain abilities to him. Finally, he produced, in the sense that his activities produced a tangible result. The result he produced did not necessarily depend on his personal qualifications as a black. Anyone could have produced the result he did using the same tactics, and many teachers did, but it is important that the tangible result was attributed to a set of mysterious qualities.

The consultant, entering the school situation, is in a position which is in many ways analogous to that held by the community relations worker. When he enters, he has no power. Much power of a kind is attributed to him. He is a "shrink" who can read minds, and will inevitably find out about people's hidden guilts and insecurities. He knows people, can tell about them by looking, and can solve problems by finding out what's troubling someone and saying a few magical words to him. The consultant is a person who really *knows*.

In ghetto situations particularly, less so in other circumstances, there is a high level of anxiety and anger. Unvoiced concerns that the school and/or the teachers are at fault abound. Somehow they are not doing the right thing, they are prejudiced, and they are frightened and angered by the surrounding community. Many are in a state of high tension because the situation is frustrating. This situation elicits angry feelings and, too often, the sense of competence is not validated by a desired result. Moreover, teaching, no less than psychotherapy is an authority, rather than empirically oriented discipline; and because it is, the first concern, just as it is with psychotherapists and their supervisors, is for reassurance that one is doing the right thing.

In the school situation, people do entertain wishes for magical solutions, and the appearance of someone who claims to know arouses such fantasies. Those who work with a consultant feel ambivalent toward him, fearful on the one hand, but also hoping against hope that he will find the answer to difficult problems. At least in the early stage of the relationship, the combination of anxiety, the magic attributed to the consultant, and the wish for him to succeed work together to permit others to attribute any change whatsoever to the consultant's magic. (Of course, these are not the only set of conditions under which one may exercise power. This set is commonly found in city schools, or in other agencies whose methods of operation are under strong pressure to change.) He has that working for him, not as actual power, but as attributed magic, when he first enters the situation. Of course, the anxiety and the attributed magical power also lead to a certain cautiousness, and to distance. Some are skeptical or openly hostile, eager to prove that nothing can be done, to validate their own previous positions. Nonetheless, in the beginning, the balance of the psychological forces is favorable for the consultant, despite the fact that his early reception will be marked by caution, suspicion, and testing.

How then does not capitalize on the situation? And toward what end, given the set of principles which I have stated above? The first step is to put oneself in such a position that one can in fact get to know the whole setting. Postulate 1: the setting is always involved. Here the problem is not unlike that of getting to know a new neighborhood and community in which you have bought a house. One explores, one talks to people, reads official documents, attends social gathering, observes, compares and contrasts with previous experiences, learns from faux pas, and tries to do little else except learn about the setting. Given the ambivalence, and the truly fantastic amount of projection onto the consultant (the consultant does his own projection of course; remember what it was like to be a little child in front of a giant, hawk-nosed, red-eyed, whitehaired, terrifying principal?), the consultant has the problem of establishing himself as nonthreatening, friendly, approachable, willing to learn, intelligent but not overbearing, and yet a definite enough person to emerge as something other than a stereotype.

One's official and unofficial reception by the setting will reveal a great deal of information about characteristics of the setting. Zachary Gussow (1964) has a valuable paper in this regard. Our own experiences suggest that different settings will greet one with attitudes ranging from apparent cooperation which masks apathy, or fear and suspicion, through apparent disorganization, (do whatever you want) which reveals a failure of leadership and demoralization, through rigid control and surveillance of one's every move. Probably the most favorable prognostic index is an attitude of cautiousness, and curiosity, mixed with modest openness. However, each situation must be viewed, at least initially, as having potential for growth and change.

The consultant also has a problem in the situation. He is uncertain of himself. He is under psychological pressure to do something to prove himself in the new situation, and he may be inclined to establish himself as the expert in ways which will result in others shoving off responsibility on to him, responsibilities he may not want at a later time. He also may feel anxious and guilty because he feels that his knowledge or skills are relevant to one situation only; or if he retains residuals of the mind-shrinking experience of graduate school, he will be certain he does not belong in the new situation because he knows nothing which is relevant in the world.

Both positions are accurate, because of the state of our knowledge. However, I have come to believe the only reasonable attitude is one which might be termed "responsible chutzpah." You rely on whatever knowledge and skills you have, and accept that you are willing and able to learn. One has to accept that errors, however painful, are inevitable, are not disasterous, and that in point of fact errors represent the best opportunity for learning. Most errors are not only *not* irretrievable, but they have a certain value. Aspects of the value of the consulting relationship, and its hazards, have been discussed in a result paper by Sarason (1967).

The consultant's uncertainty leads to another difficulty, one more or less derivable from the postulate which states that a problem in a setting is in part a function of deficiencies in the problem-solving devices in the setting. A role is defined by sociologists as the set of functions an actor performs in a setting, and as the set of expectation that others have for the actor to perform the particular functions. For purposes of the kind of practice spelled out by the five postulates, the consultant must enter the situation without a defined role. However, he will experience strong pressure from the expectations of others for him to fulfill a certain kind of problem-solving role. Based largely upon stereotypes about the consultant's profession, or upon experiences with people who had the same labels, others will exert pressure upon him to become a familiar problem-solver, by engaging in certain familiar tasks. Where is your test box? Talk to Johnny and find out what's bothering him. He's obviously sick. Can you send him to the clinic (i.e., get him out of here)? Can you give him therapy?

If the consultant also feels the need to prove himself, there is a grave danger he will respond by meeting those role expectations which are congenial for him and which give him something to do which makes him feel comfortable and competent. The difficulty is that the consultant will not learn anything new, but will find himself encapsulated in a role and set of functions which will keep him busy, and out of harm's ways. He will be doing just exactly what he had always been doing, but in a new physical setting. Parenthetically one can say the set up is a natural experiment in understanding how factors in a situation mold roles.

The fourth postulate states that the major goals and major values of the setting are important. Let me translate this postulate into the problem of leadership. I may be forcing the fit here, but bear with me as I translate the major goals and values of the setting into the question of leadership, and leadership competition. If one sees the leader as either the analogue, or the embodiment of major goals and values, then to the degree that the consultant exercises leadership, he will be in a position of competition with the existing leadership. He will be in some degree of conflict with the setting.

Typically, the consultant can expect that at some point his efforts will be misunderstood, if not handicapped, sabotaged or undercut by actions of the regular leader and others. The resistance, or the differences, or the unexpected and unwelcome action from the regular leader may be based upon rational disagreement with the proposed approach, upon bureaucratic timidity, or upon an irrational fear of losing power or of being displaced in the situation.

If one starts out with the expectation of error and conflict, and the most rational thing to do is anticipate the conflicts, and to build in a mechanism for resolving the conflict. Before doing anything else it is wise to establish a relationship, and a mechanism in which it is possible to discuss differences of opinion before they arise. The consultant may be very wise to state that he expects that he will have differences with the authority in the situation, that he expects that sometimes he will be wrong, that he is willing to change and to learn, but that the leader must also expect that the consultant will want to be free to thrash out problems with the authority in the situation. By working to build a situation of mutual respect, and by developing a reasonably positive working relationship before difficulties arise, the consultant and others in the situation can work out difficulties, not in the midst of a crisis which may push them into polarized win-lose positions, but against a background in which differences are a normal, to be expected part of the contingencies in the situation.

The third and fifth postulates have to do with the delivery of help, and the use of resources in the situation to provide the necessary form of help. If a consultant responds, either out of his anxiety, or his need to derive narcissistic gratification, by accepting an oracular role, then he will fail to recognize the competencies of others, and he will not work to create the conditions for the growth of others. He will relate to weakness, and accept dependence upon him as a sign of recognition by others of his wisdom. Rather than look toward people in the setting in terms of their potential as resources, he will tend to view only their weaknesses. When it comes to helping bring about changes, the consultant will overlook possibilities, or he will ignore people who do have ambitions and abilities, calling forth resistance and opposition to any change.

At the risk of sounding pollyannish, I am willing to assert that the strongest motive the consultant has going for him is the wish that others feel self-respect and experience increasing competence. Maslow's (1962) concepts tell us that growth motivation predominates when security needs are met, and from this viewpoint, it is essential for the consultant to maintain a supportive position, an attitude of "unconditional positive regard," for those with whom he works.

It is his job to reduce anxieties in order to release the growth potentials in others. Particularly if the consultant wishes to enter into the inner councils of the particular group, he needs to express his continued respect for everyone in the setting. He cannot, no matter how great the temptation, line himself up with a few people who are congenial or accepting. Otherwise, he will not be seen as objective and fairminded, and he will be drawn into all of the factional rivalries, the feuds, and the shifting alliances which seem to characterize so many school situations.

Let me recapitulate. The role I envisage is one that I might call a problem solving leader-catalyst. The theoretical position holds that the social setting is intimately involved in either producing the problem or in determining the form in which the problems are expressed. From this position one can argue that changes in the situation will lead to modification in the problem behavior. The consultant's role is to gain a position in the social setting such that he can understand it, and so that he can influence it or the leaders within the setting to attempt new methods of dealing with old problems, using available resources or resources which can be introduced into the setting on a systematic basis. The postulate system can be used as a rough guide to understand how one might get into this position and as an outline for understanding the difficulties one encounters in attempting to gain a position of influence. I am probably not letting any secrets out when I say that I feel that I know more about the difficulties than I do about the solutions to the difficulties. On the other hand, I am also very excited about the successes we have had and the potential for learning which access to the living situation provides. If nothing more, our concepts of how people live and work, of personality and of psychopathology, will inevitably change to become much more encompassing as we leave the confines of our own limited social settings, and enter the larger social world.

References

Gussow, Z. "The Observer-Observed Relationship as Information about Structure in Small Group Research." *Psychiatry* 27 (1964): 230-47.

Levine, M. "Some Postulates of Community Psychology Practice." In F. Kaplan and S. B. Sarason (eds.), *Collected Papers of the Psycho-Educational Clinic* (in preparation).

Levine, M. "Some Postulates of Practice in Community Psychology and Their Implications for Training." Paper read at the University of Texas Symposium on Training in Community Psychology. Austin, Texas, April 1967.

Maslow, A. H. *Toward a Psychology of Being*. Princeton, N.J.: Van Nostrand, 1962.

Sarason, S. B.; Levine, M.; Goldenberg, I.I.; Cherlin, D. L.; and Bennett, E. M. *Psychology in community settings: Clinical, Educational, Vocational, Social Aspects*. New York: John Wiley, 1966.

Sarason, S. B. "Toward a Psychology of Change and Innovation." *American Psychologist* 22 (1967): 227-33.

Scheff, T. J. *Being Mentally Ill: A Sociological Theory.* Chicago, Illinois: Aldine, 1966.

Szasz, T. S. *Law, Liberty and Psychiatry.* New York: Macmillan, 1963.

14

Social Action as A Vehicle for Learning

Seymour B. Sarason
Yale University

[Editor's Note] : *In this final chapter Seymour B. Sarason examines the long-standing conflicts that have characterized the university's stance toward the legitimacy of direct and ongoing social involvement as a relevant dimension in the education and training of social scientists. Cutting through the rhetoric of both activists and traditionalists, he indicates – perhaps more forcefully than anyone else – how self-defeating, unnecessary, and even illogical it has become to artificially separate theory from action, research from application, and reflection from intervention. Most importantly, however, Sarason places the responsibility for resolving the "contradictions" squarely on our own shoulders, for, as he puts it: "We are models for our students. If we close off avenues of experience to ourselves, we also do so for our students. If we do not take risks, neither will our students." It is entirely appropriate that this volume end on such a note: it demands that we ourselves become whole, much as we demand that our society become whole.*

The purpose of this chapter is to examine the implications of some long standing attitudes towards the role of social action in graduate education in the social sciences. These attitudes, of course, are those of the faculty and, not surprisingly, they tend to become the attitudes of the graduate student. From time to time turmoil in the larger society gets reflected in the university and when it does the role of social action by university people get raised, and three major positions emerge: it is an obligation of the university to help remedy social injustice; it is a subversion of the basic purposes of the university to direct its energies to solve practical problems; and the third position reflects different stances ranging from indifference to "this too shall pass." Anyone who has been in the university in the past decade knows what I am talking about. At the moment it appears that those who predicted that "this too shall pass" were most accurate. Compared to two or three years ago the university is a paradise for those who staunchly defended the position that its major purpose was to contribute to knowledge, i.e., "basic" knowledge illuminating the nature of man and society.

By social action as a vehicle for learning and contributing to knowledge, I refer to any instance in which an academic person takes on a socially responsible role – in government, politics, business, schools, poverty agencies, etc. –

©1973. Seymour B. Sarason.

This chapter, slightly revised, is reprinted with permission from *The Psychological Sense of Community: Towards a Community Psychology,* San Francisco: Jossey-Bass, 1974.

which will allow him to experience the "natural" functioning of that particular aspect of society. The role must be an operational one with responsibility and some decision-making powers. He becomes an insider. He is not a consultant with the luxury of giving advice without responsibility for implementation. He is at bat. He is not sitting in the stands passively observing the game and passing judgment on the players. He is in the game and he is a player. Finally, he assumes the new role not only to learn but to change and move things. He is there to win, and winning is defined in terms of ideas and theories about the game that he or others developed prior to assuming the new role. He assumes the new role to test the adequacy of ideas and theories, i.e., to see how they fit with social realities. His motivations have both an intellectually selfish and selfless quality. The period of time he spends in this role will vary, but there is no doubt in his mind that at the end of the period he must discharge the obligation to determine and communicate the general significance of his experience.

Part of winning is in contributing to new and general knowledge about man and society. Machiavelli founded political science by writing about his social-political-military experiences. He was a scholar before he was a social activist, but his social activist roles were the basis for provocative conceptualizations which are still quite relevant today. Schlesinger, Moynihan, and Kissinger are current examples of what I mean by social action. Proshansky (1972) has recently said rather eloquently some of the things I take up in this chapter. In regard to the role of social action in graduate education his plea is identical to mine.

> ... Clearly, direct involvement — whether for educational purposes or otherwise — in community problems is fraught with all of the sociopolitical difficulties with which we are familiar. But again I must say that it is the only way to provide a viable basis for new and meaningful research roles for our students. In the late 1940s, Kurt Lewin first postulated the notion of "action research," that is, research done in an actual problem context and which would be socially useful as well as theoretically meaningful. Given the recent recommendations by the National Science Foundation, the Social Science Research Council, and other groups of the need for problem-oriented social issue research, it is evident that Lewin was far ahead of his time. But to achieve Lewin's objective, we will need doctoral programs organized in terms of an interdisciplinary problem orientation, in which there is a close and continuing set of interrelationships between the community or problem setting and the students and faculty that make up these programs.

> In the last year, two very high-level community administrators of public agencies have said almost the same thing to me. Each indicated his strong belief in the value of behavioral science research in the actual context of the problems they dealt with. But each was quite wary about moving ahead in this respect because of what they had experienced in the past. Let

me paraphrase what one of them said:

> 'Too often you people come in not as problem oriented researchers but
> academic purists more interested in searching and testing what is im-
> portant for your theory than for the problem itself. But what really
> gripes me is that there is no long-term commitment. You come in, do
> your research, and then go back to the university and that's it. I am not
> asking for the solution to practical problems or what you call "quick
> and dirty research." I want a long-term commitment, because this is
> useful for us and scientifically important for you. Give us the word,
> and we will make you permanent members of the team. You can't come
> in, have your fun, and then leave — and expect us to welcome you back,
> particularly after you have left a mess'. (pp. 211-12)

If we try to understand why the university tradition is inimical to social action as a vehicle for contributing to knowledge, we must distinguish between
two arguments: the one that documents contributions stemming from basic
scholarship and research carried out without regard for their practical and social
consequences, and the one that asserts that involvement in society for the purpose of changing it is both dangerous and corrupting and had best be left to
others. Social action, however desirable and inevitable it may be, cannot be
carried out with the dispassion, objectivity, and controls that are the hallmark
of traditional scholarship and research. These two arguments are not logically related in the sense that agreement or disagreement with one determines one's
position in regard to the other. The failure to keep these arguments separate
has had the effect of obscuring issues and asking murky questions, an effect
which I shall attempt to show has effectively diluted the possibility that the
social sciences can open themselves to new and basic knowledge.

In regard to the first argument there is no need to document the conclusion
that much has been learned and illuminated by social scientists about man and
society. One can generate quite a controversy trying to get agreement about
what these basic contributions and illuminations have been, but I assume that
for some of them there would be fair agreement even among those social
scientists who disagree widely on other issues. To argue that little or nothing
of a basic sort has come out of the social sciences in the university makes no
sense to me, besides which I have not heard this argument even among the most
vociferous critics of American social science. The fact that some fundamental
contributions have emerged from university social science tends, of course, to
strengthen the attitude that research and scholarship unconcerned with application and social action are the only kind of geese that lay golden eggs. (This
is a metaphor used by Samuel Fernberger after World War II to make the point
that bringing clinical psychology into academic departments of psychology
would lower the production of golden eggs.) It is neither to deny or amend
this argument to point out that most social scientists think that most social
science research and scholarship are trivial affairs, at best, and stupefying stu-

pidities at worst. Irrelevant is the adjective I most frequently encounter. In his preface to the 1935 *Handbook on Social Psychology,* published in the middle of the Great Depression, Murchison says:

> The social sciences at the present moment stand naked and feeble in the midst of the political uncertainty of the world. The physical sciences seem so brilliant, so clothed with power by contrast. Either something has gone all wrong in the evolution of the social sciences, or their great day in court has not yet arrived. It is with something akin to despair that one contemplates the piddling, trivial superficial, damnably unimportant topics that some social scientists investigate with agony and sweat. And at the end of all these centuries, no one knows what is wrong with the world or what is likely to happen to the world. (p. ix)

And in 1970, Nisbet, in his preface to the 1971 edition of *The Quest for Community,* states:

> More than anything else it is the massive transformation of the American social scene since the Second World War that has focused attention upon the relative poverty of resources in the social sciences. Vast industrial relocations, redevelopments of central cities, city and regional planning, community organization, serious efforts on the part of civic agencies to prevent, rather than merely punish, crime, the innumerable social and psychological problems involved in the administering of both governmental and private social security systems — all of these and other problems have led to an almost desperate turning to social scientists for help.

> Of a sudden, a good deal of so-called social science was proved empty or irrelevant despite the public pretense to the contrary of some academic intellectuals. It became evident that more reliable knowledge — slim though it was — frequently lay in the experiences of social workers, businessmen, architects, city-managers, and politicians than in whole volumes of the social science journals. Several generations of social thought based upon determinism had produced very little of value to society. The familiar prescriptions of governmental ownership or management, by which liberals had for decades salved their social consequences, began to turn sour in the mouth when it became apparent that the real problem often was not *whether* the government shall render aid, but *how.*

And most recently Gouldner (1970) in his massive indictment of a good part of American social science carries the argument to the present day. And then there is C. Wright Mills. And no one said or described it better than Veblen. For those who prefer the poignant and tragic I would recommend Ernest Becker's (1971) moving account of Albion Small, one of the fathers of modern sociology. I think it is a fair assessment of the contributions stemming from the traditional stance in favor of "basic" scholarship and research unconcerned with practical problems and social action to say that it has produced a few nuggets of gold and a mountain of trivia.

Now let us turn to the argument that social action or immersion with practical problems is, for the university social scientist, a dangerous, corrupting business because it involves pressures and goals that subvert objectivity, adherence to the rules of evidence, and the attainment of generalizations of "laws" that make sense of the world of appearances. Like the first argument this one has some truth to it. We need only look at the biographies which politicians and statesmen write to agree that in the real social world truth is a frequent victim of self-interest. And each of us can probably point to an academic colleague who either assumed some sort of public position or directed his interests to solving a practical problem and who subsequently seemed unable to relate what he did in any clear way to a larger picture. That is to say, he did not contribute to basic knowledge, however successful or helpful he otherwise was. (That is a better outcome than one in which the individual became a partisan, such a blind advocate of policy and ideology, that one holds suspect anything he reports.) But this argument, like the first one, has its notable exceptions. Some of the nuggets of gold that the social sciences treasure were not mined in academia but rather by people very much in the affairs of their day. For those who need their memories refreshed on this score I suggest they read Schlesinger's (1971) *The Historian as Participant* in which he in no way denies the validity of the second argument at the same time that he convincingly demonstrates its limits.

At this point we can conclude that both arguments have very limited validity. Then why in the university is there such a strong and unreasoned tradition against social action as a possible way of learning and contributing to general knowledge of man and society? Schlesinger provides part of the answer, and although he talks about the historian it is, in my opinion, no less true of all the social sciences:

> In the later nineteenth century, however, a new question arose, I think for the first time — the question whether participation in public events might not disqualify the participant from writing about these events as a historian; whether, indeed, experience in the public world might not be incompatible with the ideal of historical objectivity. Such questions were a direct consequence of the professionalization of history. Historians were now increasingly segregated in universities, enshrined in academic chairs, surrounded by apprentices; and the crystallization of this distinct and specific status brought with it a tendency to reject, first, historians who participated in the events they described and, soon, historians who participated in anything beyond the profession of history. Indeed, it may have been unconsciously felt that eyewitness history, by involving the historical profession in ongoing conflicts, might raise threats to the hard-won new status. As Sir Walter Raleigh, one of the few historians to suffer the ultimate criticism of

the executioner's ax, had warned two and a half centuries before, "Whosoever, in writing a modern history, shall follow truth too near the heels, it may haply strike out his teeth. . . . "

Professionalization meant rigorous training in the techniques of the craft; it meant specialization; it meant specialization; it meant bureaucratization; it meant a stern insistance on critical methods as the guarantee of objectivity; it meant a deep pride in the independence and autonomy of the historical guild and an ardent conviction that the new professional techniques were winning history unprecedented new successes. "The historians of former times," wrote Acton, "unapproachable for us in knowledge and in talent, cannot be our limit. We have the power to be more rigidly impersonal, disinterested and just than they."

Such severe standards created the image of the historian as a monastic scholar, austerely removed from the passing emotions and conflicts of his own day. From this viewpoint, participation in the public world meant the giving of hostages — to parties, to institutions, to ideologies. In retrospect, it seemed that Macaulay was too deeply a Whig, Bancroft too deeply a Jacksonian, Henry Adams too deeply an Adams. The view arose that not only participant-historians but even historians who wrote about contemporaneous events were too deeply compromised to fulfill the pure historical vocation. (pp. 341-42)

I have no doubt that when the final history of the human race is written, high on the list of diseases contributing to its downfall will be professionalization which, whatever its origins in social virtue, dialectically gave rise to its own destruction.

Professionalization within the university rests on what I call the myth of contamination by society: the nonuniversity world is organized in ways and for purposes, and populated by kinds of people, that are personally corrupting, truth-killing, and crassly materialistic. That is only one part of the myth. The other is that what is true of society is not true of the university. If you go into society you get diseased. If you stay in the university, you will be healthy. What would transform the myth into a description of reality would be the recognition that the university must reflect the larger society, and staying in or venturing out of the university both possess the potential for true learning and profound corruption.

By venturing into the everyday world two ways of getting new knowledge become available to the social scientist. The first way is particularly important to those who develop theories, mini or maxi, to explain something about man and society, because the assumption is usually made that either what needs explanation "out there" is adequately described or that the description is incomplete or incorrect and the theory serves to tell one the true state of affairs "out there." For example, over the years there has been a lot of

theorizing by every brand of social scientist about what schools are like, and
the amount of theorizing increased as the schools became object of national
concern and controversy. In one way or another these conceptual efforts
were addressed to how schools should be changed, the assumption being that
what schools *are* was pretty well known. That assumption was crucial, of
course, because if what was considered valid knowledge about schools was
in error then efforts to change the schools would likely misfire. And does anyone doubt that they misfired? The reasons they failed and will likely continue
to fail are complex, but there is no doubt in my mind that a major factor is
sheer ignorance about what schools are. Ignorance is bad enough, but when in
addition the available "knowledge" is based on unexamined prejudices and
incompleteness that produces caricature, the outcome is not in doubt. I devoted
a recent book, *The Culture of the School and the Problem of Change* (1971),
to these issues and I have space only to describe briefly some of its major points.
First, those who developed theories about what schools are and how they should
change obviously had no first-hand sustained experience in schools, e.g., those
who developed the new math, the new biology, the "new" community-school
relationship. Second, those agents of change *within* the school (usually using
the concepts of the Christian Diors of academia) tended to be equally ignorant
about the culture of the school – a good example of how being in or out of
the university can make for a profound difference.[a] Third, the theoretical literature is remarkably devoid of meaningful descriptions of how schools work or
change. We have anecdotes and case histories which, almost invariably, tell us
more about the phenomenology of the change agent than about schools. Fourth,
the failure of efforts at change rarely have the effect of changing theories, but
frequently results in further criticism of the schools by "blaming" the stupidity
of recalcitrance of teachers and administrators. Fifth, when one looks carefully at instances of change it becomes apparent that the theories on which
they are based never justify the particular time perspective that is employed.

   What permitted me to make these points about change agents in the university and in the schools? That is a long story (Sarason, Levine, Goldenberg,
Cherlin, and Bennett 1966), but it all began with the decision that in our desire
to understand the culture of the school we would establish an intensive helping relationship to schools, a relationship that would require us to be *in* them
on a sustained basis for the purpose of being helpful *there*.[b] We were not
going to be participant observers, passive consultants, or so-called crisis inter-
veners. Each of us at the Yale Psycho-Educational Clinic spent at least two

---

[a] Our lack of knowledge about the actual functioning of schools is by no means peculiar to these parts of the educational scene. For example, in a four-paragraph comment on
university goverance (*Saturday Review,* January 1970) Logan Wilson states: "I don't
know of a single empirical study of a campus that delineates just how decisions are made.
In many institutions it is a kind of shell game, and I suspect that this is a source of frustration to many students who make recommendations and then are mystified about what

full days a week in a school.[c] We learned a lot. First we learned about the depth of our ignorance about what schools are and about the unexamined assumptions with which we approached them. Once the unlearning process was well under way we could begin to understand schools from the standpoints of the different groups within them. We were able to observe numerous attempts to introduce change in the schools and why in each instance failure was guaranteed because there was an amazing ignorance of "the way things are." And we learned to be intellectually alone because when we read the social science literature on schools there was pitifully little (there were a few nuggets) that we could use or that squared with our experiences. Candor requires that I report that we became increasingly hostile to colleagues in universities who in the turbulent sixties became "relevant" by becoming interested in the schools, willing to contribute their "hard science" expertise in a kind of *noblesse oblige* manner. Their motivations were as clear as their ignorance profound. They were going to share their "basic" conceptions and rigorous methodology. They were going to determine the true state of affairs, and many of them had nothing to determine because they already knew what the score was!

In his book *Maximum Feasible Misunderstanding,* Moynihan (1969) describes some of the unfortunate things that happen when academic social scientists are brought into the "public sector" to provide the basic understanding on the basis of which successful practical programs can be mounted. Fortunately, Moynihan's wit and literary style help the reader stay with his account of the ineptness of the social scientist: well-woven theories that bear the stamp of creative thinking and unexamined partisanship and social values, ignorance of how federal bureaucracy works and its ties with legislative power and politics, and the inability to forsee the practical consequences of recommendations. In fact, Moynihan's disillusionment with the social scientist is so great that he recommends that his role be restricted to evaluator of programs, not the suggester or implementor. Moynihan seems to be saying that by keeping the social scientist in his academic cage he will do less practical harm and conceivably might even do some good. Moynihan's recommendation is unfortunately superficial, if not thoughtless. How can you evaluate social action programs if you do not comprehend the social contexts of their origins

---

happens to them." This simple, clear, and justified statement should give pause to those who believe that the different efforts to change the university in one way or another are really directed to the way things are.

[b] At an earlier point I gave consideration to a more traditional methodology: questionnaires, interviews, observations. When I realized that much of what we know about personality has come from efforts to change it, I decided that it would be productive to work in schools in the same way. It is not that one approach is good and the other bad. They give you different pictures because you are experiencing the setting in different ways.

[c] The Yale Psycho-Educational Clinic no longer exists as an organized entity. The explanation for its demise is given in my book *The Creation of Settings and Future Societies* (1972), and is part of the background context from which the present chapter emerges.

as well as the contexts of their implementation? How do you evaluate
postive or negative results when you have no secure basis for knowing whether
the study was appropriate in the first place, i.e., whether the study was
directed to the right questions and would be carried out in ways that would
not be self-defeating? How can you talk about the significance of consequences if you are not deeply knowledgeable about antecedents, and how can
you be knowledgeable if you have no first-hand experience with the relevant
social contexts? Is the social scientist someone to be given data to determine
if they are statistically significant? Is the social scientist to be the servant of the
public officials who determine what needs to be done, do it, and then ask the
social scientist to find out if it was worthwhile? *And on what basis does Moynihan assume that the nonuniversity agent of change does not daily commit the
same errors of ineptness of which he accuses the social scientist?* It is strange
that Moynihan does not ask and pursue the question why the academic social
scientist is so inept when he ventures forth into the social world, especially
since I assume Moynihan knows that, his recommendation notwithstanding,
social scientists are going to be drawn into public affairs. (A less charitable way
of putting it is that they will be seduced by their own view of their expertise
as well as by public agencies who have come to believe what the university
has in recent decades told them to believe: that "basic" research pays off, like
in physics with the atomic bomb!)

Thus far I have been discussing the social scientist as he pursues social
action for the purpose of applying basic theory to the solution of the problems
of society. There is a second way, far less ambitious and more unplanned
or fortuitous, which can be illustrated by World War II experiences. It first has
to be noted that in World War II almost everyone in the university willingly
and eagerly sought to be helpful. No one was saying that the rest of society
should fight the war while the university should continue its pursuit of basic
knowledge. Academic people in or out of the armed services concentrated
on practical problems with which they frequently had no background or
previous interest. They were not seeking basic knowledge or developing new
theoretical systems. The problems were immediate, pressing, and in need
of some practical solutions. The visual problems of pilots, instilling certain
attitudes in soldiers, managing mental breakdowns near the field of battle, the
formation of groups and the maintenance of morale, teaching of heretofore
neglected foreign languages, increasing industrial efficiency and output, the
development of effective propaganda, training people for espionage, predicting reactions to stress, improving decision-making and planning processes
— this is a very small sample of the problems academic people were dealing
with. World War II had personal and professional consequences for university
people, personal in the sense that for many it simply expanded their knowledge of the larger society and its problems, and professional in the sense
that it changed the substantive nature of many fields. It is hard to over-

estimate how World War II changed the direction of basic research and theory because it was an unpredictable consequence of dealing with some practical or applied problems. Garner (1972) has recently discussed and illustrated this process in regard to experimental psychology. Let me quote one instance from Garner:

> The topic of space perception is almost synonymous with the name of James Gibson these days, so when I want to talk about concepts and research in space perception, I cannot do so without talking about James Gibson's research. He was well established as an authority on perception before World War II, but his experiences during that war, working on some applied problems, changed the nature and direction of his theorizing considerably. Specifically, his experiences led him to his "Ground Theory" of space perception as described in his book, "The Perception of the Visual World" published in 1950.
>
> As Gibson describes the experience in that book, he and some other psychologists were trying to understand how aircraft pilots estimate the distance to the ground when they are landing an airplane. He found that the traditional cues for depth perception, listed without fail in every introductory textbook on psychology, simply failed to explain the perception of depth at the distances required in flying and landing an airplane. He furthermore found that experiments had to be done in the field to get at the process, that laboratory experiments changed the nature of the process too much. So into the field he went.
>
> It was from these experiments that Gibson came to the conclusion that the prerequisite for the perception of space is the perception of a continuous background surface; thus the "Ground Theory" which evolved from this work.
>
> The important point for my thesis today is that Gibson's whole way of thinking about the problem of space perception changed when he was faced with the problem of understanding how pilots in a real-life situation actually land their airplanes without too many crashes. His theoretical notions were changed by his contact with people with problems. He did not develop these important ideas by a continuous relation to his previous work. Rather, his research and thinking, according to his own report, took a decided turn for the better as a result of this experience. (pp. 8-9)

Garner could have used his own illustrious career as an example.

It is unfortunate that it was as a consequence of a world war that theory and research in practically every university discipline changed markedly and the pace of new knowledge accelerated. The lesson, of course, is not that we should have more wars but that concern with practical problems can lead to new and fundamental knowledge. But this lesson was not drawn, so that in 1972 Garner is compelled to say:

... the quality of basic research is improved by communication between the basic research scientist and the people who have problems to solve. Thus for scientists to engage in goal-oriented research, research aimed at solving problems known to exist, is both to perform a service to society and to improve the quality of the basic research itself . . . if the scientist will talk to people with real problems, and just as important, if those people will talk to those of us who are scientists, then both those who acquire knowledge and those who apply it will benefit. The relation is truly symbiotic."

I should remind the reader that the thrust of this chapter has not been to deny the validity of the tradition that holds that research and theorizing untrammeled by practical considerations or the need to solve immediate social problems can contribute new general knowledge about man and society. I have argued against the exclusivity of this tradition and its historically unwarranted assumption that dealing with the practical problems of people and society is dangerous and unproductive. I hope that it has also been clear that I have not advocated that the academic social scientist should become involved in practical matters as an end in itself but rather as a vehicle for testing his comprehension of social realities or for the deliberate purpose of experiencing a new role in its actual fullness.

I must turn again to personal experience. One of the several major reasons I started and directed the Yale Psycho-Educational Clinic was to test myself in the role of leader. It was an inchoate kind of motivation but in some dim way I felt I had to do it if I was better to understand why new settings fail, and rather quickly so. I was painfully aware of the self-defeating character of most organizations, new and old, but I was vaguely uncomfortable in the knowledge that my understanding was from an outsider's perspective. And, frankly, the literature I read on leadership and organizations was far more effective than seconal as a sleep producer. I also found what was for me a fantastic omission in this literature: There was practically nothing on how to create a new setting even though new settings were being created at an ever accelerating rate. The more I dug into the literature the clearer it became that what we know is based on chronologically mature, malfunctioning organizations. So in my curiosity about myself as a leader I was led to the problem of the creation of settings which I defined as two or more people coming together in new and sustained relationships to attain stated objectives. As best I could, it is all described in my recent book (1972) *Creation of Settings and Future Societies.* I experienced leadership and the creation of settings in their fullness. I would like to believe that what I learned and reported are fundamental and a contribution to general knowledge. What I believe is ultimately of no significance unless others agree that what came out of ten years of planning and working — ten years of continuous, day by day, month by month responsibility, influencing and being influenced, experiencing anxiety, joy and controversy — is of general import. If my recent book was a biography of a particular clinic in a particular university in a particular city, I should not be surprised if it met with disinterest. What may be interesting to *me*, or what was the most self-transforming experience of *my* life are not benefits that can be derogated, but unless I can relate the particulars of my experiences to more general contents and issues I am not fulfilling my role as a member of a university faculty. *The more pertinent point here is that as a member of a university faculty I had an obligation to pursue knowledge even if that meant "messing" in a sustained way with the realities of modern society.* But, as I pointed out before, that sense of obligation is not shared by many people in the university who have successfully innoculated themselves against a contaminating society.

How the Tradition Is Maintained

I have described a set of beliefs inimical to the idea that immersion with practical problems (i.e., some form of social action aimed at changing something or creating something new) is a productive way of contributing new and general knowledge of a fundamental sort. Having said something about the rhetoric of this tradition, I would like briefly to comment on how the tradition is maintained. If we have any desire to change or add to this tradition, we should know how it works.

Each year I read scores of letters from colleges and universities seeking to employ young faculty members. The letters are monotonously alike. What they seek is a young person who is "rigorous in approach," "interested in a career in research," and "shows promise of being a productive contributor to the literature." Not surprising, in recent years many centers ask for someone with "community interests." Of course he should also be a good teacher and a responsible departmental citizen. I presented these sought after characteristics in the order that they are usually given in the letters.

So what is wrong? For a partial answer let us turn to how graduate students are chosen. Faculty select graduate students on precisely the same grounds they choose new faculty. If there is any basis for inferring that the prospective student is a social activist or "do-gooder" — he or she wants to be in and change the world — the chances for admission reduce almost to nil. If the application does not contain statements that the student is interested in the world of ideas, rigorous research, and theory — if he remains general and vague and has not already developed interests in a specific and restricted area familiar in the literature — the odds against admission rise. If he presents evidence that he was already an undergraduate researcher, and his recommenders attest to his devotion to basic research, the odds for him or her increase sharply. Faculty choose new faculty and graduate students in terms of how the candidates fit the dominant academic tradition, and it is a process intended to screen out "deviants." It is a process deliberately carried out to reduce the risk of choosing people who may not fit in with the dominant tradition.

In the past decade two new factors have altered either the "success" of the selection process or the population from which students are selected. The first of these factors is that undergraduates have become very knowledgeable about how to write an application to graduate school. That is to say, many of them have social activist inclinations and goals, but they know that to express them is to participate in a kiss of death. They know that they can learn much in graduate school, but they also know that they do not accept the exclusivity of the dominant academic tradition. Phenomenologically they see themselves as needing knowledge and skills, and a union card, which will permit them after graduate school to make their mark in society, not in the university. These are the ones who seek to beat the system. If they get into graduate school, their problems begin. Rarely will they find a faculty member who meets their conception of a role model, i.e., someone who is actively engaged in trying to do something about some aspect of a social problem. Even more rarely will they find a faculty member who is so engaged but for the purposes of learning and conceptualizing (i.e., not only for the purpose of doing good) and for this kind of graduate student this kind of role model is crucial, otherwise he gets lost in particulars. So what is he to do? The more appropriate question is: what is he required to do? He is required to go through a program which, instructive and stimulating though it may be, does not get to the center of the student's interests. No less than the factory worker the student feels alone and alienated: a significant part of him or her is untouched or unused in work. Some students succumb to the system with what personal consequences, short or long term, I cannot say. Some make "trouble." Some drop out.

The other factor affecting the selection process has to do with those who do *not* apply because they reject the values and substance of graduate education as they see them. For the majority of these nonapplicants the decision is a wise one in the sense that they are social activists dedicated to ideologies which are tantamount to a way of life in which the demands of untrammelled intellectual pursuits have little place. These kinds of ideology can be no less confining than the dominant academic one. But there are other nonapplicants I have known who had the appropriate mixture of social activism and the capacity to conceptualize, think critically, and generalize from their activism. Their rejection of further education is a tragic waste of human resources. What life has in store for them I find distasteful to contemplate. I hope I am wrong. I have no doubt that I am right that among them are some of the finest minds I have known.

It is clear, I hope, that I am not recommending that students be chosen because of their social activist interests. Aside from maintaining that such interests should not be a disqualification, I maintain that certain intellectual or conceptual talents and freedom have to be present — not fully formed but of a quality which can benefit from intellectual confrontation. It does not bother me if such a student comes with the "truth," or the self-assurance that is always based on oversimplification; or with the attitude that youth has a grasp of the social realities that age only weakens, or a view of past people and efforts (of social and intellectual history in general) that, at best, borders on tolerance and, at worst, reflects sheer ignorance; or with that biblical prophetic stance that says the world must be saved and they will do it. These things do not bother me if I feel I can "fight" with such a student and we both still want to continue the battle. What am I there for if not to engage in intellectual battle, to provide "out there" experiences which will help resolve the issues that divide us, to help him experience the continuity between theory and action, to aid him to see that self-change is a prerequisite to social change, and that being able to take distance from oneself is no less important a skill than taking distance from whatever it is one wants to change. I have learned the least from students with whom I have not had to do battle. I in no way subscribe to the notion that a faculty should be sensitive to the needs and interests of students in order to satisfy them. I must be sensitive to their needs and interests in order to see what the battle is going to be like: where we differ and to what extent, whether we can agree on a constitution that permits, indeed encourages, peaceful war, and whether he or she is willing to share experiences with me in the social world so that we have a degree of communality from which to view our presumed differences.

The attitudes of the university toward social action as a vehicle of learning and contributing to general knowledge have not changed very much in recent years. At the present moment universities are experiencing a financial crisis and it would appear that new programs that do not fit in with traditional attitudes toward scholarship and research will be weakened or eliminated. Indeed, I have heard some who blame the current financial plight in part as a misdirected expansion of frilly, or social-action type programs which took much needed resources away from what they consider the most intellectually substantial activities of the university. In any event, it is unrealistic to expect that graduate education in the social sciences will change in ways I have suggested. The dominant attitudes are too strongly held by too many academics, and this has been true for too long a time, to justify optimism for change. And we must not forget that these attitudes reflect a tradition with some solid achievements. Those of us who feel that this tradition is narrow and confining and is robbing the social sciences of new experiences which are the life blood of new ideas have no alternative but to fight the self-defeating exclusively of the tradition. But it should not be fought in terms of superficial good-bad, virtuous-sinful, progressive-reactionary polarities. I say this because it is conceivable that as time goes on nonuniversity-based vehicles will be created to avoid the obstacles of academic tradition and there is the real danger that these new ventures will ignore what is best in that tradition, i.e., the search for continuity and generality in face of the fact that the search is beset with serious obstacles, not the least of which are in the searcher himself.

Immersion in social action or the affairs of the social world can be justified in a number of ways but contributing to general *knowledge* of man and society is not among its most frequent justifications. Such a contribution requires at least three characteristics: the action is intended for the purposes of learning, it requires one's total involvement, and it is intended that at some point the general sense one makes of the experience will be published for critical scrutiny. I would add one more "condition": That the immersion is time limited precisely to safeguard the requirements that one organizes and presents what one has learned.

There is a contradiction between the intent to learn and total involvement, and my critics point to this as a fatal flaw. How can you be true to the intent to learn at the same time you engage in a.value-ridden, partisan action which creates pressures that deceive the self and defeat the search for truth? I borrow the principles of an answer from Freud, who, faced with the task of how to be sensitive to the conscious *and* unconscious messages contained in verbal and motor communications, recommended the stance of "listening and not listening." That is to say, one adopts a set which maximizes the chances that one becomes aware of multiple meanings. It is a control against exclusivity of attention on the other person and against the ignoring and utilizing of one's own fleeting ideas and feelings. Freud's dictum "to listen and not listen" was no foolproof control, particularly in the therapeutic context in which the desire to be a good healer and the sources of resistance in the patient to being healed can collude to unwittingly corrupt both. Freud was quite aware that partisan action, as analyst or patient, could distort the pursuit of truth, which is why he recommended that analysts be analyzed every five years. Freud, of course, is a beautiful example that one can engage in actions, very "practical" kinds of actions, and cull from them understanding and generalizations which enormously influence theory and practice in many academic fields. I would suggest that this was possible because his desire to learn equalled in strength his desire to heal. (Freud did not seem to have been an outstanding therapist, probably because he could not contain his intellectual curiosity which, in the therapeutic endeavor, is not always helpful to the therapy.)

The contradiction is a real one but it is no excuse for retreat. Our task is to learn whatever we can, to experience whatever we can, in the quest for general knowledge. We are models for our students. If we close off avenues of experience to ourselves, we also do so for our students. If we do not take risks, neither will our students. If we fear being contaminated by society, if we are afraid of testing our ideas about society by intervening in it, and if we are always the detached observer of society and rarely if ever a participant in it, we can only give our students ideas about society, not our experiences in it. We can tell our students how society ought to be but not what it is like to try to change the way things are.

The social action role as I have described it is not everybody's cup of tea. It is, however, a brew without which the social sciences will remain pallid and unduly trivial. In their quest for scientific respectability the social sciences have erected "experimentation" and the "experimental attitude" as a supreme value. An essential feature of this attitude, so obvious that it rarely receives elaboration, is that if you want to understand how things work you have to *intervene,* i.e., to introduce something new into the accustomed order of things. The additional feature of manipulating variables, contrasting control and experimental conditions, is a consequence of the basic assumption that you must *intervene and change* things in some way. Social action is a form of intervention no less than changing the feeding schedules of rats is an intervention. Where it is possible to introduce controls one should do so, of course. But the fact that such controls may not be possible, or that they may fall short of the ideal mark, is an argument for caution in interpretation and not against intervention. One does the best one can and relies on the efforts and criticisms of others to do better the next time. *But that is also true for the most rigorous experimentalist.* In the final analysis the best control is in what others say and do in response to what one claims to have learned. Rigor is no guarantee of significance and importance. Calling something social action or field work is no excuse for sloppiness. What we ask of everyone is that they do justice to themselves and the problem uninfluenced by fashion, unconstrained by narrow tradition. and unfearful of the new.

References

Becker, E. *The Lost Science of Man.* New York: Braziller, 1971.

Garner, W. "The Acquisition and Application of Knowledge: A Symbiotic Relation." *American Psychologist* 27, 10 (October 1972).

Gouldner, A. W. *The Coming Crisis of Western Sociology.* New York: Basic Books, 1970.

Moynihan, D. P. *Maximum Feasible Misunderstanding: Community Action in the War on Poverty.* New York: Free Press, 1969.

Murchison, C. (ed.). *A Handbook of Social Psychology.* Worcester: Clark University Press, 1935.

Nisbet,   . *The Quest for Community* (rev. edition). New York: Oxford University Press, 1970.

Proshansky, H. M. "For What Are We Training Our Graduate Students?" *American Psychologist* 27, 3 (March 1972): 205-212.

Sarason, S. B. *The Creation of Settings and Future Societies.* San Francisco: Jossey-Bass, 1972.

Sarason, S. B. *The Culture of the School and the Problem of Change.* Boston: Allyn and Bacon, 1971.

Sarason, S.B.; Levine, M.; Goldenberg, I.I.; Cherlin, D.L.; and Bennett, E.M. *Psychology in Community Settings: Clinical, Educational, Vocational, Social Aspects.* New York: John Wiley, 1966.

Schlesinger, A.M. "The Historian as Participant." *Daedalus* 100 (Spring 1971): 399-58.

Wilson, L. "Other Voices, Other Views." *Saturday Review* 53, 74 (January 10, 1970).

About the Editor

I. Ira Goldenberg is currently associate professor of Education and Clinical Psychology at Harvard University. Prior to coming to Harvard he was on the faculty of the Department of Psychology at Yale University. During those years (1964-70) he was directly involved in community action programs, the public schools, problems of mental retardation, and the development of community-based residential centers for adolescents. He received the B.A. from C.C.N.Y. (1958), and the M.A. (1960) and Ph.D. (1963) from the University of Connecticut. At the present time he is engaged in problems concerning the de-institutionalization of correctional facilities for adjudicated youthful offenders, is a member of the Governor's Special Commission on the Care and Treatment of Children in the Commonwealth of Massachusetts, and is doing research in the area of drug addiction, rehabilitation and employment. He is the author of *Build Me a Mountain: Youth, Poverty, and the Creation of New Settings* (MIT Press, 1971) and co-author (with S. B. Sarason, M. Levine, D. L. Cherlin and E. M. Bennett) of *Psychology in Community Settings* (Wiley & Co., 1966).